Intellectual Property Rights and Public Policy

AF739494

NIPA® GENX ELECTRONIC RESOURCES & SOLUTIONS P. LTD.
New Delhi-110 034

About the Author

Md. Zafar Mahfooz Nomani specializes in Ecology law and Intellectual Property Rights and serving as Professor of Law at Faculty of Law, Aligarh Muslim University, Aligarh. As a writer, he is receptive to trans disciplinary method of inquiry and brandies belief. His methodology partakes to systematization of legal propositions, penetrating examination of case laws and ordering of legal institutions to novelties of law, jurisprudence and human development. His thrust has always been social inquiry of visceral affinity of subjects in socio-legal context and doctrinal holism. Believing ardently that 'the life of law has not been logic rather it has been experience, he offers symbols of progressions to identify society, environment, sustainable development and social change. He authored five books and published more than 100 research papers in prestigious refereed and peer reviewed journals covering diverse areas of environmental and intellectual property and corporate laws and has been recipients of many awards and accolades.

BOOKS BY THE AUTHOR

1. ***Natural Resources Law and Policy,*** Uppal Publishing House: New Delhi; 2003[ISBN 81-7658-024-4]
2. ***Legal Control of Radiation Pollution,*** Regency Publication: New Delhi; 2004[ISBN 81-87498-89-7]
3. ***Right To Health: A Socio-Legal Perspective,*** Uppal Publishing House: New Delhi; 2003[ISBN 81-7658-023-6]
4. ***Environment Impact Assessment Law,*** Satyam Law International: New Delhi; 2009[ISBN 978-81-905852-5-5]
5. ***Law & Sustainable Forestry,*** Aligarh Muslim University Press, 2010 Aligarh

Intellectual Property Rights and Public Policy

Zafar Mahfooz Nomani
Professor
Department of Law
Aligarh Muslim University
Aligarh (U.P.)

NIPA® GENX ELECTRONIC RESOURCES & SOLUTIONS P. LTD.
New Delhi-110 034

NIPA® GENX ELECTRONIC
RESOURCES & SOLUTIONS P. LTD.

101,103, Vikas Surya Plaza, CU Block
L.S.C. Market, Pitam Pura, New Delhi-110 034
Ph : +91 11 27341616, 27341717, 27341718
E-mail: newindiapublishingagency@gmail.com
web: www.nipabooks.com

For customer assistance, please contact
Phone: + 91-11-27 34 17 17
Fax: + 91-11- 27 34 16 16
E-Mail: feedbacks@nipabooks.com

ISBN: 978-81-19215-94-2

Composed and Designed by NIPA®.

Dedicated to
my Maternal Uncle
Janab Md. Basharat Hussain

Justice K.G. Balakrishnan
Former Chief Justice of India
Former Chairperson National Human Rights Commission

59/A, Friends Colony (East),
New Delhi-110065
Ph. : 011-26326847, Mob.: 9717266700
E-mail : kgbalakrishnan45@gmail.com

Foreword

The academic book *Intellectual Property Rights & Public Policy* compiled by Professor Zafar Mahfooz. Nomani from Faculty of Law, Aligarh Muslim University, Aligarh is a judicious inquiry into the Intellectual Property Law in India and its governance in post Agreement on Trade-Related Aspects of Intellectual Property Rights (TRIPS) compliant phase. The object of the book being 'creativity and innovation being hallmark of knowledge economy', leads a keen inquiry into the frontiers of Intellectual property laws and their governance in India.

The creative space of the book is spread over to four sections containing three papers in each section. It ranges from Section I: *Intellectual Property & Public Policy Discourse;* Section II: *Copyright, Climate Change & Food Security Policy;* Section III: *Patent, Health & Public Policy;* and Section IV: *Cybernetics, Law & Public Policy.*

The content of the book lucidly illumines grey areas of Intellectual property to the readers with clarity and collusiveness.

I commend the author and the publisher for having endeavored to bring an innovative book on intellectual property and public policy in India.

Justice K.G. Balakrishnan

Contents

Section III: Patent, Health & Public Policy

Section IV: Cybernetics, Law & Public Policy

Preface

I. IMPERATIVE OF PUBLIC POLICY

The book on *Intellectual Property Rights & Public Policy* offers a multi layered narratives of IP laws and governance in the context of India's emergence of one of the fastest growing economies in the world. The time is ripe to leverage the country's knowledge-based assets to achieve inclusive and sustainable economic growth.[1] The IPR Policy, 2016[2] is the first of its kind in India which encapsulates the critical role of Intellectual Property (IP) as a custodian to transform knowledge into intellectual assets. Additionally, the policy also provides for IPs enhanced role as a competition regulator, a marketable financial asset as well as an economic tool. Although India has a significant knowledge base, a large part of it remains unprotected due to the lack of awareness about intellectual property legislations. The IP policies attempt to create an innovation ecosystem which can potentially transform knowledge into protectable and tradable 'intellectual assets'. The public policy regarding intellectual property has been shaped in the after math of supreme court pronouncement in *Novartis A.G.* v. *Union of India*[3], most notably after the accession of BJP government and their initiative of Review of IP laws and pronouncement of *National Intellectual Property Policy*, 2016. It is therefore logical to look at fall out of *Novartis* judgments in critical perspective[4] and appraisal of UPA-II Government's failure to cooperate with an investigation led by the *US International Trade Commission (USITC)* into India's IPR related issues under the title of *'Trade, Investment and Industrial Policies in India: Effects on the US Economy'* during 2013-14.[5]

---

1 OECD on New Sources of Growth: Knowledge-Based Capital: Key Analyses and Policy Conclusions - Synthesis Report, OECD, (2013).

2 Intellectual Property Rights: New Policy May Power R&D, National Growth, New Indian Express, 17 May 2016.

3 *Novartis A.G.V. Union of India*, (2007) 4 MLJ 1153 & *Novartis A.G.V. Union of India*, AIR 2013 SC 1311.

4 The Cost of Drugs: Beyond The Supreme Court Order, Economic and Political Weekly, Vol-XLVIII, No. 17, April 27, 2013.

5 Intellectual Property Issues Dominate The USITC Public Hearing on India, Third World Network, 13 February, 2014.

II. IMPLICATION ON ACCESS TO HEALTH

The Commerce and Industry Ministry maintains that in order to resolve the weak IPR protection environment in India and the ministry would soon have a policy think-tank. A new IPR policy will be brought to deal with issues raised by the developed countries like the United States a clear indication of change and ground setting before Narendar Modi's visit to United States.[6] This created rumours that the NDA Government had withdrawn powers of the *National Pharmaceuticals Pricing Authority (NPPA)* to fix or revise prices under Para 19 of *Drugs Pricing Control Order (DPCO)*, 2013.[7] It alleged that media had wrongly reported the direction given to the NPPA for withdrawing the notifications dated 10 July 2014, fixing prices of 108 non-scheduled drugs used to treat diabetes and cardiovascular diseases.[8]

Some experts had opined that the government clampdown on NPPA's power was an attempt to project India as market-friendly just ahead of the PM's visit to US. Iftikhar Gilani publisher of DNA documented that the Government's decision to decontrol prices of 108 drugs pushed up the price of Glivec *(among many others)* – an anti-cancer drug/ tablet that was denied patent protection by the Supreme Court of India in April 2013 - from Rs 8,500 to Rs 1.08 lakh. It seemed like a well-orchestrated move on the part of NDA to appease US drug companies who did not like the low-priced "generic" medicines that are manufactured in India.[9] The Ministry of Chemicals and Fertilizers [dated 25 September, 2014] also joined in such denial by saying that:

> The Government has clarified that it had not withdrawn powers delegated to the NPPA on 30th May 2013, within the framework of the National Pharmaceuticals Pricing Policy (NPPP) 2012 and the Drugs Pricing Control Order (DPCO), 2013. It is further stated that the orders dated 10.07.2014 issued by the NPPA, fixing prices of certain drugs in exercise of powers under Para 19 of DPCO, 2013 have not been withdrawn.

In the light of some writ petitions filed in Bombay and Delhi High courts, the NPPA withdrew certain internal guidelines that it had earlier

---

6 Joint Statement During The Visit of Prime Minister to USA, Prime Minister's Office, Press Information Bureau, 1 October, 2014.

7 DIPP Statement on Bilateral Mechanism for Discussing IPR Issues with USA, Press Information Bureau/ Ministry of Commerce & Industry, 3 October, 2014.

8 Delegation of Powers to National Pharmaceuticals Pricing Authority Stand, Press Information Bureau/ Ministry of Chemicals and Fertilizers, 25 September, 2014.

9 Cancer Drug Price Goes up from Rs 8,000 to Rs 1.08 Lakh, DNA, 1 October, 2014.

issued on 29.05.2014, after a consultation with the Ministry of Law and Justice.[10] The clarification comes in the wake of some media reports which indicated that the Government had withdrawn powers of the NPPA to fix or revise prices under Para 19 of DPCO, 2013.[11]

III. ENABLED EFFICACY & EVERGREENING

It may be recalled here *Novartis Judgment* teleogically interpreted Section 3 (d) of *Patent Act*, 1970 by saying that patents that do not involve real innovation that is not an invention. It is clearly not appreciative of Section 3(d) which states in relevant part that *"the mere discovery of a new form of a known substance which does not result in the enhancement of the known efficacy of that substance"* is not considered to be an *"invention"* under Indian law.[12] In fact, the *Special 301 Report*, 2014 states that the US is worried that section 3(d), as interpreted by the Supreme Court of India, *"may have the effect of limiting the patentability of potentially beneficial innovations"*, which *"would include drugs with fewer side effects, decreased toxicity, improved delivery systems, or temperature or storage stability"*.[13] The foreign pharmaceutical companies are not in agreement with the Supreme Court's tilt towards public health concerns for greater common good. Similarly, compulsory licensing provisions in the Indian Patents law aim to ensure that patent holders do not abuse patents to develop monopolies and thereby charge exorbitant prices which would result in denial of access to medicine at affordable prices to the people of India.

The US lobby might try to exert pressure to modify Section 3(d) India's Patent Act including dilution of patentability criteria, including those enshrined in Section 3(d) of the Indian *Patents Act*, limitations to the use of compulsory licensing for access to patented medicines through generic production, prohibition of the use of pre- and post-grant oppositions. the Indian judicial system would audit and secure the patent rights of foreign entities and introduction of 'data exclusivity', thus extending patent monopolies and delaying the entry of generics and to challenge fraudulent patent claims by foreign MNCs.[14] The government's

---

10 A New Order, The Business Standard, 18 September, 2014.

11 New Drug Era, The Indian Express, 27 September, 2014.

12 Nomani, M.Z.M., 'Enabled Efficacy & Ever Greening in Patenting of Drug: A Case Comment of *Novartis A.G.V. Union of India*', VII(1) *Quest for Justice* 311-331(2015).

13 2014 Special 301 Report, Office of The United States Trade Representative, Executive Office of The President of The US, April 2014.

14 Http://Indiatogether.Org/Modi-Us-Visit-Intellectual-Property-Rights-Patent-Laws-Trips-Government.

clarification on the Indo-US Joint Statement on Intellectual Property Rights issued during Modi's visit to the United States highlights the imperative of maintaining India's original stance on patent laws and refusal to yield to US demands made in its Special 301 Report. The Joint Statement on IPRs read:

> Agreeing on the need to foster innovation in a manner that promotes economic growth and job creation, the leaders committed to establish an annual high-level Intellectual Property (IP) Working Group with appropriate decision-making and technical-level meetings as part of the Trade Policy Forum.

The Joint Statement provoked many social activists and health policy experts to believe that India had succumbed to the US pressure to change its existing IPR policy, which had the provision of compulsory licensing in accordance with World Trade Organization's (WTO) *Trade-Related Intellectual Property Rights (TRIPS) Agreement*. On 3 October, 2014, the Ministry of Commerce and Industry clarified that:

> There already exists the Innovation and Creativity Focus Group in the Trade Policy Forum since 2010 to consult each other no less than twice a year on 'improving intellectual property rights protection and enforcement, enhancing awareness of intellectual property rights, fostering innovation and creativity, and increasing collaboration between US and Indian innovators'. The statement on US-India Trade Policy Forum was signed by the then Commerce and Industries Minister in March 2010 with his US counterpart.

The press release further added

> The joint statement issued now merely reiterates whatever has existed in the earlier Trade Policy Forum. IPR issues are critical for both the countries and India has been repeatedly raising the issue of copyright piracy and misappropriation of traditional knowledge with the US. India has consistently pointed out that the IPR legal regime in India is fully TRIPS compliant and that any issues to be discussed have to be discussed in bilateral forums like Trade Policy Forum. India has refused to be subjected to unilateral action proposed by US under the Special 301 report, an annual report on IPR under US Trade Act. USA agreeing to discuss IPR issues through the bilateral mechanism of the Trade Policy forum is in fact a re-affirmation of India's stand that issues need bilateral discussion and not unilateral action. The statement on the IPR issue will only strengthen the bilateral institutional mechanism.

IV. TRANSNATIONAL RAMIFICATIONS

The institution of intellectual property is important so as to give the original inventor the incentive to create new ideas or to undertake R&D. India is on the *"priority watch list"* of the US as per the *Special 301 Report*, 2014. The *Special 301 Report*, 2014 which by implication entail that India is unable to provide congenial environment to patented products by US companies. It is noteworthy here to enumerate Indian concerns:

1. Reported inadequacies in trade secret protection as well as an increasing incidence of trade secret misappropriation;
2. The continuing challenges of copyright piracy over the Internet; and
3. Market access barriers, including non-transparent, discriminatory or otherwise trade-restrictive measures, which hamper access to healthcare.

This is considered a blow to "generic" medicines manufactured in India. It is estimated that 'anywhere from 10-40 percent of drugs sold in Indian markets are counterfeit and could represent a serious threat to patient health and safety.' The *Special 301 Report*, 2014 underlines concerns regarding market access barriers affecting pharmaceutical and medical device products in India and antithetical to mandate of Section 3(d) of *Patent Act*, 1970.

This clearly indicates that the US is not comfortable with the Supreme Court decision in the *Novartis case* that cleared the way for production of "generic" drugs in India. Indian laws pose several challenges to IP protection even after a product receives a patent. The patent applications can get tied up in costly challenge proceedings for years when a person can easily *"challenge a patent through both pre-grant and post-grant opposition proceedings on any of eleven enumerated grounds, including by citing the same grounds in both pre- and post-grant challenges"* at minimal cost. The Report is explicit on this count:

> The United States urges India to provide greater transparency about its ongoing inter-ministerial process that is considering over a dozen patented medicines as candidates for government-initiated compulsory licenses, and urges India to allow opportunities for input by rights holders, as appropriate, with respect to decisions concerning compulsory licenses.

It is well known that prior to *TRIPS Agreement*, 1995 the *Drug Policy* of 1978 and the process patent system that came into being after the enactment of the *Patents Act*, 1970, encouraged the growth of the domestic pharmaceutical industry. India's IPR policy is TRIPS-compliant. India chose to use the health safeguards available in the TRIPS Agreement, to protect the interests of Indian patients as well as millions of people living in other developing countries. The law requires that patented inventions are available to the public at affordable prices as well as obligates the patent holders to work their patents in India.

V. TRADITIONAL KNOWLEDGE POLICY

The people in the unorganized sector in India tacit knowledge bases is vast repository of wisdom and endowed with tremendous innovative potential and rich experience of turning trash into treasure.[15] The tacit knowledge bases have immense cumulative value in fostering social and economic developments.[16] There is glaring evidence that *National Innovation Foundation (NIF)*, Ahmadabad, has identified more than 170,000 innovations in traditional knowledge practices. This change in perspective is not grounded in any analysis of existing efforts to protect indigenous knowledge. The Geographical Indications law has been in force for 17 years, and government initiatives to increase registrations have been reasonably successful. The *Biological Diversity Act*, 2001 is of similar vintage, but has only been enforced with seriousness in the present decade. The *ABS Guidelines*, 2014 in the backdrop of *Nagoya Protocol*, 2011 has also strengthened the TK Framework. Have these laws resulted in substantial benefits to any community which originated a form of traditional knowledge? Has legal protection spurred the regeneration of traditional knowledge?

In the absence of concrete evidence that either objective has been satisfied, it is unclear why India should carve out larger property protections in this domain. Organizations like the *World Intellectual Property Organization (WIPO)* would probably be happy if we did; they want us to believe there is a pot of gold at the end of that rainbow. But there is no gold, so we will not find it. What rich countries know is that our quest to protect traditional knowledge will ensure that we remain enthralled by the IP myth, thereby allowing their own IP to lucratively flourish in poor countries around the world. However this body is not a talismanic cure for 'new innovation paradigm' reflected in *STI Policy*, 2013 but desired to contain new sets of concurrent paraphernalia for a innovation eco-system support. It is apprehended that the 'formalization' of the informal sector without understating 'indigenous specifics' might prove to be counterproductive. Thus there is urgent need of leverages

[15] Konte, A. and Ndong, M., *Afr. J. Sci.Technol. Innov, Dev.*, 2012, 4(3): 61–97.

[16] Daniels, S., *Making Do: Innovation in Kenya's Informal Economy*, Analogue Digital Department for Infrastructure and Economic Co-Operation, 2010.

for a meaningful protection of tacit knowledge corpus.The government's IPR policy seems to lack a holistic understanding of the complexities attached with "traditional" knowledge (to be free and open for public access) vs. some kind of privately locked knowledge capital.[17]

VI. POLICY ON PATENT LAW

The National IPR Policy makes it clear that we will not roll back any aspects of Indian patent law, which was amended in 2005 to comply with World Trade Organization (WTO) regime. The Indian patent law extols a philosophy of minimalism – less is more. With the new IPR policy, this minimalism is now inexplicably shrouded in a cloak of maximalism, the lesson apparently having been revised to mean more is more. The most significant achievement of the 2005 amendment to our patent law was a high bar for innovation, thereby restoring sanity and balance to a system run amok: it was designed to reward real innovation, rather than the tweaks pharmaceutical companies the world over use to justify extending their monopolies – and their high prices. The Indian system of supporting both innovation and access to medicines was an innovation in law-making, and after a long, hard, slog, culminating in a Supreme Court ruling in April 2013 that ratified our law, the world sat up and took notice. Later that year, South Africa announced its decision to amend the country's patent law along the lines of Indian law, and Brazil launched a bill supported with exactly the same intent. To follow through, what these countries require is the unwavering confidence of the Indian government in its own patent law. Unfortunately, you would have to read between the lines to find that confidence in this policy. This is a shame, for we could have used our patent law to take a bold, strong leadership position across the world.[18] The main concern that had been expressed during the policy formation period was that the policy might tilt the country's approach to IP towards a maximalist position, undermining its social and economic development needs, notably the goal of providing access to affordable medicines. The pharmaceutical companies used the opportunity to influence the policy in their favour to undermine public interest safeguards in *Patent Act*, 1970.[19]

---

[17] Deep Anshu Mohan on 0 8/0 8/2016 • 1 Comment Social Utility Needs to be Part of The Debate on Intellectual Property Rights in India, THE WIRE, 20.12.2016].

[18] Achal Prabhala & Sudhir Krishnaswamy, Patently A Missed Opportunity, The Hindu Daily].

[19] K.M.Gopakumar, Why New IPR Policy is Inadequate: Pressure from us is Unstated Reason', 51(21),*Economic&Politicalweekly*, 21May, 2016 [Http://Www.Epw.In/Journal/2016/21/Commentary/Why-New-Ipr-Policy-Inadequate.Html?0=Ip_Login_ No_ Cache%3d6e2657f38faaa85e21cc30c52065000f].

VII. SCIENCE, TECHNOLOGY & INNOVATION POLICY

Before we delineate on the legal dynamics of *IPR Policy*, 2016, it is relevant to see from legal parlance the strides made by *Science, Technology and Innovation (STI) Policy*, 2013 in inculcating innovation culture in India. The goal of *STI Policy*, 2013 is to foster scientific researches and development, technological inventions and innovation in organized and unorganized sectors of knowledge.[20] In this context it is appropriate to refer Indian's *STI Policy*, 2013 which favour of 'formalized' lab science approach in contrast to informal learning and informal economy model.[21] The *STI Policy* maintains that the policy document is solely developed to support 'structural innovation' and there is no mention of how to transform the whole innovation system.[22] The pronouncements of *Science, Technology and Innovation Policy*, 2013[23] lays greater thrust on innovation, establishing research institutions and creating a robust national innovation system(NIS) for formal and informal sectors of knowledge.[24] The *STI Policy* aims to position India among the top-five scientific powers in the world by 2020.[25] 'Science, technology and innovation for the people' and in the 'new innovation paradigm' reflected in the policy necessitates a congenial environment and paraphernalia for its organic growth. For a vigorous innovation ecosystem it is incumbent to develop informal knowledge system.[26] The *STI Policy* needs leverages to recognize and harness the innovative potential of the informal knowledge sector and economy.[27] It is apprehended that the excessive 'formalization' of *STI*

---

20 Bhaduri, S. and Sheikh, F. A., Community Innovations in The Informal Sector: Study of Kashmir Pashmina Shawls. Paper Presented in Globelics Academy, Rio De Janerio, Brazil, 2012.

21 Lundvall, B.Å., National Systems of Innovation: Towards A Theory of Innovation and Interactive Learning, Pinter, London, 1992.

22 Abrol, D., 'New Science, Technology and Innovation Policy', XLVIII(9) *Economic & Political Weekly*, 10-13 (2013).

23 See *India Science & Technology*, Vol 3, CSIRNISTADS, 2015 for The Details of The Co-Evolving Scenario in Respect of The Generation and use of IP in India.

24 Gault, F., Innovation Strategies for A Global Economy: Development, Implementation, Measurement and Management, Edward Elgar, UK and IDRC, Ottawa, Canada, 2010.

25 Mani, Sunil., (2014): "Doesn't India Already Have An IPR Policy?" *Economic & Political Weekly*, Vol 49, No 47, Pp 10-13.

26 Jaffe, Adam B & Josh Lerner,*Innovation and Its Discontents: How Our Broken Patent System is Endangering Innovation and Progress and What to do About It* (2007) Princeton: Princeton University Press.

27 Becker, K.F., Fact Finding Study: The Informal Economy, Swedish International Development Cooperation Agency, 2004, Pp. 3-52.

Policy the informal sector without understating it's 'specifics' might prove to be counterproductive.[28] India innovation model has to come out of ponds and shells of 'V. Bush model of innovation', 1945 and 'linear model of innovation'.[29] Thus knowledge generated in the informal sector especially tacit and localized by 94% of India's working population is completely excluded from the purview of this policy report. Thus in sludge hammer manner the rich innovative potential of subaltern knowledge are ignored in innovation policy making.[30] The *STI Policy* has no satisfying solutions to such vital questions as to how to incubate, develop and generate value from such grass root innovations?

VIII. IPR POLICY

Before we actually liberated from the enigma of *STI Policy*, 2013 and its consequential fall outs of India's innovation laws in infancy, the government pronounced *IPR Policy*, 2016. In its vision statement, the policy necessitates the transformation of knowledge into an intellectual asset to accelerate economic development and to make further advancements in science and technology, and arts and culture, thereby facilitating knowledge dissemination.[31] The objectives of the government's new *National Intellectual Property Rights (IPR) Policy*, 2016[32] is strengthening of the legal and legislative framework of IP and reinforcing the enforcement and adjudicatory mechanisms for Intellectual Property (IP) infringements. The policy seeks to address the issue of the enforcement of IPRs, presently thought of as a formidable challenge by Indian as well as foreign enterprises. The policy acknowledges the importance of maintaining a predictable and an efficient IPR regime and attempts to streamline the processes. Some of the measures provided by the policy include a five pronged strategy to revamp IP law and enforcement regimes are as under:

---

[28] Sheikh, F.A., 'Science, 'Technology and Innovation Policy 2013 of India and Informal Sector Innovations', 106(1) *Current Science*, 21-23 (10 JANUARY 2014).

[29] Godin, B., 'The Linear Model of Innovation: The Historical Construction of An Analytical Framework', 31(6) *Sci. Technol. Hum. Val.*, 639-667 (2006).

[30] Chesbrough, H., Open Innovation: The New Imperative for Creating and Profiting from Technology, Harvard University Press, Boston, 2003.

[31] The Policy Document is Available in The Website of DIPP, URL : Http://Dipp.Gov.In/English/Schemes/Intellectual_Property_Rights/National_IPR_Policy_ 12.05.2016. Pdf (Accessed On 8 June 2016).

[32] "National Intellectual Property Rights Policy," Ministry of Commerce and Industry, Depart. of Industrial Promotion, Http://Dipp.Gov.In/English/Schemes/Intellectual_ Property_Rights/National_IPR_Policy_12.05.2016.Pdf.

1. Modernization and standardization of infrastructure of IP offices
2. Enhancement of transparency and efficiency in the enforcement of IPRs
3. Establishment of Department of Industrial Policy & Promotion (DIPP) as a nodal agency to streamline processes and ensuring improved services to users
4. Establishment of a Cell for IPR Promotion and Management (CIPAM) to facilitate promotion, creation and commercialization of IP assets
5. Improvement in the adjudicatory mechanism to combat IPR infringements.

Although the legislative framework provides adequate legal remedies by way of injunctions and penal and pecuniary damages, the lack of a coherent enforcement mechanism has resulted in widespread availability of counterfeit products. According to a FICCI-CASCADE Report 'the total loss of revenue to the government due to the sale of counterfeit products was pegged at approximately USD 6 billion in Financial Year (FY) 2013-14. The policy seeks to usher in multiple reforms in the enforcement framework to combat the sale of counterfeit products.'[33]

In consonance with strategic outlook, the IPR Policy is underpinned in these seven professed objectives. They are as under:

i) IPR awareness: outreach and promotion-to create public awareness about the economic, social and cultural benefits of IPRs among all sections of society;

ii) Generation of IPRs: to stimulate the generation of IPRs laws;

iii) Legal and legislative framework: to have strong and effective intellectual property rights laws, which balance the interest of rights owners with larger public interest

iv) Administration and management—to modernize and strengthen service-oriented IPR administration;

v) Commercialization of IPRs—get value for IPRs through commercialization;

[33] Illicit Trade Leading to Alarming Revenue Loss: FICCI-CASCADE Report, *The Hindu*, Published on 15 October 2015.

vi) Enforcement and adjudication—to strengthen the enforcement and adjudicatory mechanisms for combating IPR infringements; and

vii) Human capital development—to strengthen and expand human resources, institutions and capacities for teaching, training, research and skill building in IPRs.

A logical analysis of the seven professed objectives can be broadly be culled out into three categories:

i) Those dealing with popularization and strengthening the administrative machinery for dealing with IPR issues (objectives 1, 4 and 7);

ii) Those dealing with the generation and commercialization of IPRs (objectives 2 and 5); and

iii) Those dealing with legal aspects, enforcement, and adjudication (objectives 3 and 6).

Of the above three categories, the third category the more substantive which relates to legal and legislative framework and effective intellectual property rights laws which can balance the interest of rights owners with larger public interest and germane to this paper.

IX. LEGAL IMPLICATIONS OF POLICIES

Whereas Although the legislative framework on IP protection is compliant with the *Trade-Related Aspects of Intellectual Property Rights* (TRIPS) regime a decade ago, the *IPR* Policy has attempted to provide a cohesive road map, covering the wide-ranging aspects of the IP value chain *i.e.*, from IPR generation to commercialization. The *IPR Policy*, 2016 rightly identifies the growing importance of IP in a knowledge economy and also aims to address several IPR challenges during the generation, protection and commercialization stages of IP. The IPR Policy endeavours for effective legislative framework of intellectual property laws which can balance the interest of IP holders and public interest. This entails that extending the term of protection, expanding the scope of IP protectable subject matter, increased penalties, facilitating enforcement, expediting litigation, or enhancing the quality of IP. The policy in prescription and policy in implementation is extremely significant in revamping *Copyright Act*, 1957; *Patents Act*, 1970, 1997 and 2005; *Trade Marks Act*, 1999; *Design Act*, 2000; *Geographical Indications of Goods Act*, 2001; *Protection of Plant Varieties and Farmers' Rights Act*, 2001; *Semiconductor Integrated Circuits Layout Design Act*, 2001 and *Biological Diversity Act*, 2002. The onset of IP law reform will meaningfully forge new vistas in inventiveness and innovation. The slew of reform under the exuberance of IPR Policy will have significant impact on pharmaceuticals, software, electronics and communications, seeds, environmental goods, renewable energy, agricultural and health biotechnology, information and communication. In addition to legal adjustments in key statutes of IP law, the IPR Policy recommends amendments to the *Cinematography Act*, 1952 to fix criminal liability clause for infringement and mutilation of music and films. This may result in undermining the limitations and exceptions that have been provided in Sections 51 and 52 of the *Copyright Act*, 1957 to ensure *doctrine of fair use* of copyrighted works. The *IPR Policy* also recommends further studies and research on the interplay between IP laws and other laws to remove ambiguities and inconsistencies. However, the policy does not make it clear in case of inconsistency between IP law and other law, which law is going to prevail. The *IPR Policy* also dovetails IP law and competition law and the formulation of guidelines on administration and endorsement of patents. These measures threaten the dilution of stringent requirements of and biodiversity diversity related rights under *sui generis* system and access and benefit sharing[34] contained in the *Convention on Biological Diversity*, 1992, *Bonn Guidelines*, 2001, *Nagoya Protocol*, 2009 and India's *Conservation of Biological Diversity Act*, 2002.[35] The policy has attempted to promote a holistic framework to enable the stakeholders to not only realize the full potential of IP but aims to bring in a paradigm shift on the perception of IP. It foster an IP culture, which is likely to enable innovators to realize the commercial potential of IPRs, thereby facilitating wealth creation, knowledge dissemination, employment opportunities and business development on the pattern of Organization for Economic Co-operation and Development (OECD), 'knowledge based capital'.[36]

X. LEGAL ADJUSTMENT & COMPATIBILITIES

The *IPR Policy*, 2016 recommends a review of existing laws with the purpose of updating and improving these and to remove anomalies and inconsistencies. This would expose India to the pressure to undertake

---

34 Nomani, M.Z.M., 'Biological Diversity, IPR &Sustainable Development: A Critical Appraisal of Access & Benefit Sharing Models of U.S., Australia & India',VI911&12) *International Journal of Environmental Consumerism*, 40-55 (2010).

35 Gopakumar, K. M., 'Why New IPR Policy Is Inadequate Pressure from US is Unstated Reason', LI (21) *Economic & Political Weekly* 18-19 (May 21, 2016).

36 Http://Indianexpress.Com/Article/Business/Business-Others/Intellectual-Property-Rights-New-Policy-May-Power-Rd-National-Growth-2804419/

"TRIPS-plus" obligations and limits public interest safeguards during free trade agreement negotiations. The policy has to be seen in the context of the pressure from the United States (US) government under the country's Special 301 law.[37] Contrary to the statement of the finance minister that the *IPR Policy* does not recommend any changes in the existing law, but the new policy does open up the door for changes in the law. To this end, it also attempts to address the anomalies in the existing framework and has taken significant measures to balance the interests of individuals' rights with the public interest. Thus the policy may be used as a springboard by stakeholders to take proactive measures to transform their innovation capabilities.

It would be interesting here to make an effort to understand the economics of intellectual property, its impact on emerging market structures and highlight the limitations of legal jurisprudence on it.[38] It is also critical to question the envisioned optimal regulation of "intellectual property" from the standpoint of an economics of law that draws parallels between intellectual and tangible property based on its' usability, while approaching concepts of innovation, public goods and marginal cost pricing with strong evidence. It should also be viewed in the context of the *Trans-Pacific Partnership (TPP)* gaining in favour amongst Ministry of Commerce and Industry officials. The partnership has several TRIPS (Trade-Related Aspects of Intellectual Property Rights)-plus provisions. It is also being argued that it is not possible for India to keep out of mega regionals. This implies that the *IPR Policy* adopts an IP maximalist agenda of maximum possible incentive for IP owners to drive the future course of development of industry, publicly-funded research and development organizations educational institutions and government departments.[39]

XI. KNOWLEDGE MANAGEMENT & PUBLIC POLICY

The *IPR Policy*, 2016 ostensibly designed to strengthen India's IPR regime by fostering creativity and innovation. It clearly spells out the interests of intellectual property owners, global knowledge asset above

---

[37] The Government's IPR Policy Needs More Clarity Https://Thewire.In/57318/Thegovernmentspolicyonintellectualpropertyrightsneedsmoreclarity/3/6osner05.Pdf)].

[38] Posner, Richard., *Intellectual Property: The Law And Economic Approach*,(2005) (Http://People.Ischool.Berkeley.Edu/~Hal/Courses/Strattech09/Lectures/IP/Papers/P12/20/2016.

[39] Abrol, Dinesh., 'The Wrong Incentive: The National Intellectual Property Rights Policy Must Be Opposed, LI(18) 24 *Economic & Political Weekly*, 24 (JUNE 11, 2016).

that of public interest. Though some of the salubrious provisions of IPR Policy are laudable, it is clear that the policy objectives are not evidence-based and are tailor made to suit the requirements of the northern industrial developments.[40] From the legal stand point, the policy does not address the question of how gains from a stronger IP would be distributed between corporate and community in equitable manner. The policy framework is cloaked with a one-size-fits-all approach. This is eventually going to disturb the fine balance between public interest and IP that the courts and laws have struggled to maintain after the adoption of TRIPS Agreement.[41] It is critical for the government to hone out strategies for a suitable legislative and regulatory framework which could allow stakeholders to secure their intellectual assets and realize the commercial potential of their innovation in multi stake holding manner.[42]

The IPR Policy in its pursuit to innovation encourages the privatization of indigenous knowledge. The IPR policy was an opportunity to embrace the spirit of India's time tested with an emphasis on indigenous innovation, access and equity. Unfortunately IPR Policy egregiously fails to provide impetus to innovation culture by doing tokenism to inventiveness in research and development and their public accessibility for greater common good. India endeavours to recalibrate knowledge economy without reflecting on the complexities of knowledge society and overcoming systematically institutional deficit for generating innovative policies. One of the fundamental flaws is that our knowledge society does not differentiate between information, knowledge and heuristics. By confusing information and knowledge, we lack critical thinking and meta languages that go into the definition of knowledge. This central confusion permeated in *Knowledge Commission Report*, 2006 which equated the knowledge revolution to the education revolution and confused technology with epistemology.

XII. KNOWLEDGE AS METAPHORE OF POWER

In this context, it becomes all the more important to discover the Knowledge and power relationship in public policy diametric. A brilliant

40 Sunil Mani., 'New IPR Policy 2016: Not Based on Evidence', XXVIII(38) *Economic & Political Weekly*, September 17, 2016.

41 Abrol, Dinesh., 'Who Will Gain from The National IPRS Policy?: Policy Brief', Institute For Studies in Industrial Development, New Delhi.

42 KPMG, 'National Intellectual Property Rights Policy: Analysis In The Light Of Inclusive Innovation', [Risk Consulting]August 2016KPMG.Com/In

backgrounder is provided by Shiv Vishvanathan as he believes that it is necessary to understand the new relations between knowledge and power.[43] Linking the two is the field called policy. It also creates two kinds of intellectuals, the policy intellectual and the public intellectual. According to him the distinction is critical. The policy intellectual serves as an extension of the state which strictly cater to policy interests of the state or of corporations. A public intellectual is a figure who provides a wide-ranging critique of policy, and looks more creatively at the relation between knowledge and power.

> The policy intellectual usually takes his expertise for granted. The public intellectual questions the nature of expertise, probing deeper into the ethics and genealogy of ideas. In the post-liberalisation period, India has had more policy than public intellectuals with think tanks like the Centre for Policy Research and the Observer Research Foundation dominating the scene.[44]

The think tanks and their attempts to formulate policy raise the whole question of the relation between knowledge and the public sphere. Policy formulation has not really articulated the views of the public sphere. In fact, the first challenges to policy came from the social movements, and from civil society which identified policy and experts as mere extensions to the state. This is substantiated by the movements that grew around the Bhopal gas victims, the Narmada dam; the narratives of displacement and dispossession raised deep questions about policy and expertise, and about the public consumption of policy. Thus, Shiv Nathan is right in his public policy perception when he asserts that:

> Governance is now seen no longer as a statist exercise and the question of governmentality involves civil society articulating new epistemologies, notions of citizenship, ideas about the democratization of knowledge and the assessment of public policy impacts. Governance has become tied to democracy, with the public sphere becoming crucial and public policy a critical field.[45]

The field of the future belongs to the fact as to what makes public policy exciting, protean and potentially inventive is the contested nature of the public sphere. It is anchored in a diversity of perspectives which challenges the dominance of one subject. The new demands of democracy

---

43 Shiv Vishvanathan, 'A New Public Policy for A New India', *The Hindu Daily: New Delhi Edition*, Monday April 6, 2015 Editorial Page.

44 *Ibid.*

45 *Ibid.*

entail an enlightened broadening of public policy perspective. It is not out of context to exemplify the public sphere debating of biotechnology of Genetically Modified (GM) crops (bt. brinjal) initiated by Mr. Jairam Ramesh in 2010 multi stake holding public consultations. It is under this backdrop the book on *Intellectual Property & Public Policy* subsumes IPR policy in shaping IP laws and governance in India. A collection of 12 essays reflect on the core and periphery of IPR diametric and discourse. The volume cannot be epitomized rather to be taken a modest attempt to underline the epistemology and heuristics of IPR. I hope the contributions of the book is to enlarge the amplitude of public policy in IP arena in understanding deeply the tacit and explicit knowledge system of India legally ordained and fashioned by legislature and courts alike.

Aligarh **Zafar Mahfooz Nomani**

31.5.2017

List of Contributors

Dr. Anis Ahmad presently serving as Assistant Professor Department of Law, School for Legal Studies, Babasaheb Bhimrao Ambedkar University (A Central University) Lucknow. Before that he has worked as Lecturer in Institute of Law and Research, Faridabad (Haryana) from 2002 to 2008. He did his Master Degree L.L.M from Aligarh Muslim University Aligarh and obtained Ph.D. Degree from Faculty of Law, M.D University, Rohtak, Haryana. His areas of interest are: Environmental Law, Agriculture Law, Intellectual Property Law and Jurisprudence. Dr. Ahmad has more than 13 years of teaching and research experience and published several research papers in reputed national and international journals. He has authored a book entitled Agro-Environmental Sustainability and Intellectual Property Rights, Mittal Publications, New Delhi (2016). He has guided 25 L.L.M Dissertations on various environmental and other issues. He is a member of the advisory board of Clean up & Recycle for Environment (CURE) Jaipur (Rajasthan) a reputed NGO working on E-waste. *Email: anisbbau@gmail.com*

Professor (Dr.) Autar Krishen Koul is an eminent scholar of international trade law and intellectual property. He has not only taught the subject of International Trade Law but also appeared as legal counsel in the Supreme Court of India in vexed matters related to International Trade Law. He has the credit of teaching and research the subject of International Trade Law and Business Law in the law schools of USA also. Professor Koul has published more than 13 books on various issues of law including WTO and GATT. Professor Koul has been visiting scholar of various universities of India and abroad. Professor Koul has published more than 40 articles in national and international journals besides attending 100 conferences and paper presentations. He served as Dean of Campus Law Centre University of Delhi and Vice Chancellor of National Law University, Jodhpur and National University of Legal Studies & Research, Ranchi

Dr. Azim Pathan is a Senior Assistant Professor and Program Head for Taxation, Banking and International Law Programs, in University of Petroleum and Energy Studies, College of Legal Studies, Dehradun, U.K. He has obtained four gold medals in B.A.LL.B.

and L.L.M. Degree from Amravati University and RTM Nagpur University respectively. He has been awarded with Ph.D. on the topic of "Emerging Concept of Global Warming at International Level and Effect of Climate Change on Environment: A Critical Study with Reference to UNFCCC, 1992". He is offering and teaching the subjects like Environmental Law in Energy Sector, Public Law and Administrative Law in College of Legal Studies, UPES. *Email: abpathan@ddn.upes.ac.in / pathanazim9@gmail.com.*

Dr. Faizanur Rahman specializes in Intellectual Property Rights and serving as Assistant Professor at Faculty of Law, Jamia Millia Islamia, New Delhi. After he earned his Degree in Law at the Law Faculty of the Aligarh Muslim University in Aligarh in 2007, he continued with his studies in AMU (LL.M. in 2007) besides completing Doctoral studies in Aligarh (Ph.D. in 2014). Dr. Rahman has to his credit several research papers in Trade Secrets Law, Competition Law and IPRs. His research work is cited in national and international reputed refereed journals. While Dr. Rahman is, at the core, a scholar, his work has also achieved remarkable acceptance by practitioners across multiple fields. *Email: faizan.faizylaw@ gmail.com*

Professor (Dr.) Gurusharan Varandani did his LL.B and LL.M. from campus Law centre of Delhi University and was member of Teaching Faculty of campus Law centre of Delhi University. Subsequently he joined Law faculty of Kurukshetra University in the year 1975 and elevated to the position of Professor, Chairman and Dean of Law faculty of Kurukshetra University. Dr. Varandani also served as Professor; Dean & Head of the P.G. Department of Law of Sambhalpur University, Sambhalpur for one year in the year 1990. Dr. Varandani has the privilege of being Director of Dogra Law College, Jammu from September 2005 to September 2008. Dr. Varandani contributed in the field of Labour Laws, Intellectual Property Laws, Copyright and Neighboring rights, Laws protecting disabled persons, Defamations etc. Besides this he has been visiting professor of many Universities and Institutes including ILI, New Delhi and Dean, Faculty of Law Jagan Nath University, Jaipur.

Professor (Dr.) Imtiaz Ghulam Ahmed specializes in Jurisprudence, Corporate Law, Human Rights and Family Law. He did his LL.M. from U.K. he served as visiting professor at National Law University, Bangalore and developed family law courses and alleviated to dean faculty of law Calcutta University, Calcutta. He is now serving as a Professor of law at the Department of Law and Dean of School of Social Sciences in Sikkim Central University, Sikkim *Email: igahmedlaw@cus.ac.in*

Mr. Justice Ram Prakash Sethi, Born on 7th July, 1937 and started practice in Law in 1961. Remained a Special Public Prosecutor in the cases under the Enemy Agents Ordinance and also served as an Additional Advocate General of the Jammu and Kashmir State in 1976. He had been the Standing Counsel of the Union of India in the Jammu Wing of the High Court. He was appointed Additional Judge of the Jammu and Kashmir High Court on 30.5.86 and permanent Judge on 5.8.87. He then transferred to Punjab & Haryana High Court on 18.10.93. Later he was appointed Chief Justice Karnataka High Court on 29.6.96. And finally, he was appointed as a Judge of Supreme Court of India on 8.1.1999 and retired on 6.7.2002. Author of commentaries on the Hindu Marriage Act and Editor of Urdu Weekly Shagaf besides being the Regional Editor of more than 12 Law Magazines published from various parts of the country. He also participated in various Seminars, Symposiums and authored articles on burning topics relating to law.

Dr. Raman Mittal. He has been working as Associate Professor, Campus Law Centre, Faculty of Law, University of Delhi. He went to Germany and worked as a Visiting Faculty at the Max Planck Institute for Intellectual Property, Competition and Tax Laws, Munich, Germany. He also worked at the Indian Law Institute, New Delhi, first as Assistant Professor and then as Associate Professor. Indian Law Institute is the premiere centre for legal research and teaching in India. Main job responsibilities included research and teaching in the field of cyber and Intellectual Property laws and editing of the Journal of Indian Law Institute. He has also worked as Research Associate with Cyber and Space Telecom Inc. which is an international legal research and consulting organisation. He also worked as an intern in the Cyber & Space Law division of 'Winthrop Stimson Putnam & Roberts'- an international law firm at its Washington, DC office. *Email: mittalraman@gmail.com*

Professor (Dr.) S. K. Verma (S. J. D. from Harvard University, L.L.M. from Banaras Hindu University and University of California, Berkeley) is former professor in Faculty of Law, University of Delhi. She has been Director of Indian Law Institute, Delhi (1998-2001), Dean and Head of Faculty of Law, University of Delhi (1997-98). She has lectured at numerous universities, including Banaras Hindu University (1968-75), Delhi University (1975-87), University of Zambia, Lusaka (1982-1985), S. P. Mahila University, Tirupati (1993), Max-Plank-Institut fur Patenntrecht, Munich, Germany (1994 and 1997), University of Alberta and University of Calgary, Canada

(1998) and University of Washington (2001). She has more than 35 years of teaching and research experience. She has authored/edited several books and published more than 75 research articles in the areas of public international law.

Dr. S.Z. Amani was educated at Aligarh Muslim University by completing his L.L.B. (Hons.) and L.L.M. (Commercial Law) in 1980. He was associated with the Faculty of Law, Aligarh Muslim University as Lecturer since 1984. He later joined the Faculty of Law of the Jamia Millia Islamia, New Delhi in 1990.At present Dr. Amani is serving as Associate Professor. He obtained his Ph. D. degree from Jamia Millia Islamia, New Delhi. During his 28 years of teaching experience, Mr. Amani published dozens of articles on numerous legal issues in various law journals, magazines and gazettes. He authored Justice Hidayatullah on Commercial Laws. He is versatile teacher of International Economic Institutions, International Trade Law, and Intellectual Property. Apart from his academic pursuits, Dr. Amani also meaningfully contributed to the corporate life of the university in various administrative and supervisory capacities. *Email: amani_sz@yahoo.com*

Professor (Dr.) S.S. Hasnat Azmi is a well known Commercial Law specialist and contributed significantly in the field of Sale of Goods and Evolution and Development of Consumer Law. He happens to be an erudite scholar and his seminal contribution lies in writing case comment on leading cases of commercial law decided by the Supreme Court and the High Courts. Professor Dr. Azmi has been a former Chairman and Dean, Faculty of Law, A.M.U., Aligarh.

Professor Zafar Mahfooz Nomani specializes in Ecology Law and Intellectual Property Rights and engaged in teaching and research since last 22 years. He authored five books and published more than 100 research papers in prestigious refereed and peer reviewed journals covering diverse areas of environmental and intellectual property and corporate laws. *Email: zafarnomani@rediffmail.com.*

Section-I
Intellectual Property and Public Policy Discourse

1

Intellectual Property and Public Policy Under TRIPS Agreement and Beyond

Autar Krishen Koul

I. PUBLIC POLICY CONCERNS

The working of the *Trade Related Aspects of Intellectual Property Rights Agreement (TRIPS) Agreement,* 1995 along with World Intellectual Property Organization (WIPO) and the jurisprudence developed for the last twenty years is a testimony to the fact that although TRIPS is geared to promote the protection of intellectual property rights internationally, yet some controversial public policy issues need to be addressed and solutions devised for addressing these public policy issues otherwise there is a possibility of seeing the demise of *TRIPS Agreement* or sidetracking it by some other methods which may not be conducive for maximizing the welfare of the international trading community. As all of us know that intellectual property and international trade are mutually inclusive and the minimum standards set forth in the *TRIPS Agreement* are economically value oriented. The trade offs among and between the members of the WTO need to be balanced on an even keel, otherwise the possibility of camaflouging the *TRIPS Agreement* and the attendant jurisprudence becomes real. The *TRIPS Agreement* addresses seven categories of IP rights such as; Copyright and related rights; Patents; Trademarks and Service marks; Geographical Indications; Undisclosed Information or Trade Secrets; Industrial Designs ; and Layout Designs of Integrated Circuits and read with other WIPO Treaties obligates the members of the World Trade Organization (WTO) to reduce distortions and impediments to international trade by taking into account the effective and adequate protection of intellectual property rights as well as the procedures for the enforcement should not become barriers to international trade. The *TRIPS Agreement* also recognizes the need to cater to the special needs of the developing and least developed countries.

II. NATURE OF PROTECTION

A cursory look at the various IP rights in the *TRIPS Agreement* makes it abundantly clear that all the rights are tradable and trade specific having being recognized and legally protected and universally enforceable in public policy realm. Copyright for instance recognizes originality and tangibility as key concepts in literary works. Dramas, choreography, pictorial, graphic and audiovisual works, musical works (including sound recordings), and architectural works and computer programmes TRIPS excludes moral rights of author[1] yet includes neighbouring rights[2] and

---

1 Article 9.1 of *Agreement on Trade-Related Aspects of Intellectual Property Rights,* 1995 entails: Members shall comply with Articles 1 through 21 of the Berne Convention (1971) and the Appendix thereto. However, Members shall not have rights or obligations under this Agreement in respect of the rights conferred under Article 6*bis* of that Convention or of the rights derived there from.

2 Article 14 of *Agreement on Trade-Related Aspects of Intellectual Property Rights,* 1995 provides: *Protection of Performers, Producers of Phonograms (Sound Recordings) and Broadcasting Organizations*: (1) In respect of a fixation of their performance on a phonogram, performers shall have the possibility of preventing the following acts when undertaken without their authorization: the fixation of their unfixed performance and the reproduction of such fixation. Performers shall also have the possibility of preventing the following acts when undertaken without their authorization: the broadcasting by wireless means and the communication to the public of their live performance. (2) Producers of phonograms shall enjoy the right to authorize or prohibit the direct or indirect reproduction of their phonograms.(3) Broadcasting organizations shall have the right to prohibit the following acts when undertaken without their authorization: the fixation, the reproduction of fixations, and the rebroadcasting by wireless means of broadcasts, as well as the communication to the public of television broadcasts of the same. Where Members do not grant such rights to broadcasting organizations, they shall provide owners of copyright in the subject matter of broadcasts with the possibility of preventing the above acts, subject to the provisions of the Berne Convention (1971). (4) The provisions of Article 11 in respect of computer programs shall apply *mutatis mutandis* to producers of phonograms and any other right holders in phonograms as determined in a Member's law. If on 15 April 1994 a Member has in force a system of equitable remuneration of right holders in respect of the rental of phonograms, it may maintain such system provided that the commercial rental of phonograms is not giving rise to the material impairment of the exclusive rights of reproduction of right holders. (5) The term of the protection available under this Agreement to performers and producers of phonograms shall last at least until the end of a period of 50 years computed from the end of the calendar year in which the fixation was made or the performance took place. The term of protection granted pursuant to paragraph 3 shall last for at least 20 years from the end of the calendar year in which the broadcast took place. (6) Any Member may, in relation to the rights conferred under paragraphs 1,2 and 3, provide for conditions, limitations, exceptions and reservations to the extent permitted by the Rome Convention. However, the provisions of Article 18 of the Berne Convention (1971) shall also apply, *mutatis mutandis,* to the rights of performers and producers of phonograms in phonograms.

no registration is required. Inventions of all kinds can have patent protection both in products and processes in all field of technology, provided they are new, involve inventive step and are capable of industrial application. Patents are territorial and by way of monopoly confer the right of exploitation of the patent holder for a limited period once the country where the application of patent has been filed, grants the patent. International Conventions such as *Paris Convention*, 1968 and *Patent Cooperation Treaty*, 1970 amended from time to time help in filing a patent in more than one jurisdiction by filing a single application and obtaining a priority date. Trademarks are defined as any sign, or any combination of signs, capable of distinguishing goods or services of one undertaking from those of other undertakings, which are capable of constituting a trademark. Trademarks include personal names, letters, numerals, figurative elements, and combination of such signs. The purpose of this protection is to safeguard the integrity of products and to prevent product confusion, and unfair competition (passing off). Geographical indications are those indications, which identify goods as originating in the territory of a member of WTO, or region or locality in that territory, where a given quality reputation or other characteristics of the good is essentially attributable to its geographical origin.[3] Members are obligated to prevent the misuse of geographical indications. Trade Secrets or Undisclosed Information are rights such as formula, pattern, compilation, progamme, method, or technique, process, or device that have economic value and with regard to which reasonable efforts have been made to keep it

[3] Article 22 of *Agreement on Trade-Related Aspects of Intellectual Property Rights,* 1995 provides: *Protection of Geographical Indications*: (1) Geographical indications are, for the purposes of this Agreement, indications which identify a good as originating in the territory of a Member, or a region or locality in that territory, where a given quality, reputation or other characteristic of the good is essentially attributable to its geographical origin. (2) In respect of geographical indications, Members shall provide the legal means for interested parties to prevent: (a) the use of any means in the designation or presentation of a good that indicates or suggests that the good in question originates in a geographical area other than the true place of origin in a manner which misleads the public as to the geographical origin of the good; (b) any use which constitutes an act of unfair competition within the meaning of Article 10*bis* of the Paris Convention (1967). (3) A Member shall, *ex officio* if its legislation so permits or at the request of an interested party, refuse or invalidate the registration of a trademark which contains or consists of a geographical indication with respect to goods not originating in the territory indicated, if use of the indication in the trademark for such goods in that Member is of such a nature as to mislead the public as to the true place of origin. (4) The protection under paragraphs 1, 2 and 3 shall be applicable against a geographical indication which, although literally true as to the territory, region or locality in which the goods originate, falsely represents to the public that the goods originate in another territory.

confidential. For marketing of pharmaceutical or of agricultural chemical products, which utilizes new chemical identities, the submission of undisclosed test or other data, the origination of which involves a considerable effort, is equally protected against disclosure. Industrial Designs, which are independently created and are new or original or significantly differ from known designs and have industrial application, are equally protected.[4] Finally, the protection to layout designs (topographies) of integrated circuits or layout designs as reflected in *Intellectual Property In Respect of Integrated Circuits Treaty*, (IPIC Treaty) 1981. Thus the term of protection of these IPRS under TRIPS varies from one IPR to another.

III. NATURE OF OBLIGATIONS

The nature and scope of the obligations of WTO members under TRIPS are; give effect to the provisions of TRIPS; recognize and implement the varieties of IPRs; extend treatment to nationals both natural and legal persons in the laws governing the IPRs in the member countries; not to derogate from the existing obligations arising under *Berne, Paris, Rome conventions* and IPIC Treaty; extend national treatment to nationals of other members of WTO; abide by most favored nations treatment of GATT; exceptions could be made under certain specified circumstances to the obligations of TRIPS either under the specific exceptions as provided in TRIPS or measures necessary to protect public health nutrition and promoting the public interest in sectors which are of vital importance to the members socio-economic and technological development; exceptions can be provided to prevent the abuse of intellectual property right holders who resort to practices which unreasonably restraint trade and effect international transfer of technology. In addition TRIPS establishes civil, criminal, and administrative standards and subjects IPRS to WTO dispute settlement system and certain common procedural standards that each member states must meet concerning the administration and maintenance of IP rights.

---

[4] Article 25 of *Agreement on Trade-Related Aspects of Intellectual Property Rights*, 1995 provides: *Requirements for Protection* (1) Members shall provide for the protection of independently created industrial designs that are new or original. Members may provide that designs are not new or original if they do not significantly differ from known designs or combinations of known design features. Members may provide that such protection shall not extend to designs dictated essentially by technical or functional considerations. (2) Each Member shall ensure that requirements for securing protection for textile designs, in particular in regard to any cost, examination or publication, do not unreasonably impair the opportunity to seek and obtain such protection. Members shall be free to meet this obligation through industrial design law or through copyright law.

IV. PUBLIC POLICY AND TRIPS

Gleaning through the preamble of the TRIPS and the cases brought before the *WTO Dispute Settlement Understanding* (DSU) and the customary law of the members, the public policy perspectives of members are amply demonstrated by the twin role which IPRs provide for members development and technological progress. IPRs, as already mentioned are commodities by themselves across the members and protection afforded to these commodities are *per se* protections to technology, trade and commerce. Therefore public policy options of members need to be reconciled with the rights and obligations as contained in TRIPS. TRIPS recognizes these public policy options, by protecting and enforcing IP rights in a manner conducive to social and economic welfare of the members besides contributing to the promotion of technological innovations and transfer of technology to the mutual advantages of producers and users of technological knowledge.[5] Public policy options from the point of view of globalized markets and from the perspective of developed and developing countries trade relations raise certain important issues, which are as under:

a) Whether public policy options of less developing and least developed members of WTO are simply marriages of convenience within the spigot bowl of WTO to serve the business interests of the TNCs of the developed countries;

b) Whether the TRIPS enhance the piracy of traditional knowledge of the developing and least developed members in sectors such as traditional medicines and cultural art works etc;

c) Whether the TRIPS undermine the *UN Convention on Biological Diversity (CBD)*, 1992 which recognizes the right of the members to safeguard the biological resources within the sovereign borders of the members in sustainable and equitable manner.

d) Whether TRIPS endanger human health in poor countries by providing stronger IPRs and monopoly to medicines of pharmaceuticals of developed countries to fight health crises and pandemic diseases such as HIV and AIDS;

---

5 Article 7 of *Agreement on Trade-Related Aspects of Intellectual Property Rights*, 1995 provides the objectives: The protection and enforcement of intellectual property rights should contribute to the promotion of technological innovation and to the transfer and dissemination of technology, to the mutual advantage of producers and users of technological knowledge and in a manner conducive to social and economic welfare, and to a balance of rights and obligations.

e) Whether the TRIPS threaten food production globally by extending the IPRs over food plants and seeds, denying such rights to farmers in developing countries, as they cannot afford to pay prices demanded for them.

These public policy choices to some extent have been taken care of by domestic and international legislations yet there is no evidence to prove or disprove the benefits arising from public policy choices legislated domestically or internationally.[6] TRIPS definitely serve the interests of TNCS of the rich nations. For developing and least developed, there is hardly any empirical evidence to show that TRIPS serve their public policy choices. The preambular justification of TRIPS that it will boost investment, trade, and capital formation in the poor countries as well as develop training and research, fostering creativity in inventions and dissemination of technology in these countries has hardly happened.

V. PUBLIC POLICY & CBD

The piracy of traditional knowledge, cultural artefacts and folklore continues unabated and it is not yet clear in what form the traditional knowledge or folklore can be recognized and protected. Could traditional knowledge be recognized as a variant of patents, copyright or undisclosed information? Traditional knowledge to some extent is recognized in CBD Convention as a biological resource. But the dispute between TRIPS and CBD has yet to be resolved and the dispute recognizes the fact that members have sovereign rights over their genetic resources of plants and animals and the members have rights to exploit these resources. For this purpose the developed countries are under an obligation to provide technology to the poor countries for exploitation of these resources. The TRIPS and CBD have a serious conflict zone for environment, biotechnology, pharmaceuticals and agriculture.

Biotechnology, pharmaceuticals and agriculture are interlinked both in terms of use of genetic resources which appear to be abundant in the

---

[6] Article 8 of *Agreement on Trade-Related Aspects of Intellectual Property Rights,* 1995 provides the Principles: (1) Members may, in formulating or amending their laws and regulations, adopt measures necessary to protect public health and nutrition, and to promote the public interest in sectors of vital importance to their socio-economic and technological development, provided that such measures are consistent with the provisions of this Agreement. (2) Appropriate measures, provided that they are consistent with the provisions of this Agreement, may be needed to prevent the abuse of intellectual property rights by right holders or the resort to practices which unreasonably restrain trade or adversely affect the international transfer of technology.

poor countries, as well as manufacturing of new medicines and new varieties of seeds to suit all sorts of environment and consequently impacting the agriculture in a big way. Poor countries have few choices in either refusing access to their genetic resources or imposing heavy prices for the exploitation of their resources. Even if a country is interested to impose conditions on access to genetic and other resources Article 15 of the *CBD Convention*,1992[7] yet conditions of mutually agreed terms did not muster the WTO and GATT if we peruse Article 1 [8] read with Article 3 of GATT[9] and the conditions and prohibitions would be discriminatory

---

[7] Article 15 of the *CBD Convention*, 1992 provides for access to genetic resources (1) Recognizing the sovereign rights of States over their natural resources, the authority to determine access to genetic resources rests with the national governments and is subject to national legislation. (2) Each Contracting Party shall endeavour to create conditions to facilitate access to genetic resources for environmentally sound uses by other Contracting Parties and not to impose restrictions that run counter to the objectives of this Convention. (3) For the purpose of this Convention, the genetic resources being provided by a Contracting Party, as referred to in this Article and Articles 16 and 19, are only those that are provided by Contracting Parties that are countries of origin of such resources or by the Parties that have acquired the genetic resources in accordance with this Convention. (4) Access, where granted, shall be on mutually agreed terms and subject to the provisions of this Article. (5) Access to genetic resources shall be subject to prior informed consent of the Contracting Party providing such resources, unless otherwise determined by that Party. (6) Each Contracting Party shall endeavour to develop and carry out scientific research based on genetic resources provided by other Contracting Parties with the full participation of, and where possible in, such Contracting Parties. (7) Each Contracting Party shall take legislative, administrative or policy measures, as appropriate, and in accordance with Articles 16 and 19 and, where necessary, through the financial mechanism established by Articles 20 and 21 with the aim of sharing in a fair and equitable way the results of research and development and the benefits arising from the commercial and other utilization of genetic resources with the Contracting Party providing such resources. Such sharing shall be upon mutually agreed terms.

[8] Article I of GATT provides for general condition for most-favoured-nation treatment: With respect to customs duties and charges of any kind imposed on or in connection with importation or exportation or imposed on the international transfer of payments for imports or exports, and with respect to the method of levying such duties and charges, and with respect to all rules and formalities in connection with importation and exportation, and with respect to all matters referred to in paragraphs 2 and 4 of Article III,* any advantage, favour, privilege or immunity granted by any contracting party to any product originating in or destined for any other country shall be accorded immediately and unconditionally to the like product originating in or destined for the territories of all other contracting parties.

[9] Article III of GATT provides for national treatment on internal taxation and regulation: (1) The contracting parties recognize that internal taxes and other internal charges, and laws, regulations and requirements affecting the internal

and *ultra virus* to the WTO. Article XX (g) of the GATT[10] also imposes obligations on to members of WTO not to discriminate by imposing bans on foreign firms as against local firms.

---

for sale, purchase, transportation, distribution or use of products, and internal quantitative regulations requiring the mixture, processing or use of products in specified amounts or proportions, should not be applied to imported or domestic products so as to afford protection to domestic production. (2) The products of the territory of any contracting party imported into the territory of any other contracting party shall not be subject, directly or indirectly, to internal taxes or other internal charges of any kind in excess of those applied, directly or indirectly, to like domestic products. Moreover, no contracting party shall otherwise apply internal taxes or other internal charges to imported or domestic products in a manner contrary to the principles set forth in paragraph 1.

10 Article XX of of the GATT provides for General Exceptions. It reads as under: Subject to the requirement that such measures are not applied in a manner which would constitute a means of arbitrary or unjustifiable discrimination between countries where the same conditions prevail, or a disguised restriction on international trade, nothing in this Agreement shall be construed to prevent the adoption or enforcement by any contracting party of measures: (a) necessary to protect public morals; (b) necessary to protect human, animal or plant life or health; (c) relating to the importations or exportations of gold or silver; (d) necessary to secure compliance with laws or regulations which are not inconsistent with the provisions of this Agreement, including those relating to customs enforcement, the enforcement of monopolies operated under paragraph 4 of Article II and Article XVII, the protection of patents, trademarks and copyrights, and the prevention of deceptive practices; (e) relating to the products of prison labour; (f) imposed for the protection of national treasures of artistic, historic or archaeological value; (g) relating to the conservation of exhaustible natural resources if such measures are made effective in conjunction with restrictions on domestic production or consumption; (h) undertaken in pursuance of obligations under any intergovern-mental commodity agreement which conforms to criteria submitted to the contracting parties and not disapproved by them or which is itself so submitted and not so disapproved; (i) involving restrictions on exports of domestic materials necessary to ensure essential quantities of such materials to a domestic processing industry during periods when the domestic price of such materials is held below the world price as part of a governmental stabilization plan; Provided that such restrictions shall not operate to increase the exports of or the protection afforded to such domestic industry, and shall not depart from the provisions of this Agreement relating to non-discrimination; (j) essential to the acquisition or distribution of products in general or local short supply; Provided that any such measures shall be consistent with the principle that all contracting parties are entitled to an equitable share of the international supply of such products, and that any such measures, which are inconsistent with the other provisions of the Agreement shall be discontinued as soon as the conditions giving rise to them have ceased to exist. The contracting parties shall review the need for this sub-paragraph not later than 30 June 1960.

VI. PUBLIC POLICY & PATENT

The policy choices in patentability have gone beyond the cliff as Article 27 of the TRIPS[11] allows patenting of all sorts of inventions in products and processes, and technology including micro- organisms etc. thereby allowing patenting of genetically modified micro-organisms, animal genes, human DNA, gene sequencing, human protein and human genes. This extended definition of patentability has virtually allowed the science and technology, a monopoly of the rich countries to exploit the trading relations of the international community for their betterment. Policy choice of human health and TRIPS imposes an obligation on the members of the WTO to respect the rights of patent holders of drugs and pharmaceuticals at the same time allow the access to medicines for human health especially for infectious diseases such as HIV/AIDS, tuberculosis, and malaria which are the scourge of poor countries. The insistence of the poor countries that TRIPS does not allow the members of WTO to take corrective measures of providing cheaper generic or patented medicines for public health purposes since the TRIPS were negotiated and the subsequent *Doha Declaration,* 2001 and the Decision of the General Council of August 2003, the concerns of public health have been to a large extent mitigated. This Decision of General Council of

---

[11] Article 27 of *Agreement on Trade-Related Aspects of Intellectual Property Rights,* 1995 provides for *Patentable Subject Matter*: (1) Subject to the provisions of paragraphs 2 and 3, patents shall be available for any inventions, whether products or processes, in all fields of technology, provided that they are new, involve an inventive step and are capable of industrial application.[2] Subject to paragraph 4 of Article 65, paragraph 8 of Article 70 and paragraph 3 of this Article, patents shall be available and patent rights enjoyable without discrimination as to the place of invention, the field of technology and whether products are imported or locally produced. (2) Members may exclude from patentability inventions, the prevention within their territory of the commercial exploitation of which is necessary to protect *order public* or morality, including to protect human, animal or plant life or health or to avoid serious prejudice to the environment, provided that such exclusion is not made merely because the exploitation is prohibited by their law. (3) Members may also exclude from patentability: (a) diagnostic, therapeutic and surgical methods for the treatment of humans or animals; (b) plants and animals other than micro-organisms, and essentially biological processes for the production of plants or animals other than non-biological and microbiological processes. However, Members shall provide for the protection of plant varieties either by patents or by an effective *sui generis* system or by any combination thereof. The provisions of this subparagraph shall be reviewed four years after the date of entry into force of the WTO Agreement.

TRIPS defines a pharmaceutical product as any patented product, or product manufactured through patented process of the pharmaceutical sector needed to address public health problems affecting the poor countries and the poor countries are eligible importing members by notifying to the General Council of TRIPS of their intention to use the system as importers (Whether in general or for example, only in the case of a national emergency or other circumstances of extreme urgency).

VII. PUBLIC POLICY ON HEALTH

This to a large extent obviates the onerous responsibilities of the members under compulsory licensing procedures and parallel impositions under *TRIPS Agreement*.[12] However one must note the conditions for using the system which include the following:

a) Council of TRIPS has to be notified of the eligible importing members names and expected quantities of the required pharmaceutical products and not a least developed country it should establish that it has insignificant or no manufacturing capacity in the product in question, if the product is manufactured in the member country, the compulsory license may be granted in accordance with Article 31 of the TRIPS for imports.[13]

---

[12] Article 6 of *Agreement on Trade-Related Aspects of Intellectual Property Rights,* 1995 provides for *Exhaustion:* For the purposes of dispute settlement under this Agreement, subject to the provisions of Articles 3 and 4 nothing in this Agreement shall be used to address the issue of the exhaustion of intellectual property rights.

[13] Article 31 of *Agreement on Trade-Related Aspects of Intellectual Property Rights,* 1995 provides for *Other Use Without Authorization of the Right Holder*: Where the law of a Member allows for other use[3] of the subject matter of a patent without the authorization of the right holder, including use by the government or third parties authorized by the government, the following provisions shall be respected: (a) authorization of such use shall be considered on its individual merits; (b) such use may only be permitted if, prior to such use, the proposed user has made efforts to obtain authorization from the right holder on reasonable commercial terms and conditions and that such efforts have not been successful within a reasonable period of time. This requirement may be waived by a Member in the case of a national emergency or other circumstance of extreme urgency or in cases of public non-commercial use. In situations of national emergency or other circumstances of extreme urgency, the right holder shall, nevertheless, be notified as soon as reasonably practicable. In the case of public non-commercial use, where the government or contractor, without making a patent search, knows or has demonstrable grounds to know that a valid patent is or will be used by or for the government, the right holder shall be informed promptly; (c) the scope and duration of such use shall be limited to the purpose for which it was authorized, and in the case of semi-conductor technology shall only be for public non-commercial use or

b) The compulsory license must specify the amount required by the importing member which has to be manufactured; the entirely of the production under license must be exported to that member and the products under the license must be clearly identified by specific labeling;

c) The exporting member must notify the TRIPS Council of the grant of license and the attached conditions, including the quantity to be manufactured and the country of export; and

d) Eligible importing members must take reasonable measures within their means proportionate to their administrative capacities and to the risk of trade diversion to prevent re-exportation of the products that have been actually imported.

---

to remedy a practice determined after judicial or administrative process to be anti-competitive; (d) such use shall be non-exclusive; (e) such use shall be non-assignable, except with that part of the enterprise or goodwill which enjoys such use; (f) any such use shall be authorized predominantly for the supply of the domestic market of the Member authorizing such use; (g) authorization for such use shall be liable, subject to adequate protection of the legitimate interests of the persons so authorized, to be terminated if and when the circumstances which led to it cease to exist and are unlikely to recur. The competent authority shall have the authority to review, upon motivated request, the continued existence of these circumstances; (h) the right holder shall be paid adequate remuneration in the circumstances of each case, taking into account the economic value of the authorization; (i) the legal validity of any decision relating to the authorization of such use shall be subject to judicial review or other independent review by a distinct higher authority in that Member; (j) any decision relating to the remuneration provided in respect of such use shall be subject to judicial review or other independent review by a distinct higher authority in that Member; (k) Members are not obliged to apply the conditions set forth in subparagraphs (b) and (f) where such use is permitted to remedy a practice determined after judicial or administrative process to be anti-competitive. The need to correct anti-competitive practices may be taken into account in determining the amount of remuneration in such cases. Competent authorities shall have the authority to refuse termination of authorization if and when the conditions which led to such authorization are likely to recur; (l) where such use is authorized to permit the exploitation of a patent ("the second patent") which cannot be exploited without infringing another patent ("the first patent"), the following additional conditions shall apply: (i) the invention claimed in the second patent shall involve an important technical advance of considerable economic significance in relation to the invention claimed in the first patent; (ii) the owner of the first patent shall be entitled to a cross-licence on reasonable terms to use the invention claimed in the second patent; and (iii) the use authorized in respect of the first patent shall be non-assignable except with the assignment of the second patent.

The *Doha Development Decision* on *Public Health and TRIPS,* 2003 has created uncertainties both in respect of its legal status and interpretation. Can the Decision be taken as a waiver to certain TRIPS obligations as well as enhancing the opportunities of members to have access to medicines when needed in dealing with grave public health problems'? The decision *per se* appears to be favorable for those members who have political or other clout to make an exporter member oblige the importing member who is facing public health crises.

VIII. REGIONAL GROUPINGS & PUBLIC POLICY

So far TRIPS and bilateral regional groupings are concerned, the public policy choices appear to be TRIPS minus. The general frame of bilateral treaties especially between those countries where one of the parties have fairly developed IPRS and chemical biological processes well developed pharmaceutical industry would conclude the bilateral in such a way that IPRS as goods and technology need not necessarily follow the TRIPS mandate. The same appears to be true of trade areas or regional economic groupings amongst developing countries. Although the regional agreements need to conform to the criteria as set forth in Article XXIV of the GATT and the criteria is still controversial, yet the possibility of giving go by to the TRIPS mandate is real. The bilateral or regional approaches to patents may assist the developing countries in gaining access to generic and patented medicines provided the countries in bilateral or regional settings have sufficient resources to satisfy the requirements of drugs and medicines. Public policy choices as recognized in Article 6 of the TRIPS which gives options to the WTO members to adopt a rule or a system of either national exhaustion or international exhaustion. The wording in Article 6 makes it clear that subject to the general obligations of national treatment and *most favoured nation treatment,* for the purposes of dispute settlement nothing shall be used to address the exhaustion of IPRs.

Obviously members may choose to adopt a rule of either national exhaustion or international exhaustion. National means that by authorization of first sale of a product in a given country, the owner of IP rights in that product exhausts those rights in that country only, whereas international exhaustion means that first sale exhausts the IP rights associated with the product worldwide, allowing parallel imports of the product after the first sale. In national exhaustion, a product legitimately sold in one country cannot be imported into another country without the authorization of the IP owner. Imports in parallel to the authorized distribution network may infringe the IP owner's rights in the importing country. The public policy choice of importing a pharmaceutical, which may be necessary either due to lack of production facility or for serious public health concerns such as AIDS/HIV, malaria etc, cannot be allowed in both the exhaustions, national or international. However, if regional patents are granted across the WTO members, the patent rights at the first sale, it may be possible for the regional patent system to import products without violating the patent holders rights. This may increase both the manufacturing capacity and purchasing power in the region by generating economies of scale.

IX. PUBLIC POLICY & FREE TRADE

The public policy and free trade in the context of unilateralism and Special 301 reveals some interesting facts for analysis. The public policy choices of some of the Free Trade Areas especially between US and other countries a TRIPS plus trend is discernable which may greatly enhance the IPR protection beyond TRIPS. The recently concluded FTAs between USA and Jordan, Australia-US Free Trade Agreement, US-Peru Trade Promotion Agreement, US-Al Salvador, and other FTAs, strengthen the IP rights beyond the requirements of the TRIPS which is a serifs concern and might impact the WTO members including India. The IP provisions in these agreements may affect the developed countries equally and may foreclose the reform in the TRIPS Agreement. There is an urgent need to understand these FTAs in the context of their implications for and towards the minimum standards established under TRIPS for IPRS.US being the super power, the other WTO members cannot venture to challenge the US FTAs' in the WTO DSU, rather their continued uncertainty under Article XXIV of the GATT may further help US FTAs not be declared *ultra-virus* the WTO.[14]

Under Special US 301 of the Omnibus Trade and Competitiveness, 1988 as amended in 1994, USTR has a right to identify those countries

---

[14] Article XXIV of the GATT provides for Territorial Application – Frontier Traffic – Customs Unions and Free-trade Areas: The provisions of this Agreement shall apply to the metropolitan customs territories of the contracting parties and to any other customs territories in respect of which this Agreement has been accepted under Article XXVI or is being applied under Article XXXIII or pursuant to the Protocol of Provisional Application. Each such customs territory shall, exclusively for the purposes of the territorial application of this Agreement, be treated as though it were a contracting party; *Provided* that the provisions of this paragraph shall not be construed to create any rights or obligations as between two or more customs territories in respect of which this Agreement has been accepted under Article XXVI or is being applied under Article XXXIII or pursuant to the Protocol of Provisional Application by a single contracting party.

that deny adequate and effective protection for IPRs or deny fair and equitable market access for persons that rely on intellectual rights protection. The USTR has a right to designate the countries as 'priority' foreign countries, which have the most onerous or egregious acts, policies or practices and whose acts, or policies, or practices have greatest adverse impact (actual or potential) on the relevant US products. It is fairly well known how US use and misuses the Special 301 both as a measuring yardstick of complying with the US IP laws, TRIPS and US FTAs. The US has used Special 301 as a sword of Damocles to make the nations complaint to its IPRs policies and practices. The inclusion of a member in the watch list or priority watch list entails a threat either of a dispute settlement challenges at the WTO, or review of tariff preferences. At best it is a tool to conform to US standards of IPRs. India before complying with the TRIPS requirements was on the watch list of USTR and currently there are forty- six of the seventy eight countries examined by USTR on the Watch list.

X. CONCLUSION & SUMMATIONS

The public policy choices as reflected above is putting TRIPS under tremendous strain which *albeit,* cannot be ignored. At the same time it is important to keep in mind that a multilateral treaty like TRIPS shall always be susceptible to the various pressure groups of national and individual types. There are other threats and disappointments looming large on TRIPS and the political and economic choices of member nations are equally daunting for TRIPS to survive. But these threats and disappointments should not be advanced for the burial of TRIPS, as TRIPS is an important tool in the developing and furthering welfare economics nationally and internationally. TRIPS should be further strengthened and the policy choices and options of member nations should be made compatible to the TRIPS innovations in developing international standards for the protection of intellectual in the members of WTO. India's public policy choices need to be crafted in its domestic IPRs laws to the extent that without formally violating the normative order of the TRIPS public priorities are taken care of.

2

Legal Challenges to Copyright & Patent in India: Public Policy Perspective

S.K. Verma

I. ROLE OF INTELLECTUAL PROPERTY

The international community has set itself the target of reducing the proportion of people below poverty line to half by 2015, along with associated specific targets for improving health and education and environmental sustainability. The *Millennium Development Goals*, adopted at various international fora, recognize the crucial importance of reducing poverty and hunger, improving health and education, and ensuring environmental sustainability. It is important to know whether and how intellectual property rights (IPRs) could play a role in helping the world meet these targets – in particular by reducing poverty, helping to combat diseases, enhancing access to education and contributing to sustainable development, protecting our cultural heritage, safeguarding the food security for the country. It is also necessary to deliberate whether and how they create obstacles to meeting those targets and, if so, how those obstacles can be removed.

There are strong views from both sides on the protection and enforcement of IPRs though there is no data to check these views objectively. Some argue strongly that IPRs are necessary to stimulate economic growth, which in turn, helps in poverty reduction. By stimulating invention and new technologies, IPRs help to increase agricultural or industrial production, promote domestic and foreign investment, facilitate technology transfer and improve the availability of medicines necessary to combat diseases. They are also of the view that there is no reason why a system that has worked for developed countries would not work for developing countries. Others argue equally vehemently the opposite. IPRs do little to stimulate invention in developing countries, because the necessary human and technical capacity may be absent there. In assessing these opposing arguments, it is important to remember the technological disparity between developed and developing countries as a group. What role the intellectual property can play to plug this gap is a serious subject for every developing nation? For this, it is also pertinent to know about the IPRs, the challenges they pose to the legal system in general and to the Indian legal system in particular, and their basic rationale to take a considered approach in their implementation.

II. CONCEPT AND SIGNIFICANCE

Intellectual Property Rights broadly means the legal rights which result from intellectual creativity in the industrial, scientific, artistic and literacy fields. IPRs refer to a bundle of legal doctrines which regulate the use of information, in the form of ideas, expressions etc. The various branches of IP law - patents, trademarks, designs, copyright, trade secrets etc., confer legal exclusivity to the holder in the market place. Intellectual property is nothing but legal concept of ownership applied to intangibles. It is not a property right (as is understood for tangibles) but monopoly right limited in time and space. IPRs are statutory rights, which are territorial in nature, and negative in their ambit, excluding others thereby from exploiting or encroaching upon those rights. Like all monopolies, intellectual property is also liable to be abused, if not safeguarded against. As they are private economic rights, they need to be managed properly by their owners. Main reasons for their protection are two-fold: (i) to give statutory expression to the moral and economic rights of creators in their creations and such rights of the public in access to those creations and (ii) to promote, as a deliberate act of government policy, creativity and the dissemination and application of its results and to encourage fair trading which would contribute to economic and social development.

IPRs are assuming increasing importance worldwide due to their economic importance as well as its role in enhancing and cultivating the creative potential of the society. IPRs make it possible for the creators and innovators to establish themselves more readily, to penetrate new markets with a minimum of risk, and to amortize the investments made in the research that led to the innovations in the first place. For example, the right to obtain a patent for an invention stimulate the investment of money and effort in research and development; the grant of a patent encourages investment in the industrial application of the invention. It also encourages R & D activities in a country, which ultimately help in its growth. On the fiip side, these rights block competitors and are used to improve one's bargaining position in the market. Many academic observers, for this reason, remain determinedly ambivalent as to whether the social benefits of IPRs exceed their costs. Typical of these is the following example:

It is almost impossible to conceive of any existing social institution (like the patent system) so faulty in so many ways. It survives only because there seems nothing better to do.[1] In the case of developing countries, several recent reports by international agencies have refiected on the likely impact of the globalization of IP protection on developing countries which may result into heavy costs, but with less perceivable benefits for them. Intellectual property is traditionally divided into two branches: "industrial property" and "copyright". Industrial property covers within its breadth all the IPRs, except copyright.

III. MANDATE OF TRIPS

The *Agreement on Trade-Related Intellectual Property Rights (TRIPS),*1995 covers within its ambit: (i) copyright and related rights; (ii) trademarks (including service marks); (iii) geographical indications; (iv) industrial designs; (vi) patents, (vi) layout designs (Topographies) of integrated circuits; and (vii) trade secrets. It has also introduced the IP protection for plant varieties. Prior to the TRIPS, two international conventions, the *Paris Convention for the Protection of Industrial Property,* 1883 and the *Berne Convention for the Protection of Literary and Artistic Works,* 1885, were concluded to administer these rights. Now these conventions, along with 21 other international conventions on different IPRs, are administered by the *World Intellectual Property Organization* (WIPO) which was constituted in 1967. *TRIPS Agreement* is outside the purview of the WIPO. Whereas the *Paris* and *Berne Conventions* laid down the broad framework for the protection of IPRs, leaving it to the members to lay down the standards thereto, TRIPS requires all WTO Members to provide minimum standards of protection for a wide range of IPRs, though they are free to exceed them. These standards have to be given effect through national legislation. A special body, the Council for TRIPS (commonly known as the TRIPS Council), on which each WTO Member is represented, has been established to administer the operation of the TRIPS. The TRIPS Council is responsible for reviewing various aspects of TRIPS as mandated in the agreement itself and also as requested by the biennial WTO Ministerial Conference, the last of which was held in Cancun in September 2003. TRIPS has however, provoked a lot of discussion in developing countries, particularly in India.

---

1 J.Jewkes, D.Sawers & R.Stillerman, *Sources of Invention,* (1955).

IV. INTEREST OF DEVELOPING COUNTRIES

TRIPS took effect on 1 January 1995. WTO Members considered as developed countries were given one year to comply whilst developing countries and transition economies were given until 1 January 2000 although developing countries required to extend product patent protection to new areas such as pharmaceuticals, a further five years was provided before such protection had to be introduced. Among the most debatable issues raised by1 TRIPS are as under:

- Whether the objective set out in Article 7[2] that IPRs should contribute to the transfer of technology is achievable, particularly in respect of developing country members of the WTO.
- The perceived tensions between Article 8[3] which allows countries to adopt measures necessary to protect public health, and to prevent abuses of IP rights, provided they are TRIPS consistent, and other requirements in the agreement. These include the requirements to provide patent protection for pharmaceutical products, limitations on the conditions for issuing of compulsory licenses (Article 31)[4] and on the scope of provisions providing exceptions to patent rights (Article 30).[5] The *Doha Declaration on TRIPS and Public Health* adopted at the WTO Ministerial Meeting on 14 November, 2001, is an attempt to address the issue. The Declaration covers within its ambit the public health problems of developing countries resulting from HIV/ AIDS, TB, malaria and other epidemics, and allows them to take necessary measures.

---

2 Article 7: The protection and enforcement of intellectual property rights should contribute to the promotion of technological innovation and to the transfer and dissemination of technology, to the mutual advantage of producers and users of technological knowledge and in a manner conducive to social and economic welfare, and to a balance of rights and obligations.

3 Article 8: Members may, in formulating or amending their laws and regulations, adopt measures necessary to protect public health and nutrition, and to promote the public interest in sectors of vital importance to their socio-economic and technological development, provided that such measures are consistent with the provisions of this Agreement.

4 Article 31: Where the law of a Member allows for other use[4] of the subject matter of a patent without the authorization of the right holder, including use by the government or third pAries authorized by the government, the following provisions shall be respected:

5 Article 30: Members may provide limited exceptions to the exclusive rights conferred by a patent, provided that such exceptions do not unreasonably conflict with a normal exploitation of the patent and do not unreasonably prejudice the legitimate interests of the patent owner, taking account of the legitimate interests of third parties.

- The requirement to protect test data against "unfair commercial use" in Article 39,[6] which deals with, undisclosed information (trade secrets).
- The justification for providing additional protection for geographical indications for wines and spirits, (Article 23)[7] and whether this additional protection should also be extended to cover other or all geographical indications, *viz., Basmati,* Darjeeling Tea etc.
- The extent to which patents should be allowed on inventions relating to living forms, for example microorganisms (Article 27.3 (b)[8]), and the requirement to provide IP protection for plants. In that context, the compatibility of TRIPS with agreements such as the Convention on Biological Diversity (CBD) has been raised.
- The cost of meeting the requirements of TRIPS for many developing and least developed WTO Members in relation to the administration of IP rights and their effective enforcement (Article 67).[9]

---

6 Article 39: In the course of ensuring effective protection against unfair competition as provided in Article 10*bis* of the Paris Convention (1967), Members shall protect undisclosed information in accordance with paragraph 2 and data submitted to governments or governmental agencies in accordance with paragraph 3.

7 Article 23.1: Each Member shall provide the legal means for interested parties to prevent use of a geographical indication identifying wines for wines not originating in the place indicated by the geographical indication in question or identifying spirits for spirits not originating in the place indicated by the geographical indication in question, even where the true origin of the goods is indicated or the geographical indication is used in translation or accompanied by expressions such as "kind", "type", "style", "imitation" or the like.[7]

8 Article 27 (3) (b): plants and animals other than micro-organisms, and essentially biological processes for the production of plants or animals other than non-biological and microbiological processes. However, Members shall provide for the protection of plant varieties either by patents or by an effective *sui generis* system or by any combination thereof. The provisions of this subparagraph shall be reviewed four years after the date of entry into force of the WTO Agreement.

9 Article 67: In order to facilitate the implementation of this Agreement, developed country Members shall provide, on request and on mutually agreed terms and conditions, technical and financial cooperation in favour of developing and least-developed country Members. Such cooperation shall include assistance in the preparation of laws and regulations on the protection and enforcement of intellectual property rights as well as on the prevention of their abuse, and shall include support regarding the establishment or reinforcement of domestic offices and agencies relevant to these matters, including the training of personnel.

10 Article 65.1: Subject to the provisions of paragraphs 2, 3 and 4, no Member shall be obliged to apply the provisions of this Agreement before the expiry of a general period of one year following the date of entry into force of the WTO Agreement.

Least Developed Countries (LDCs) are expected to enact TRIPS by 2006 although the *Doha Ministerial Declaration on Public Health* allowed them a further 10 years in respect of pharmaceutical products, till 2016 (Article 65).[10] India is a party to WTO TRIPS Agreement; hence its IP laws have to be TRIPS compliant.

V. CHALLENGES TO COPYRIGHT

The two most important forms of IP rights are patents and copyright. Any serious enquiry into the subject of IP and development, however, has to consider the crucially important role of copyright and the copyright-based industries (including publishing, film, television, radio, music and now computer software too) in the production and dissemination of knowledge and knowledge-based products. These industries supply the intellectual "raw material" for science and innovation, as well as for education and instruction in general, and they have helped to bring about dramatic increases in productivity through aiding the creation of information-based products like desk-top publishing software, electronic mail or sophisticated scientific computer databases. Moreover, the copyright-based industries have developed into a huge source of wealth and employment creation in the knowledge-based global economy. In the US, for example, their overall combined value has increased at such a rapid rate in the last thirty years, that together they currently contribute more than $460 billion to US gross domestic product and sold almost $80 billion in exports in 1999.

India is counted among the top seven publishing nations of the world with a sizeable portion of her publications being in English and is known all over the world for its excellence in software technology, though developed countries, *viz.*, US, UK, Germany, France and Italy between themselves produce nearly two-thirds of global exports of books. We also have a thriving music and film industry, which look towards its protection from onslaught of piracy. It is one of the largest markets for audio and video cassettes. India has a huge potential in the field of computer software. The software industry has been growing at an amazing rate of over 50%, since the last decade. Between 1994-95 and 2001-2002, the industry's gross earnings expanded from $787 million to $ 10.2 billion. Besides protecting creative potential of the society, copyright contributes to a nation on economic-front as well. The copyright based industries and industries based on neighbouring rights, together are huge

[10] Article 65.1: Subject to the provisions of paragraphs 2, 3 and 4, no Member shall be obliged to apply the provisions of this Agreement before the expiry of a general period of one year following the date of entry into force of the WTO Agreement.

generators of employment world-over. The national exchequer benefits from the contribution made by these industries in the form of excise duty, sales tax, income tax etc. from the production and sale of right-related products. *Copyright protection* covers all "literacy and artistic works" such as writings, including scientific and technical texts and computer programs; databases that are original due to the selection or arrangement of their contents; musical works, audio-visual works, works of fine arts, including drawings and paintings; and photographs. It protects authors' original forms of expression and does not protect ideas (which are protected by patents).

VII. RELATED AND NEIGHBOURING RIGHTS

Related or neighbouring rights protect the contributions of others who add value in the presentation of literacy and artistic works to the public, *viz.*, performing artists, such as actors, dancers, singers and musicians; the producers of phonograms, including CDs and broadcasting organizations. The subject-matter of copyright and related rights include every production in the literary, scientific and artistic domain, whatever the mode or form of expression, provided the work is original intellectual creation. But it is not necessary that the work should pass the test of imaginativeness or inventiveness. The protection is independent of the quality or the value attached to the work, as well as even the purpose for which it is intended, because the use to which a work may be put has nothing to do with its protection and also when it has little in common with literature, art or science, such as purely technical guides or engineering drawings, or even maps. By giving creators incentives in the form of recognition and fair economic rewards by way of royalties and protecting their moral rights, which involve the right to claim authorship of a work, and the right to oppose changes to it (mutilation) that could harm the creator's reputation or integrity, copyright and related rights help in human creativity and thus in the growth of the society.

Like other IPRs, copyright is a limited monopoly. It is limited in the 'scope' of the rights granted and in terms of 'time'. In India, the copyright subsists in any work of art for 60 years, including computer programme, as against the TRIPS' 50 year period (Section 38 of the *Copyright Act*, 1957). The most worthy criticism of IPRs in general and copyright in particular is that they tend to create monopolies which are loathed in a socialistic set up like that of ours. In order to strike a balance between the society's need for access to knowledge and the need to rewarding creators, limited uses of copyright protected works are permitted without authors consent. These *limitations and exceptions* (made a part of the *Berne Convention* and evolved over-time) are not only to give the author sufficient incentive to produce new works to satisfy the public interest, but also to ensure that parts of existing creative works are available to build upon in the creation of new works by the society. The *Berne Convention* provides limitations or exceptions to exclusive rights in accordance with "three-step test", *i.e.,* they must be:

1. Confined to certain special cases;
2. That these cases do not confiict with the normal exploitation of a work; and
3. That they must not unreasonably prejudice the legitimate interests of the right owner.

The doctrine of 'fair use' of copyright has been given legal recognition in many jurisdictions. Reproduction of a work exclusively for the personal and private use, including research study, teaching or amusement; making quotations from a protected work, after duly acknowledging it; fair dealing with the protected work for the purposes of reporting current events in print or electronic media, criticism and comment etc. come under "fair use". Section 52 of Indian *Copyright Act* permits certain activities which do not amount to infringement of copyright. Important in this 'exception list' are reproduction of literary, dramatic, musical or artistic works for educational purposes, *e.g.,* research, review, reporting in newspapers, magazines and periodicals etc.' But for determining "fair use", it must take into account: whether or not it has a commercial nature or is for non-profit making educational purposes, the nature of the copyrighted work as a whole and the effect of this use on the potential market for or value of the copyrighted work. This is perfectly in accordance with the societal needs to educate the vast masses and to give a fillip to research activities.

Though the growth of copyright system has always kept pace with the growth of technology, the recent technological developments of computers, internet, and digitization have posed unprecedented challenge to copyright law which has led to the unauthorized creation of unlimited, perfect and costless copies of protected works as also their instantaneous and worldwide distribution. Digitization (through DVD, CD-Rom and broad base) has also enabled the rapid development of the multi-media product, combining written text with sounds and images, still and moving. All these developments have threatened the rights of authors and copyright holders. They have also jeopardized the traditional concept of territoriality of IPRs. In the digital environment, the *most fundamental issue* that has emerged in the field of copyright is the scope of protection, *i.e.,* how these rights are defined, and what exceptions and limitations are permitted. Other important issues include:

- How these rights are enforced and administered in this environment;
- Who in the chain of dissemination of infringing material can be held legally responsible for the infringement; and
- Questions of jurisdiction and applicable law.

Issues of enforcement and licensing of copyright are not new, but take an added dimension and urgency when works are exploited on digital networks. In order for legal protection to remain meaningful, right holders must be able to detect and stop the dissemination of unauthorized digital copies. It is necessary to protect the economic interests of the right holder and moral interests of the author of the work. And, in the context of e-commerce, workable systems of online licensing must evolve; in which consumers can have confidence. The answer to these challenges to a great extent will lie in the technology itself. The US Congress has introduced the bill called *BALANCE Act,* 2003 (Benefit Authors without Limiting Advancement or Net Consumer Expectation) addressing some of these issues.

Technological control measures, such as encryption and anti-circumvention measures, supplemented by contract law and *sui generis* forms of databases protection, give copyright holders the capacity to limit non-public performances, but they also threaten society's interests and fair use rights of individuals. In order to address these issues, in 1996, the WIPO adopted two treaties: the *WIPO Copyright Treaty (WCT)* and *WIPO Performers and Phonograms Treaty (WPPT),* known as Internet Treaties, to deal with the challenges of internet to the copyright and to prevent unauthorized access to and use of creative works on the internet or other digital networks. Both these treaties have now come into force in March and May 2002 respectively. In India, attempts are underway to amend the Copyright Act, I957, as amended in 1994, 1999 and 2014 to insert appropriate provisions to give effect to these treaties by amending Section 52[11] of the *Indian Copyright Act,* 1957.

---

[11] Article 52 (1): The following acts shall not constitute an infringement of copyright, namely: (1) The following acts shall not constitute an infringement of copyright, namely:

a) A fair dealing with a literary, dramatic, musical or artistic work 1[not being a computer programme] for the purposes of – 1[(i) Private use including research;] [(aa) the making of copies or adaptation of a computer programme by the lawful possessor of a copy of such computer programme from such copy-1[(aa) the making of copies or adaptation of a computer programme by the lawful possessor of a copy of such computer programme from such copy– "3[(ab) the doing of any act necessary to obtain information essential for operating inter-operability of an independently created computer programme with other

VIII. INTERNATIONAL REGIME ON PATENTS

In the area of patents, beside the *TRIPs Agreement*, 1995 India became a party to *Paris Convention* and also to the *Patents Cooperation Treaty (PCT)*

---

programmes by a lawful possessor of a computer programme provided that such information is not otherwise readily available; 3[(ab) the doing of any act necessary to obtain information essential for operating inter-operability of an independently created computer programme with other programmes by a lawful possessor of a computer programme provided that such information is not otherwise readily available;"(ac) the observation, study or test of functioning of the computer programme in order to determine the ideas and principles which underline any elements of the programme while performing such acts necessary for the functions for which the computer programme was supplied; (ad) the making of copies or adaption of the computer programme from a personally legally obtained copy for non-commercial personal use;]

b) A fair dealing with a literary, dramatic, musical or artistic work for the purpose of reporting current events—

c) The reproduction of a literary, dramatic, musical or artistic work for the purpose of a judicial proceeding or for the purpose of a report of a judicial proceeding;

d) The reproduction or publication of a literary, dramatic, musical or artistic work in any work prepared by the Secretariat of a Legislature or, where the Legislature consists of two Houses, by the Secretariat of either House of the Legislature, exclusively for the use of the members of that Legislature;

e) The reproduction of any literary, dramatic or musical work in a certified copy made or supplied in accordance with any law for the time being in force;

f) The reading or recitation in public of any reasonable extract from a published literary or dramatic work;

g) The publication in a collection, mainly composed of non-copyright matter, bona fide intended for the use of educational institutions, and so described in the title and in any advertisement issued by or on behalf of the publisher, of short passages from published literary or dramatic works, not themselves published for the use of educational institutions, in which copyright subsists: Provided that not more than two such passages from works by the same author are published by the same publisher during any period of five years. Explanation — In the case of a work of joint authorship, references in this clause to passage from works shall include references to passages from works by any one or more of the authors of those passages or by any one or more of those authors in collaboration with any other person;

h) The reproduction of a literary, dramatic, musical or artistic work—

i) The performance, in the course of the activities of an educational institution, of a literary, dramatic or musical work by the staff and student of the institution, or of a cinematograph film or a 6[sound recording], if the audience is limited to such staff and students, the parents and guardians of the students and persons directly connected with the activities of the institution 7[or the communication to such an audience of a cinematograph film or sound recording]; 8[(j) the making of sound recordings in respect of any literary, dramatic or musical work,

in September, 1998 to facilitate world-wide search on a patent application. The important international treaty on patents is the *Paris Convention*, 1883, which created a Union among its members for the protection of technological inventions. But it evolved a passive regime rather them a prescriptive regime of TRIPS, which has specific provisions on duration,

---

k) The causing of a recording to be heard in public by utilising it,—

l) The performance of a literary, dramatic or musical work by an amateur club or society, if the performance is given to a non-paying audience, or for the benefit of a religious institution;

m) The reproduction in a newspaper, magazine or other periodical of an article on current economic, political, social or religious topics, unless the author of such article has expressly reserved to himself the right of such reproduction;

n) The publication in a newspaper, magazine or other periodical of a report of a lecture delivered in public;

o) The making of not more than three copies of a book (including a pamphlet, sheet of music, map, chart or plan) by or under the direction of the person in charge of a public library for the use of the library if such book is not available for sale in India;

p) The reproduction, for the purpose of research or private study, or with a view to publication, of an unpublished literary, dramatic or musical works kept in a library, museum or other institution to which the public has access: Provided that where the identity of the author of any such work or, in the case of a work of joint authorship, of any of the authors is known to the library, museum or other institution, as the case may be, the provisions of this clause shall apply only if such reproduction is made at a time more than 9[sixty years] from the date of the death of the author or, in the case of a work of joint authorship, from the death of the author whose identity is known or, if the identity of more authors than one is known from the death of such of those authors who died last;

q) The reproduction or publication of—

r) The production or publication of a translation in any Indian language of an Act of a Legislature and of any rules or orders made thereunder—

t) The making or publishing of a painting, drawing, engraving or photograph of a sculpture, or other artistic work falling under sub-clause (iii) of clause (c) of section 2, if such work is permanently situate in a public place or any premises to which the public has access;

u) The inclusion in a cinematograph film of—

v) The use by the author of an artistic work, where the author of such work is not the owner of the copyright therein, of any would, cast, sketch, plan, model or study made by him for the purpose of the work: Provided that he does not thereby repeat or imitate the main design of the work; 11[***]

x) The reconstruction of a building or structure in accordance with the architectural drawings or plans by reference to which the building or structure was originally constructed: Provided that the original construction was made with the consent or licence of the owner of the copyright in such drawings and plans;

y) In relation to a literary, dramatic or musical work recorded or reproduced in any cinematograph film, the exhibition of such film after the expiration of the term of copyright therein: Provided that the provisions of sub-clause (ii) of

coverage and criteria of patentability. Article 33[12] require a patent term of twenty years from the date of filing of a patent application. Patents are available for any inventions, whether products or processes, in all fields of technology, including biotechnology. Inventions may be excluded from patentability for reasons of *public order*, morality, including protection of human, animal or plant life or health, or avoiding prejudice to the environment, as long as the exclusion is not made merely because such exploitation is prohibited by national law.[13] The other permitted exclusions are: diagnostic, therapeutic and surgical methods for humans or animals; plants and animals, other than micro-organisms, essentially biological processes for the production of plants and animals other than non-biological processes. Plant varieties are to be protected by patents or a sui generis system or by any combination thereof Article 27(3).[14] To be patentable, an invention must be new, involve an inventive step (*i.e.* non-obvious) and is capable of industrial application (*i.e.* useful). Patents shall be available and patent rights enjoyable without discrimination as to whether products are imported or locally produced. It means that revocation of a patent or compulsory licence based on non-working in

clause (a), sub-clause (i) of clause (b) and clauses (d), (f), (g), (m) and (p) shall not apply as respects any act unless that act is accompanied by an acknowledgement—

za) The performance of a literary, dramatic or musical work or the communication to the public of such work or of a sound recording in the course of any bona fide religious ceremony or an official ceremony held by the Central Government or the State Government or any local authority. Explanation.—For the purpose of this clause, religious ceremony including a marriage procession and other social festivities associated with a marriage.]

(2) The provisions of sub-section (2) shall apply to the doing of any act in relation to the translation of a literary, dramatic or musical work or the adaptation of a literary, dramatic, musical or artistic work as they apply in relation to the work itself.

12 Article 33: The term of protection available shall not end before the expiration of a period of twenty years counted from the filing date.[2]

13 Article 27(2): Members may exclude from patentability inventions, the prevention within their territory of the commercial exploitation of which is necessary to protect *order public* or morality, including to protect human, animal or plant life or health or to avoid serious prejudice to the environment, provided that such exclusion is not made merely because the exploitation is prohibited by their law.

14 Article 27 (3): Members may also exclude from patentability: 3. Members may also exclude from patentability:(a) diagnostic, therapeutic and surgical methods for the treatment of humans or animals;(b) plants and animals other than micro-organisms, and essentially biological processes for the production of plants or animals other than non-biological and microbiological processes. However, Members shall provide for the protection of plant varieties either by patents or by an effective *sui generis* system or by any combination thereof. The provisions of this subparagraph shall be reviewed four years after the date of entry into force of the WTO Agreement.

the country concerned cannot be granted if the patented product is available in that country through importation. Article 5A (l) of the *Paris Convention*, which is a part of the *TRIPS Agreement* through reference by virtue of Article 2[15] of the Agreement, mandates that importation into the country where the patent has been granted of articles manufactured in any of the countries of the Union shall not entail forfeiture of the patent.

Under the TRIPS Agreement, patentee receives the exclusive rights for product patents- making, using, offering for sale, selling and importing a product; and for process patent- using the process or using, offering for sale, selling or importing a product obtained directly by that process[16]. The patentee has the right to assign or transfer by succession and to license the patent[17]. Thus, the patentee shall not only enjoy rights to exclude others from manufacturing, selling and using his patented invention or creation, but also the right to exclude others from importing the patented products in the country of grant. The burden of proof in an infringement action has been shifted from the plaintiff (the complainant) to the defendant that he has not infringed the right. It provides that in the absence of proof to the contrary, if the subject matter of the patent is a process for obtaining a product, the presumption will be that the defendant has made the product by a patented process, if one of the following two conditions is fulfilled: (i) that the product obtained by the patented process is new; and (ii) that there is substantial likelihood that the product was made by the process and the owner has been unable to determine the process actually used[18]. Due to shifting of the burden of proof, a manufacturer will be required to provide the details of the manufacturing process to rebut the presumption of infringement of a process patent.

---

15 Article 2(1): In respect of Article II, III and IV of this Agreement, Members shall comply with Article 1 through 12, and Article 19, of the Paris Convention (1967).

16 Article 28(1): A patent shall confer on its owner the following exclusive rights:

a) where the subject matter of a patent is a product, to prevent third parties not having the owner's consent from the acts of: making, using, offering for sale, selling, or importing[7] for these purposes that product;

b) where the subject matter of a patent is a process, to prevent third parties not having the owner's consent from the act of using the process, and from the acts of: using, offering for sale, selling, or importing for these purposes at least the product obtained directly by that process.

17 Article 28.2: Patent owners shall also have the right to assign, or transfer by succession, the patent and to conclude licensing contracts.

18 Article 34. 1: For the purposes of civil proceedings in respect of the infringement of the rights of the owner referred to in paragraph 1(b) of Article 28, if the subject matter of a patent is a process for obtaining a product, the judicial authorities

IX. COMPULSORY LICENSING & PATENT

The regime of compulsory license for the non-working of a patent has also been made very regimental under the *TRIPS Agreement*. Under Article 5[19] of the *Paris Convention* for the non-working of a patent, a non-exclusive and non-transferable compulsory licence could be given after the expiration of four years from the date of filing the patent application or three years from the grant of the patent whichever period expires last. Such a licence can be issued without the patentee's permission and without compensating the patentee. The licence can be refused if the patentee justifies his inaction by legitimate reasons. Forfeiture of the patent is not allowed except where the grant of a compulsory licence is not sufficient for the working of the patent. However, no proceedings for the forfeiture or revocation of a patent can be initiated before the expiration of two years from the grant of the compulsory licence. Article 31[20] of the TRIPS, lays down the procedural requirements for the issuance of compulsory licence although it does not talk about the forfeiture or revocation of the patent. The conditions for the issuance of compulsory licence include *inter alia* that, the proposed user of the patent must first make efforts to obtain authorisation from the right holder; the scope and duration shall be limited to the purpose for which the compulsory licence was authorised (principally to supply the domestic market); the licence shall be non-exclusive and non-assignable, and will be terminated if circumstances which led to its issuance cease to exist and are unlikely to recur. Subject to the adequate protection of the interests of the person authorised to use the licence, the right-holder shall be compensated; the grant of licence and the amount of compensation shall be subject to judicial review.

But these requirements will not be applicable where compulsory licences are granted to remedy anti-competitive practices. In the case of

---

shall have the authority to order the defendant to prove that the process to obtain an identical product is different from the patented process. Therefore, Members shall provide, in at least one of the following circumstances, that any identical product when produced without the consent of the patent owner shall, in the absence of proof to the contrary, be deemed to have been obtained by the patented process.

19 Article 5.1: Importation by the patentee into the country where the patent has been granted of Articles manufactured in any of the countries of the Union shall not entail forfeiture of the patent.

20 Article 31: Where the law of a Member allows for other use[3] of the subject matter of a patent without the authorization of the right holder, including use by the government or third parties authorized by the government, the following provisions shall be respected.

semi-conductor technology, the compulsory licence shall be available only for public non-commercial use or to remedy an anti-competitive practice after judicial or administrative determination. The anti-competitive practices, however, are not specified; they are obviously left to be defined under national legislation. TRIPS provide a transitional period of five years, which may further be delayed by five years if product patent is to be provided in a particular area. However, paragraphs 8 and 9 of Article 70[21] of the TRIPS Agreement have drastically curtailed this transitional period. Para 8 of Article 70[22] requires a member to provide a means by which applications for patents for such inventions can be filed. The exclusive marketing rights (EMRs) have to be granted for a period of five years from 1995 onwards under Para 9. Para 8 & 9 together, require members to provide pipeline (mail-box) protection and exclusive marketing rights in the fields of technologies related to pharmaceuticals and agricultural chemical products, which were not patentable on the date of its entry into force in a particular member country. The

---

21 Article 70: 8. Where a Member does not make available as of the date of entry into force of the WTO Agreement patent protection for pharmaceutical and agricultural chemical products commensurate with its obligations under Article 27, that Member shall:

a) notwithstanding the provisions of Article VI, provide as from the date of entry into force of the WTO Agreement a means by which applications for patents for such inventions can be filed;

b) apply to these applications, as of the date of application of this Agreement, the criteria for patentability as laid down in this Agreement as if those criteria were being applied on the date of filing in that Member or, where priority is available and claimed, the priority date of the application; and

c) provide patent protection in accordance with this Agreement as from the grant of the patent and for the remainder of the patent term, counted from the filing date in accordance with Article 33 of this Agreement, for those of these applications that meet the criteria for protection referred to in subparagraph (b).

9. Where a product is the subject of a patent application in a Member in accordance with paragraph 8(a), exclusive marketing rights shall be granted, notwithstanding the provisions of Article VI, for a period of five years after obtaining marketing approval in that Member or until a product patent is granted or rejected in that Member, whichever period is shorter, provided that, subsequent to the entry into force of the WTO Agreement, a patent application has been filed and a patent granted for that product in another Member and marketing approval obtained in such other Member.

22 Article 70.1: This Agreement does not give rise to obligations in respect of acts which occurred before the date of application of the Agreement for the Member in question.

Government of India was found to be defaulted on its international commitment on this obligation by the Dispute Settlement Board (DSB) of the WTO on 19th December, 1997, on a complaint filed by the United States with the TRIPS Council. India gave effect to the decision of the Appellate Body of the WTO through the *Patents (Amendment) Act,* 1999 on 26th March, 1999. This was the first amendment to the 1970 *Patents Act* by adding chapter IVA, comprising of section 24 A to F.

X. PATENTS (AMENDMENT) ACT, 2002

In order to bring its patent law in line with the *TRIPS Agreement,* the Act was again amended through the *Patents (Amendment) Act,* 2002; on the lines as delineated above to make it TRIPS compliant. The 2002 amended Act, however, has not provided for the product patents-for chemicals and pharmaceuticals. A Bill to further amend the Act is presently before the Parliament to give effect to this, along with other amendments on procedural matters, by the end of 2004. In the patent field the main challenges posed before the Government of India under the TRIPS are in the fields of pharmaceuticals, chemicals, biotechnology, plant variety protection and the protection of undisclosed information. Indian *Patents Act,* 1970 did not provide product patents for pharmaceutical and chemicals. In the new Act, section 53[23] of the *Patents Act,* 1970 stands amended by omitting the distinction between product and process patent It provides a uniform term of twenty years for all categories of inventions But the patents granted before the Act of 2002, if they cease to remain operative due to non-patent of renewal fee or on expiry of the term, the subject-matter covered by the said patent will not be entitled to any further protection. The Act has provided necessary safeguards for the protection of public interest, national security, bio-diversity, traditional knowledge, etc. Being the party to the PCT, the amended Act also tries to harmonise the procedure for grant of patents in accordance with international practice. Chap. II A of the *Patents Rules,* 1972 as amended on 2 Dec. 1998 is pointer to this effect.

Whereas the new Act align the provisions relating to compulsory licensing of the TRIPs, the provisions relating to licenses of rights have been omitted from the 1970 *Patents Act.* But unlike *TRIPS Agreement,* the

[23] Section 53: Subject to the provisions of this Act, the term of every patent granted, after the commencement of the *Patents (Amendment) Act,* 2002, and the term of every patent which has not expired and has not ceased to have effect, on the date of such commencement, under this Act, shall be twenty years from the date of filing of the application for the patent.

new Act retains the provision on the revocation of patents by the Controller of Patents for non-working; Section 85 provides:

> Where, in respect of a patent, a compulsory licence has been granted, the Central Government or any person interested may, after the expiration of two years from the date of the order granting the first compulsory licence, apply to the Controller for an order revoking the patent on the ground that the patented invention has not been worked in the territory of India or that reasonable requirements of the public with respect to the patented invention has not been satisfied or that the patented invention is not available to the public at a reasonably affordable price.

Plants and animals are excluded from patentability. Similarly, any process for the medicinal, surgical, curative, diagnostic therapeutic or other treatment of human beings is not entitled to a patent. Where the patent is sought for biological material, it is necessary to deposit the biological material along with the specifications with depository institution, disclosing the source and geographical origin of the biological material used in the invention (Section 10 (d)). It provides provisions relating to parallel import of patented products (exhaustion of right), by giving the right to patent holder to prohibit third parties who do not have his consent from making, using, offering for sale, selling or importing for those purposes that product or process in India[24]. It also incorporates provisions for the protection of biodiversities and traditional knowledge by refusing to grant patent or revoke a patent if the application wrongfully mention the source or geographical origin of biological material (Section 64 (p) & (q).[25] Section 64 (p) that the complete specification does not disclose or wrongly mentions the source or geographical origin of biological material used for the invention;

The provision has also been made for an Appellate Board, which shall be the same as created under the *Trademarks Act,* 2000. The Board

---

[24] Section 48: – Subject to the other provisions contained in this Act and the conditions specified in section 47, a patent granted under this Act shall confer upon the patentee– (a) where the subject matter of the patent is a product, the exclusive right to prevent third parties, who do not have his consent, from the act of making, using, offering for sale, selling or importing for those purposes that product in India;

[25] Section 64 (p) that the complete specification does not disclose or wrongly mentions the source or geographical origin of biological material used for the invention;

q) that the invention so far as claimed in any claim of the complete specification was anticipated having regard to the knowledge, oral or otherwise, available within any local or indigenous community in India or elsewhere.

shall have the power to hear appeals against any order or decision of the Controller of Patents and all such cases pending before any High Court shall be transferred to the Appellate Board (Chap. XIX, sections 116 to 117 H). The new provision has been added on the national security. [26] The Government shall not disclose any information relating to any patentable subject matter, which it considers prejudicial to the security of India. The Government is empowered to revoke any patent, which it considers necessary in the interest of the security of India.

Similarly section 108[27] of the 1970 has been amended to provide additional reliefs to the patentee in case of infringement of the patent by giving power to the courts for destruction of goods and implements used for production of such goods. The patentee may also be entitled injunction, as well as damages or an account of profits in a suit for infringement. A new provision has been added, relating to certain acts which are not to be considered infringements.[28] Any act of making or using a patented product for the purpose of development and submission of information to a regulatory authority regulating marketing approval of the product, shall not constitute an infringement ("Bolar exception"). This provision is aimed to ensure that generic drug should be available in Indian market immediately after the expiry of the term of the concerned patents. The importation of patented product from the person who is duly authorised by the patent holder similarly shall not constitute an infringement. This provision is incorporated to ensure availability of the patented product in the Indian market at minimum international market price. However, the Act does not provide for international exhaustion, and thus the parallel imports of patented product are not allowed without the authorization of the right-holder. The new amended Act has also retained the provision on granting of patent subject to certain conditions

---

[26] Section 157A: Notwithstanding anything contained in this Act, the Central Government shall – (a) not disclose any information relating to any patentable invention or any application relating to the grant of patent under this Act, which it considers prejudicial to the interest of security of India;

[27] Section 108: The reliefs which a court may grant in any suit for infringement includes an injunction (subject to such terms, if any, as the court thinks fit) and, at the option of the plaintiff, either damages or an account of profits.

[28] Section 107A: For the purposes of this Act, – (a) any act of making, constructing, using, selling or importing a patented invention solely for uses reasonably related to the development and submission of information required under any law for the time being in force, in India, or in a country other than India, that regulates the manufacture, construction, use, sale or import of any product.

(Section 47),[29] which among others, allows the Government to use any process patent for its own use; and that it can import any drug or medicine under patent for its own use or for distribution in any dispensary, hospital or medical institution maintained by or on its behalf.

XI. NEW CHALLENGES IN PATENT REGIME

The patent system is designed as a tool to provide an incentive to technical progress. The effectiveness with which this can be done depends upon the relationship between the nature of the incentive and the processes by which technological development takes place. However, whereas the patent system has uniform criteria to judge patent applications, the pattern of technical progress may vary significantly in different fields. The patent system fits best as a model of progress where the patented product, which can be developed for sale to consumers, is the discrete outcome of a linear research process. The safety razor and the ballpoint pen are examples, and new drugs also share some of these characteristics. A good patent system can work on a good supportive premise of R&D. The local R&D has to be encouraged to boost innovation and inventiveness at the local level without which a well intended patent regime will only serve the interests of foreign patentees who will use India as a captive market. It is, therefore, necessary to coin a patent system which can ensure a fillip in R&D activities and to attract necessary finance thereto. This could, however, happen only after the social utility of the monopoly created through patents becomes visible. Since the level of inventiveness and innovation is not adequate in the country presently, a system of granting utility models, on the lines of certain European countries as well as in China, Japan and Korea, for petty inventions may be provided. Since most of the R&D in developing countries particularly in India, is undertaken by the public sector institutions, they should not lose sight of the objectives of public policy for research. In the area of new technologies, *viz.*, computer software, biotechnology, India needs to take a pro-active approach. Article 27(1)[30] of the *TRIPS Agreement* mandates for the grant of patents in all areas of technology. Under the

[29] Section 47: The grant of a patent under this Act shall be subject to the condition that— (1) any machine, apparatus or other article in respect of which the patent is granted or any article made by using a process in respect of which the patent is granted, may be imported or made by or on behalf of the Government for the purpose merely of its own use;

[30] Article 27.1: Subject to the provisions of paragraphs 2 and 3, patents shall be available for any inventions, whether products or processes, in all fields of technology, provided that they are new, involve an inventive step and are capable of industrial application.[3] Subject to paragraph 4 of Article 65, paragraph 8 of

Patents Act, 2002, chemical processes, including biotechnological and microbiological processes are entitled to process patent (Section 5). Once the Act is amended again, they will be entitled to product patent. But computer software, under the Act is not entitled to patent protection. Section 3(k)[31] of the Act does not allow patents on "a mathematical or business method or a computer program *per se* or algorithms" as they are not considered to be inventions.

It is now a well established fact that the US is leading in the grant of software patents and even business methods have been granted patents. In the EU, despite the clear provision against the grant of software patents (Article 52(2) of the EPA), the patents are liberally being granted if a computer program involves a "technical effect". As India's software industry is very vibrant, it is necessary to devise legislative and administrative measures to grant software patents. The proper guidelines on biological and software patents need to be issued by the appropriate authorities, to be followed by the patent examiners. For an effective IP regime, a good infrastructural support is a *sine qua none* which require not only good legislation, but workable administrative machinery and physical facilities, which are presently not of an appropriate level. To make the patent regime workable in the interest of the country, one may refer to the CIPR Report (2002), which provides that 'the developing countries (like India) while giving effect to their international obligations on patents may:

- Provide for international exhaustion of patent rights.
- Provide an effective compulsory licensing system and adequate government use provisions.
- Provide broadest possible exceptions to patent rights including adequate research exemption exception and explicit "Bolar exception".
- Apply strict standards of novelty, inventive step and industrial application or utility (consider higher standards than currently applied in developed countries).

Article 70 and paragraph 3 of this Article, patents shall be available and patent rights enjoyable without discrimination as to the place of invention, the field of technology and whether products are imported or locally produced.

31 Section 3 (k): a mathematical or business method or a computer programme per se or algorithms;

- Make use of strict patentability and disclosure requirements to prevent unduly broad claims in patent applications.
- Provide a relatively low cost opposition or re-examination procedure.
- Provide means to prevent the granting or enforcement of patents comprising biological material or associated traditional knowledge obtained in contravention of access legislation or the provisions of the CBD.
- Consider providing alternative forms of protection to encourage sub-patentable type local innovation.

Thus a proper safeguard policy must be devised in the patent law, which should further the national interests, while ensuring compliance with international obligations. Patent system should meet the objectives of regular supply of quality goods at reasonable prices and help in the technological development of the country.

XII. CONCLUSION AND SUGGESTION

This is an era of knowledge economy. Knowledge-economy is one in which, in addition to capital and labour, technology and knowledge upon which such technology is based is the third factor of production. Earlier knowledge was to be shared, with the increasing use of IPRs, now it is to be capitalized and monopolized. Societal concerns are taking a back seat. But good IPR system has to draw a balance between these confiicting interests. Knowledge is intangible and non-rivalrous. It does not lessen by sharing with others. It was aptly said by Thomas Jefferson:

> He, who receives an idea from me, receives instruction himself without lessening mine; as he who lights his toper at mine, receives light without darkening me.

According to Alvin Toffier the world is now witnessing a trisection of power. The poor First wave nations, the mass manufacturing Second wave ones and the knowledge economies of the Third wave - all are interacting with each other. India according to him is divided into all the three waves. Though we have entered the digital age, our thinking and outlook continues to remain in the analogue mode. We are accustomed to deal with the problems posed by new technology (whether telecommunications biotechnology, computer software etc.), by adopting an only sector-wise approach. We are apprehensive about the future. Hence we try to draw parallels from the past. Metaphors sometime can be misleading. We need to take a comprehensive and holistic approach. While framing legislation on any IPR aspect, *viz;* software patents, biotechnological inventions, plant variety, etc. the national interests, public policy, morality and protection of environment should be kept in view. At the International level attempts are underway to further harmonize the substantive patent law, and a draft WIPO Substantive Patent Law Treaty is ready for negotiation. Among others, it aims at the grant of patent rights worldwide, once a patent has been granted by any country, thus displacing the concept of territoriality of IPRs. India should identify a strategy for dealing with the risk that WIPO harmonization will lead to standards not in its national interests. It may oppose them, but, in the meantime, it is also essential that India should take a pro-active approach by putting its own system in order to meet the international challenges while being competitive.

The time has, however, come to think of a new paradigm on intellectual property, to make it an engine of innovation and inventiveness to cater the needs of vast humanity around us. Assessment of our strength, weaknesses, opportunities and threat (SWOT) analysis indicate that in the emerging knowledge economy we have a vital stake. We gave the Zero to the world. Without Zero, bits and bytes of the digital revolution would not have become reality. We have a vast pool of trained skilled English speaking manpower. Our computational skills are well acknowledged. Our indigenous and traditional knowledge is very rich. Had we put in place a strong IPR regime without loss of time, our *basmati,* turmeric and *neem* would not have been pirated? Our entertainment industry is vibrant. We have a vast pool of content creators in the entertainment and information sectors. The challenges posed by internet and digital medium are fascinating, which has dazzled the law and policy makers and put many questions, which still remain unanswered. We have to meet the new challenges by putting in place a workable intellectual property regime in our national interest. At present, we are in the transition phase. The tension between new and old is always high at moments of transition. We have to go through this transition and mould the system in our best interests without losing any further time.

3

Jurisprudential Justifications and Practical Implications of Intellectual Property Rights

Imtiaz Ghulam Ahmed

I. INTRODUCTION & OVERVIEW

Intellectual property rights may be defined as the legal relationships that arise out of an individual's creative gifts and the communication to society of his or her intellectual creations. Intellectual property is challenging as well as rapidly widening horizon of law. The purpose of law is to encourage and reward creativity and intellectual effort. The prominence of this branch of law in India is partly due to India's economic structure and its geographical position in the world. Many international companies operate in India either directly or through licensees or agents. Numerous goods, services, and technological developments have overseas origins. Foreign companies often control their interests through contract but they invariably do so by means of copyright law, obtaining of patents or by registration of trade-marks and designs. It follows that in particular circumstances intellectual property remedies are most convenient method of maintaining control, or at least a useful adjunct to other remedies based on contract. Another important factor is the upsurge in "piracy" that is occurring not only in India but also in almost every other part of the world. Piracy may originate outside India, or, it may also originate in India. While devising legal apparatus for the welfare and protection of creative people, we must not lose sight of the public interest in the greatest measure of access to information and culture. Intellectual property rights are significant wealth- creating assets and their protection and commercialization are of increasing economic significance. In past the value of such rights was often overlooked and it is only in recent years that the economic potential of intellectual property has started receiving greater recognition. The dawn of the third millennium which has led to the emergence of knowledge capitalism with emphasis on intangible assets such as knowledge, competencies and intellectual property is a defining movement in the history of mankind. It is a defining moment in the history of mankind because the historical forces set in motion by the digital revolution has spawned a new civilization characterized by path breaking inventions and technological innovations and the opening up of the electronic frontier. It is an age of digital renaissance which combines the marvels of the Age of Discovery and the excellence of medieval Renaissance rolled into one. As a result of the information technology revolution there is a transition from industrial society to information society. Convergence of computer networks and communication technologies facilitated by the digital revolution has given birth to Cyberspace which in turn has ushered in knowledge economy. Hence, the intellectual property law faces challenges. In this background the concept, nature and development of intellectual property rights are proposed to be examined. The paper will be divided into V more parts. Part II of the paper will outline the meaning concept of intellectual property and range of subject matter protected by law, part III will examine the jurisprudential justifications of intellectual property protection, part-IV will explore the evolution and development of intellectual property rights under international law, part-V will demonstrate the evolution and development of intellectual property rights under Indian law. And part-VI will conclude the subject.

II. SUBJECT MATTER OF INTELLECTUAL PROPERTY

Traditionally, a number of intellectual properties were known collectively as industrial property. Such rights include patents, trademarks and designs. When other rights such as copyright are added to industrial property the phrase used to describe the entirety of rights is intellectual property. Thus, intellectual property refers to rights in creation of the human mind which arise under the laws of patents, copyrights, trademarks, trade secrets, unfair competition and related laws. Article 1(2) of the *Paris Convention for the Protection of Industrial Property*, 1883 (as revised, most recently at Stockholm in 1967) stated: "The protection of industrial property has as its object patents, utility models, industrial designs, trademarks, service marks, trade names, indications of service or appellations of origin and the repression of unfair competition." In modern times, however, "intellectual property" has acquired a compendious meaning, including all the rights enumerated in Article 1(2) above as well. This expanded meaning is discernible form Article 2(viii)of the *Convention Establishing the World Intellectual Property Organisation*, 1970, which defines "intellectual property" as including the rights relating to: (i) literary, artistic and scientific works; (ii) performances of performing artists, phonograms, and broadcasts; (iii) inventions in all fields of human endeavor; (iv) scientific discoveries; (v) industrial designs; (vi) trademarks, service marks, and commercial names and designations; (vii) protection against unfair competition; and (viii) all other rights resulting from intellectual activity in the industrial, scientific, literary or artistic fields. Thus, intellectual property rights are the legal rights given to creators of intellectual property. Intellectual property rights usually give the creator of intellectual property the right to exclude others from exploiting the creation for a defined period of time. Intellectual property laws provide the incentives that foster innovation and creativity, and strive to ensure that the competitive struggle is fought within certain bounds of fairness. The protection of intellectual property rights contributes significantly to technological progress, competitiveness of businesses and our country's well-being. Generally, the subject matter protected by intellectual property law are: (i) copyright, (ii) Patents, (iii) Trademarks, and (iv) Designs etc.

i) *Copy right:* The essence of a copyright is to confer certain exclusive rights on the owner to deal with the work in certain ways. Copyright protects the particular form of expression but not the ideas and thoughts on which the expression is based. Others are free to write about the same subject matter or theme. Traditionally, copyright has embraced literary, dramatic, artistic and musical works, as well as sound recordings, films sound and television broadcasts and published editions of works. However, in recent times, the range of copyright has expanded, e.g., the word "literary" has been stated to include computer software and electronic databases, artistic works have extended to technical drawings, sound recordings and films have included videos and CDs. More recently, performers'rights have been recognized and moral rights regime has been installed within the framework of the copyright system.

ii) *Patents:* A patent confers exclusive rights in new inventions or new manner of manufacture. It gives a legal right to prevent others from exploiting the invention for a fixed time, normally up to 20 years.

iii) *Trademarks:* Trademarks give exclusive rights in marks or symbols used to market goods and services so long as they are distinctive and do not otherwise cause deception or confusion.

iv) *Designs:* Design law confers an exclusive right to apply a design to an article of manufacture. The proprietor enjoys a monopoly. By design is meant shape or appearance, incorporated in an industrial product or applied to it, which gives the product an attractive appearance. Like patents and trade-marks, design protection is dependent on registration.

In addition, there are various *sui generis* regimes that grant rights akin to intellectual property rights, e.g., grant of proprietary rights to breeders of certain new varieties of plants, protection of certain layouts for integrated circuits. Furthermore, intellectual property rights are also protected under the law by an action for breach of confidence. Now question arises what are the jurisprudential justifications of intellectual property protection?

III. JURISPRUDENTIAL JUSTIFICATIONS FOR INTELLECTUAL PROPERTY

All justifications for intellectual property protection must contend with a fundamental difference between ideas and tangible property. Ideas, by definition, are less tangible. They exist in the mind and work of humans. Legal protection for intellectual work evolved much later in the development of human society than did protection for tangible property. The protection of such "intellectual property" raises complex philosophical questions. Should the first person to discover a way of performing an important task – for example, a procedure for closing a wound – be entitled to prevent others from using this procedure? Should the first person to pen a phrase or hum a melody be entitled to prevent others from copying such words or singing the song? Should such "intellectual property rights" be more limited than traditional property rights (i.e., the fee simple in England)? Tangible property, whether land or chattels, is composed of atoms, physical things that can occupy only one place at any given time. This means that possession of a physical thing is necessarily "exclusive"- if l have it, you don't. Jurists have to justify the exclusive rights in ideas. The principal basis for such protection is utilitarian or economic incentive justification. Nonetheless, other theories – most notably the natural rights, personhood and social requirements justifications – have been important in understanding the development and scope of intellectual property protection. *John Lock* and *Immanuel Kant* are two predominant philosophers justify exclusive rights in ideas under "intellectual property" within the framework of "*natural rights*". According to *John Lock* "though the earth and all inferior creatures be common to all men, yet every man has a property in his own person". This nobody has any right to but himself. The "labour of his body and the work of his hands, we may say, are properly his. Whatsoever, then, he removes out of the state that Nature hath provided and left it in, he hath mixed his labour with it, and joined to it something that is his own, and thereby makes it his property. It being by him removed from the common state Nature placed it in, it hath by this labour something annexed to it that excludes the common right of other men. For this labour being the unquestionable property of the labourer, no man but he can have a right to what that is once joined to, at least where there is enough, and as good left in common for others". Thus, *Lock's* theory of "natural right real property" can be applied to intellectual property including copyright "if ideas are fixed in a tangible property". *Immanuel Kant* argues that it is the "natural obligation" to respect the author's ownership of his works. On the other hand, it is the "natural right" of the author to control the use of his work and to be rewarded for it is one of significant underpinnings of the copyright jurisprudence. Thus, according to natural right philosophers every man has a natural right over the results of his labour and so the author who has put in effort to produce to work shall have a right to enjoy the fruits of his labour and object to any unauthorized modification or other attack on the integrity of the work. "*Personhood theory of jurisprudence*" has developed a relationship between property and personhood and justifies intellectual property rights of inventor or authors. According to *Margaret Jane Radin* the proposition underlying the personhood perspective is that to achieve proper self-development ~ to be a person - an individual needs some control over resources in the external environment. The necessity as assurances of control takes the form of property rights. Most people possess certain objects they feel are almost part of themselves. These objects are closely bound up with personhood because they are part of the way we constitute ourselves as continuing personal entities in the world. *Hegel* had developed the "personhood" concept in his *Philosophy of Right* and maintained that "property for personhood". *Hegel* concludes that the person becomes a real self only by engaging in a property relationship with something external. Such a relationship is the goal of the person. *Hegel* says: "The person has for its substantive end the right of placing its will in any and every thing, which thing is thereby mine; [and] because that thing has no such end in itself, its destiny should take on my will. [This constitutes] mankind's absolute right of appropriation over all things." Thus personhood framework of right developed a relationship between property and personhood. For the protection of personhood the recognition of property right is required and there is no difference between tangible property and intangible property. Therefore, intellectual property right is a justified right and very essential property right for the protection of personhood. One of the predominant philosophical frameworks of intellectual property protection is utilitarian or economic incentive framework. According to economic incentive theory the intellectual property law is often justified on the basis that it stimulates investment of time and money in the creation of new works. Most authors of works of copyright rely on the income they derive from the publication of their works for their livelihoods. If such investment is not adequately protected, any person will be free to misappropriate the fruits resulting from such investment. This acts as a disincentive to the author to engage in such initiatives. On the other hand if such investment of labour and skill is rewarded it will stimulate creativity. Therefore it is necessary to provide an adequate reward by protection of intellectual property. *Social Requirements* is another philosophical justification for protecting intellectual property. According to this theory, law protects intellectual property in the interest of society. Therefore, it is in the interest of the society that authors and creators should be encouraged to create more, as well as publish their works, since new works are additions to the cultural stock of society. Intellectual property law with its market monopoly benefits the author and creators with economic reward which would instigate them to create and publish more and more works. The legal protection of intellectual property provides an incentive to the creation and dissemination of works to the benefit of the creator as well as the society as a whole. Now question arises when and how intellectual property rights have been evolve and developed?

IV. EVOLUTION AND DEVELOPMENT UNDER INTERNATIONAL LAW

The evolution and development of intellectual property rights under international law dates back to 1883. The *International Convention for the Protection of Industrial Property,* commonly known as the *Paris Convention,* revised from time to time (and last revised at Stockholm, 1967) and the *Berne Convention for the Protection of Literary and Artistic Works,* 1886 (as last revised at Paris 1971) have established an international regime for the protection of intellectual property. There are also number of other conventions and treaties dealing with specific categories of intellectual property under the patent regime : (i) *Patent Co-operation Treaty,* Washington, 1970, (ii) *Strasbourg Agreement Concerning the International Patent Classification,* 1971, and (iii) *Budapest Treaty on International Recognition of the Deposit of Micro Organisms for the Purposes of Patent Procedures,* 1980 are important treaties. In the late nineteenth and beginning of twentieth century a number of international conventions were adopted on copyright law. They include : *Rana Convention for the Protection of Performers, Produces of Phenograms and Broadcasting Organisations,* 1961; *Geneva Convention for the Protection of Producers of Phonograms against Unauthorized Duplication of their Phonograms,* 1971, *Brussels Convention relating to the Distribution of Programme Carrying Signals Transmitted by Satellite,* 1974. Under the trademarks regime the *Trademark Registration Treaty* adopted by the *Vienna Diplomatic Conference* in June 1973 and the *Vienna Agreement* establishing an" *International Classification of the Figurative Elements of Marks* of June 1973 are important. The *Hague Agreement concerning the International Deposit of Industrial Designs*, 1960 and *Locarno Agreement establishing an International Classification Industrial Designs*, 1971 are important treaties on international designs law. The overall promotion, administration and supervision of the above treaties and other instruments is in the hands of *World Intellectual Property Organisation* (WIPO) established by a Convention at Stockholm in 1967 as one of the specialized UN agencies. The *Paris Convention for the Protection of Industrial Property*, 1967, which has a membership of 100 countries, mainly guarantees the right to national treatment, the right of priority and the rights and obligations of natural persons and legal entities for which the member nations may legislate and also provides an administrative framework for the implementation of the Convention. By 'national treatment' [articles 2 and 3] is implied that each country of the Paris Union must accord the nationals of other Convention countries the same protection, advantage and privilege as it accords to its own nationals. By right of priority is meant that once an application has been filed in one of the member countries, the applicant (or its or his successor in title) may within a period of say 6 to 12 months apply for protection in all other member countries. These later applications will be regarded as if they have been filed on the same day as the first (or earlier) application enjoying a prior status with respect to all applications relating to the same invention filed after the date of the first application. The *Berne Convention for the Protection of Literary and Artistic Works*, 1971 protects, in an effective and uniform manner, the rights of authors in their literary and artistic works in the member States of the Berne Union. The Berne Union requires the member countries to grant moral as well as economic rights to authors such as the right to object any distortion, mutilation or other modification of or other derogatory action in relation to, his work which would be prejudicial to an author's honour or reputation. The *Berne Convention* also provides for; a) national treatment, according to which works originating in one of the member States are to be given the same protection in each of the member States as the latter grant to works of their own nationals; b) automatic protection according to which national treatment is not dependent on any formality; and c) independence of protection according to which enjoyment and exercise of rights granted is independent of the existence of protection in the country of origin of the work. Although Article 2 of the *Berne Convention* contains an illustrative list of works protected, yet it is a matter of legislation in the countries of the Berne Union to determine the protection to be granted to other works. The exclusive rights granted to authors under the Berne Convention include the right of translation [Article 8], the right to reproduction in any manner or form which includes any sound or visual recording [Article 9], the right to perform dramatic, dramatico-musical and musical works [Article II],the right to broadcasting and communicating to the public by wire, by broadcasting or by loudspeaker or any other analogous instrument of the broadcast of the work [Article II],the right of public recitation [Article II], the right of making adaptations, arrangements or other alterations of a work [Article 12] and the right of making a cinematographic adaptation and-reproduction of a work [Article 14].

Intellectual property regime as discussed above was suddenly found connected with international trade and consequently matter to be brought on the agenda of GATT's (General Agreement on Tariffs and Trade) *Uruguay Round of Multilateral Trade Negotiations*, 1986 (URMTN) on the insistence of the developed industrial countries, especially of United States. This has proved to be one of the most contentious agenda of URMTN. GATT found itself concerned with intellectual property rights when ministerial declaration of GATT contracting parties called for an examination of the counterfeiting goods in the world trade. GATT articles by and large cannot accommodate the intellectual property regime as GATT was never conceived to deal with international intellectual property problems. The basic principles of GATT such as most- favoured nations treatment, national treatment, protection through tariffs, transparency and differential and more favourable treatment for LDCs applies to international trade in products while, in the case of intellectual property regime, it is the rights of persons which are protected and are intangible in character. However, the developed countries impress that all the above obligations should apply to intellectual property rights also. Now there is a new development that GATT, through the completion of its Uruguay Round in April 1994, has created a World Trade Organisation (WTO) situated in Geneva) which, among other things, will administer a highly significant instrument, the Agreement on Trade- related Aspects of Intellectual Property Rights, including Trade in Counterfeit Goods (TRIPS). The TRIPS, at present, covers 9 (Nine) categories of intellectual property. They are : Copyright, trademarks, trade secrets, Designs, Patent, etc., In order to understand the function of WTO, the four fundamental principles are of immense importance. They are : (i) non-discrimination (ii) reciprocity, (iii) market access and (iv) fair competition. All" states which subscribe to the WTO become bound to a mutual recognition of intellectual property rights at a high level of protection, in various respects going beyond the range of international obligation achieved in the Conventions mentioned in the previous paragraph. Thus, the GATT was replaced by WTO in 1995 and 145 counties have become the members of it as of today. India was a founder member of GATT.

Besides the above development, another development took place in the field of intellectual property is that of technological development. The revolution of information technology in the late 20th century and beginning of 21st century poses problems in intellectual property law. In 1994 eminent thinkers including. *Alvin Toffler*, *George Gilder* and *Esther Dyson* put forward a *Magna Carta* for digital civilization. According to them the central event of the 20th Century is the overthrow of matter. In technology, economics and politics of nations, wealth in the physical resources has been losing value and significance. The Powers of the mind are everywhere, ascendant over, the brute force of things. Nearly a decade after this idea was put forward by the eminent thinkers, the world community gathered at Geneva Unanimously Adopted a Declaration at the *World Summit on Information Society* (WSIS) Civil Society Plenary "*Shaping Information Societies for Human Needs*" – on 8 December 2003. The Declaration lays emphasis on the following principles, namely:

a) The need for a rich public domain of knowledge which must be available to all to enable sustainable information societies, to bridge the digital and to provide the grounds for a positive development of intellectual creativity, technological innovation and effective use of that technology;

b) Limited intellectual monopolies, also known as intellectual property rights, are granted only for the benefit of society, most notably to encourage creativity and innovation. The benchmark against which they must be reviewed and adjusted regularly is how well they fulfil this purpose.

c) The vast majority of humankind has no access to the public domain of global knowledge, a situation that is contributing to the growth of inequality and exploitation of the poorest people and communities. Yet instead of extending and strengthening the global domain, recent developments are restricting information more and more to private hands. Copyright periods have been extended again and again, making them practically indefinite and defeating their original purpose.

d) Human knowledge is the heritage of all humankind and the reservoir from which all new knowledge is created. The preservation of cultural and linguistic diversity, the freedom of the media and the defence and extension of the public domain of global knowledge are as essential, for information and communication societies, as the diversity of our natural environment.

V. EVOLUTION AND DEVELOPMENT UNDER INDIAN LAW

Intellectual property law made its way into the Indian subcontinent when the *English East India Company* extended the English Copyright Act of 1842 into India. The Act was modified in 1911 and later, in 1914, a new Copyright Act was enacted. The main provisions of the Act were as under: (1) the authors right was born immediately when the work was created; (2) Protection was meant for the material which was original and not to ideas ; (3) The term of the right extended up to 25 years after the death of the author. By virtue of the provisions of Article 372 (1) of the Constitution of India, it remained applicable even after the India attained independence in 1947. With a view to consolidating and amending the old law, the Copyright Act was re-enacted in 1957. The salient provisions of the new Act were: (l) Establishment of the Copyright Board. (2) Enlargement of definition of Copyright. (3) Right of the author to re-acquire his right after seven years but before expiry of ten years of assignment. (4) Issue of general or special licenses for public performances. (5) Issue of license to a library to make copy of any book. _ (6) Regulation of the activities of the performing arts societies including the fees or royalties charged. The Act was further amended in 1983 and in 1984 with a view to preventing growing piracy. These checks, however, proved ineffective necessitating formation of a Working group in 1987 with a mandate to study and recommend suitable changes, taking into consideration the advancement in communication technology. The recommendation of the Working group was incorporated in the Act through the 1994 amendment which, inter-alia, include the following: (l) Protection of performing rights covering any visual or artistic presentation. (2) Constituent of Copyright societies for the promotion of collective administration of the rights of the authors, composers and other creative artists. (3) Assignment of copyright by an author or artist to protect the interests of both assignor and assignee. The Act was further amended in 1999 which empowered the Central Government to apply the provisions relating to broadcasting organizations and performers in certain other countries as well as to restrict their rights. The Indian *Patent Act* was enacted in 1859 to grant exclusive privileges to inventors. The aim of the Act was to enable English patent holders to acquire control over the Indian markets. The 1882 saw the enactment of the *Patent and Designs Protection Act* followed by the *Inventions and Designs Act*, 1888. The enactments aimed at the protecting the interests of the industrialists, manufactures and importers. The *Patents and Designs Act* was passed in 1911 which was the first comprehensive law on the subject. It remained in force until the passing of the *Patent Act* of 1970. The salient features of the 1970 Act are: (l) The patents are granted to encourage inventions and to secure that the inventions work on a commercial scale. (2) The patents are not granted to enjoy a monopoly in important matters. (3) It recognized two kinds of patents products and process patents. (4) No product patent can be granted to medicines, food items and chemicals except to their manufacturing process. The *Patents (Amendment) Act,* 1999 added a new chapter to the Act dealing with the exclusive marketing rights to sell or distribute an article or substance in India. To comply with the TRIPS agreement and to protect the indigenous products such as rice, turmeric and neem etc. from foreign companies the *Geographical Indications of Goods (Registration and Protection) Act,* 1999 was passed. The *Trade and Merchandise Marks Act,* 1958 provided for the registration of existing and the future trademarks. This Act was replaced by the *Trademarks Act,* 1999. It not only amended and consolidated the 1958 Act, but also seeks to provide for better protection of trademarks for goods and services besides preventing the use of fraudulent trademarks. The *Designs Act* 2000 aims at the protection of the shape, construction, features or configuration of the registered designs. It amended and consolidated the law relating to the designs, developed after the enactment of the *Designs Act,* 2000, leading to a considerable progress in the field of science and technology. The Act also promotes the design activity in the production process.

VI. CONCLUSION & SUMMATION

Intellectual property is going to be the real estate of the third millennium. With the convergence of new technologies, courts will be dealing with untried and untrusted legal issues. The Judges who have grown up with legal concepts shaped by traditional values will have to open up their minds to new ways of thinking about law and technology. The rapid development of internet has created a fertile ground for innovation. Legislatures and courts have tried to squeeze relatively new medium into paradigms and precedents better suited to older form of communication technology and media. Intellectual property is a serious business for the Indian Judiciary. Since India has become a member of the WTO, it is now obligatory on her part to implement the provisions of *TRIPS Agreement* in its entirety. In order to bring the Indian Patent Law in conformity with the WTO directives, the *Patent Act,* 1970 has undergone radical change. The 'product patent' has been permitted now in addition to 'process patent'. The *Patent (Amendment) Act,* 1999 has inserted a new chapter as IVA which provides for, *inter alia,* (a) Exclusive Marketing Rights and (b) Mail Box System. Would these provisions be helpful in India? New technologies and new means of dissemination of knowledge are also causing enormous changes to copyright law. The principal purpose of copyright law is to give to authors their "just rewards" for the benefits they bestow on the society and also to encourage the making of future creative works.

Since the rights conferred by copyright are in the nature of a monopoly, it is important to ensure that the rights are not abused and that free flow of information and knowledge are not unduly hampered. Clearly, the rules pertaining to ownership should confirm to this underlying philosophy of copyright law. Further difficulties arise from the fact that under the copyright system, it is essential to show that the work originated from the author and that it was "original". Can an artistic practices dating back possibly millennia, be subject to protection as an original work? And who could claim authorship and ownership of such works? The all pervasive information technology revolution which marked the closing years of the 20th Century has heralded the third millennium as a digital epoch wherein the law of intellectual property rights will have to confront and grapple with challenges of unprecedented dimensions and magnitude where no systematic application of the traditional principles and concepts of law with wildest stretch of imagination will be able to solve the problems and answer the questions raised. New intellectual tools, techniques and concepts will have to be formulated and evolved in order to enact new laws at a national level, or, may be perhaps preferably, at an international level as a global code of digital law.

REFERENCES

1. Arthur R. Miller and Michael H. Davis. Intellectual Property: Patents, Trademarks and Copyright. West Publishing Co., USA (1983).
2. B. L. Wadehra. Law Relating to Patents Trademarks, Copyright, Designs and Geographical Indications. Universal Law Publishing Co. Pvt. Ltd., Delhi (2002).
3. David l Bainbridge. Cases and Materials on Intellectual Property Law. Pitman Publishing, London (1995).
4. David I Bainbridge. Intellectual Property, Pearson Education, Delhi (2002).
5. Hilary E Pearson and Clifford G Miller. Commercial Exploitation of intellectual Property. Universal Law Publishing Co. Pvt. Ltd., Delhi (1997).
6. John Locke. Two Treaties on Government. Third edition (1698).
7. Margaret Janet Radin. "Property and Personhood", 34 Stan. L. Rev. (1982).
8. P. Narayana. Copyright Law. Eastern Law House, Calcutta (1986).
9. P. Narayana. Patent Law. Eastern Law House, Calcutta (1998).

10. P. Narayanam. Law of Trade Marks and Passing Off. Eastern Law House, Calcutta (2000).

11. Paul Torremans and Jon Holyoak. Intellectual Property Law. Butterworths, London (1996).

12. Robert P. Merges. Intellectual Property in the New Technological Age. Aspen Law and Business, New York (2000).

13. Rodney D Ryder. Intellectual Property and the Internet. Butterworths, New Delhi (2002).

14. W. R. Cornish. Cases and Materials on Intellectual Property. Sweet and Maxwell, London (1999).

15. W.R. Cornish. Intellectual Property. Universal Law Publishing Co. Pvt. Ltd., Delhi (2001).

Section-II
Copyright, Climate Change & Food Security Policy

4

Techno-legal Dimensions of Carbon Emissions & Climate Change: An Intellectual Property Rights Perspective

Azim B. Pathan

I. INTRODUCTION

Nations are growing with pace in technology and technological advancements. Till the end of 20th century development was the priority of entire planet earth but in the ending of the 20th century it was realized by almost all countries that development cannot go alone but it has to have the social, economic and environmental concerns. It was realized by the United Nations in *Rio Conference on Environment and Development*, 1992 that there is need of sustainable development. Now in 21st century the technological advancements are needed to be utilized for saving the planet earth from the curse of climate change and global warming reducing the carbon emissions across the entire planet earth. The argument in this paper is based on, how far technological advancements and technology transfer, by developed countries to developing countries can be facilitated in reduction of the carbon emission and greenhouse gases, through legally binding norms? How there should be synergy in between technologies reducing carbon emission and IPR issues?

The sun continuously bathes the Earth with energy in the form of sunlight. Much of this energy is absorbed by the Earth, and then emitted as infrared radiation, or heat. Greenhouse gases prevent the Earth from discarding as much of this heat as it otherwise would back into space. Without naturally occurring greenhouse gases, the Earth would be a much colder place, inhospitable to modern human existence. But by the same token, the additional greenhouse gases added to this store by humans is slowly increasing the average temperature of the Earth system. Due to the quantity in which it is emitted by humans, its longevity in the atmosphere, and its effects in trapping heat, carbon dioxide is the most important of the greenhouse gases currently causing changes in the Earth's climate. While the growth of human carbon dioxide emissions slowed in

2008, a slight reprieve attributed to the global financial crisis, they are still tracking above the worst-case scenario considered by the *Intergovernmental Panel on Climate Change (IPCC)* in their 2007 report. In fact, atmospheric levels of the greenhouse gases carbon dioxide (CO_2), methane (CH_4) and nitrous oxide (N_2O) are higher now than at any time since modern humans have evolved. This growing store of greenhouse gases, is leading to extremes in our weather and changing the long-term climate. Summers are becoming hotter, and droughts are longer and drier. The oceans are becoming more acidic. Sea levels are rising as glaciers melt and the warmer water expands. If we do not act now, the newest and best science indicates that the average global sea level in 2100 will be 75 to 190 centimeters above 1990 levels, and continue to rise thereafter. In Australia, extreme fire danger days are already becoming more numerous in many parts of the country, and floods and cyclones more intense. Research by the CSIRO indicates that the frequency of days with very high and extreme Forest Fire Danger Index ratings is likely to increase by 15 to 70 per cent by 2050 in southeast Australia. With much of Earth's biosphere already 'feeling the heat', the Great Barrier Reef ecosystem is in grave danger both due to increased water temperatures, and increased acidification as the ocean absorbs some of the additional carbon we have placed in the atmosphere. Changes have been observed in the breeding and migratory patterns of birds, fish and animals; and plant species have spread into latitudes that were previously too cold for them.[1]

Every time we burn fossil fuels (gas, coal or oil) carbon dioxide and other greenhouse gasses (GHGs) are released into the atmosphere. Normally carbon dioxide is safely re-absorbed by plants and trees. But we are burning fossil fuels at such a rate that the trees and plants cannot soak up all the carbon dioxide. All this extra carbon dioxide in the atmosphere makes the temperature of the planet increase. This is called global warming. Global warming makes weather more unpredictable and extreme. Globally, we can expect more floods and hurricanes, heat waves and droughts. To reduce the risk of extreme weather, we need to reduce the amount of fossil fuel we are now burning.[2]

1 Why we must act now to reduce greenhouse gas emissions ABC - Australian Broadcasting Corporation, http://www.abc.net.au/science/articles/2009/11/25/2753561.htm (last visited Dec 25, 2016).

2 Why We Need to Reduce Carbon Emissions Why We Need to Reduce Carbon Emissions, http://www.bournemouth.gov.uk/environment-and-sustainability/Why We Need To Reduce Carbon Emissions Why We Need To Reduce Carbon Emissions. aspx (last visited Dec 23, 2016).

II. CLIMATE CHANGE AND INTELLECTUAL PROPERTY RIGHTS

The recent years have seen a worldwide consensus over the protection of environment and mitigation of climate change. In industrialized and developing countries alike, the interface between international intellectual property and environmental protection is widely perceived as one of fundamental conflict.[3] When one asks oneself how intellectual property laws cater for the protection of the environment and especially for the reduction of CO_2 in the atmosphere, the first thing that comes to mind is to look into the intellectual property international treaties and conventions.[4] The issues related to climate change and mitigation of carbon emission policy is relatively new and therefore, no such mention related to these have been made in the old conventions like the *Paris Convention* of 1883 which is the oldest convention dealing with patenting rights. Article 5A (2) (4) of the *Paris Convention* provides that "countries can impose compulsory licenses if there is an abuse of the exclusive right e.g. failure to work the patented invention". The *Trade-Related Aspects of Intellectual Property Rights ("TRIPS") Agreement*, part of the Final Act of the *Uruguay Round of Multilateral Trade Negotiations*, concluded on December 15, 1993.[5] TRIPS also seek to stimulate rapid international economic development that will likely produce a virtual technological transformation of human society and perhaps much of the natural world.[6] *TRIPS Agreement* sets forth specific standards concerning the availability, scope and use of intellectual property rights.[7] The *TRIPS Agreement* provides a "minimum" standard for domestic intellectual property laws of WTO members as there was a lack of international enforceability of IPRs due to a lack of stringent dispute settlement before the *TRIPS Agreement*.[8] IPRs play an important role as an incentive for technology development and innovation, but also influence the transfer and diffusion of technologies.[9] The objective of the *TRIPS Agreement* (Article 7) stipulates

3 Charles R Mc Manis, The Interface Between International Intellectual Property and Environmental Protection: Biodiversity and Biotechnology, http://openscholarship.wustl.edu/cgi/viewcontent.cgiparticle=1516&context=law_lawreview.

4 Estelle Derclaye, Intellectual Property Rights and Global Warming Marquette Intellectual Property Law Review, http://scholarship.law.marquette.edu/cgi/viewcontent. cgi?article=1114&context=iplr.

5 *Supra* 2.

6 *Ibid.*

7 *Ibid.*

8 Susanne Droege et al., The trade system and climate action: ways forward under the Paris Agreement, http://climatestrategies.org/wp-content/uploads/2016/10/Trade-and-climate-ways-forward-1.pdf.

9 *Ibid.*

that *"the protection and enforcement of intellectual property rights should contribute to the promotion of technological innovation and to the transfer and dissemination of technology, to the mutual advantage of producers and users of technological knowledge and in amanner conducive to social and economic welfare, and to the balance of rights and obligations."* Access to environmentally beneficial and climate-friendly technologies and know-how is a key driver of mitigation, and increasingly also of adaptation activities and the *TRIPS Agreement* strengthens the position of developers of climate-friendly technologies, but also demands a better dissemination via technology transfer.[10] According to Article 7, IPR should work *"in a manner conducive to social and economic welfare"* and requires *a balance between rights and obligations of intellectual property right holders.*[11] It is in article 27 of TRIPs where provisions for the respect of the environment and therefore implicitly the more specific problem of global warming can be found.[12] Paragraph 2 allows Members to prohibit the patentability of inventions in order to protect morality including to "avoiding serious prejudice to the environment provided that such exclusion is not made merely because the exploitation is prohibited by their law".[13] Article 27.2 of TRIPs however has no specific reference to the protection of the environment, certainly because at the time it was adopted, in 1973, this concern had not yet emerged.[14]

TRIPS-consistent measures may also be undertaken to prevent the abuse of IPRs by right holders, or *"the resort to practices which unreasonably restrain trade or adversely affect the international transfer of technology"*. As affirmed by the 2001 *Doha Declaration on the TRIPS Agreement and Public Health,* each member has the right to grant compulsory licenses and the freedom to determine the grounds upon which such licenses are granted.[15] This is particularly important for increasing emission reductions fast by transferring new technologies to as many countries as possible, without securing a minimum amount of research and development cost coverage.[16]

Article 31 of TRIPs, as it does not oblige countries to provide for compulsory licenses internally (in their intellectual property laws) does not do much for the protection of the environment and in particular the reduction of CO_2 emissions.[17] But if a country decides to provide for

---

10 *Supra 7.*
11 Supra 3.
12 *Ibid.*
13 *Ibid.*
14 *Ibid.*
15 Supra 7.
16 *Ibid.*
17 Supra 3.

compulsory licenses then it has to abide by Article 31, which lays down the conditions under which members must comply if they decide to provide compulsory licenses in their laws.[18] As the latter's provisions are not exhaustive and do not refer to the environment, they give room for Members to adopt provisions which force patentees to grant licenses when an invention helps to prevent global warming.[19] Most relevant to the reduction of CO_2 are paragraphs (b) and (l) of article 31. Paragraph (b) allows Members to require patentees to grant a license if they have not worked it (similar to article 5A of the *Paris Convention*).[20] Paragraph (l) allows Members to provide that the holder of a first patent grants a license to the holder of the second patent if (i) the second invention "involves an important technical advance of considerable economic significance in relation to the invention claimed in the first patent; (ii) the owner of the first patent shall be entitled to a cross-license on reasonable terms to use the invention claimed in the second patent; and (iii) the use authorized in respect of the first patent shall be non-assignable except with the assignment of the second patent."[21]

In 2005, a UN report from the Department of Economic and Social Affairs on Sustainable Forest Management claimed that 'policies promoting development and diffusion of technologies are probably among the most important factors affecting environmental protection. Moreover, technology transfer is one of the major factors shaping global income distribution'.[22] There is often a duality of purpose behind the inclusion of technology transfer provisions in environmental treaties, namely the achievement of development as well as various aspects of environmental protection or remediation.[23] IP rights are conferred by states and give significant power to private entities and this power is subject to some limits, but the system remains in conflict with the commons.[24] Valuable attempts have been made to limit the impact of IP through initiatives which proceed in parallel with IP, such as through the Eco-Patent Commons project.[25] The global goods perspective suggests that

---

18 Supra 3.

19 *Ibid.* 20 *Ibid.* 21 *Ibid.*

22 Karen Sullivan, Technology Transfer and Climate Change: Additional Considerations for Implementation Under the UNFCCC, http://www.lead-journal.org/content/11001.pdf.

23 *Ibid.*

24 Dr Abbe E. L Brown, A New Opportunity for Delivering the Commons: Exploring the Interface between different Legal Fields", http://biogov.uclouvain.be/iasc/doc/full%20papers/Brown.pdf.

25 *Ibid.*

international technological cooperation should be maximized in an effort to decarbonize the global economy.[26] Low-carbon/environment-friendly technologies urgently required to mitigate GHG emissions emerging from fast-growing emerging economies and less developed countries to avoid further lock-in have been developed primarily in industrialized countries.[27]Thus, financing and building up technological capacity needs to be supported by developed countries if climate change concerns are to be tackled as future greenhouse gas emissions are expected to emerge predominantly from less developed economies and their share is set to increase to over 70% of global emissions in the next three decades.[28] The developed nations have a historical responsibility as early industrialized and polluting nations towards less developed ones, which find resonance within the *United Nations Framework Convention on Climate Change (UNFCCC)*.[29] The UNFCCC was adopted in 1992 at the Rio Conference on Environment and Development and the Paris Agreement has established a new international framework for the parties to the *United Nations Framework Convention on Climate Change (UNFCCC)* from 2020 onwards.[30] Climate policy will be based on national contributions to mitigation, adaptation, and financial, technological and capacity-building support.[31] The UNFCCC remains the central pillar of the climate change regime, and the Cancun Agreements that emerged from its meeting it define *technology development and transfer* through the entire technology cycle.[32] *International technological cooperation implies financial and technical assistance that support and undertake joint actions with actors and institutions across national borders directly looking to impact a technology's innovation cycle.*[33] International bodies and non-governmental organizations have floated ideas for possibly drastic limitations on TRIPs for such technologies on the grounds of encouraging their adoption in developing countries and of international equity considerations.[34]

---

26 Shikha Bhasin, Enhancing International Technology Cooperation for Climate Change Mitigation Lessons from an Electromobility Case Study, https://www.die-gdi.de/uploads/media/DP_26.2014.pdf.

27 *Ibid.* 28 *Ibid.* 29 *Ibid.*

30 *Supra* 7.

31 *Ibid.*

32 *Supra* 25.

33 *Ibid.*

34 Timo Goeschl & Grischa Perino, The Climate Policy Hold-Up: Green Technologies, Intellectual Property Rights, and the Abatement Incentives of International Agreements Discussion Paper Series No. 591 April 2015, http://www.uni-heidelberg.de/md/awi/forschung/dp591.pdf.

Adjustments to IPRs necessary for stimulating access to and the diffusion of Environmentally Sound Technologies (ESTs) should be coordinated with other policy initiatives to supply a range of incentives for firms to develop, use and transfer ESTs.[35] Further, alternative incentive models must be considered to address particular problems, such as small markets where IPRs are unlikely to induce innovation, the differentiated adaptation costs for ESTs in Developed Countries (DC) and Least Developed Countries (LDC) economies, and the need for sustainable long-term investments in R&D to ensure the commercialization of climate change adaptation and mitigation technologies.[36] The role of fiscal-policy measures that can induce relevant and development-appropriate innovation in industrialized countries for the deployment and use of technologies in DCs and LDCs should not be overlooked either.[37] In sum, differentiated conditions across countries and sectors will require flexibility in the range and design of the domestic and international policy options necessary to ensure adequate access to ESTs.[38]

III. CLIMATE CHANGE LAW

A. ***United Nations Framework Convention on Climate Change (1992):*** The first major international agreement on climate change was the UNFCCC, which was introduced in 1992 following growing concern within the UN about the potential impact of climate change. It entered into force in 1994, and today almost every country in the UN is signatory to the agreement. The UNFCCC is the foundational agreement for future agreements, including the Kyoto protocol and others. The original UNFCCC did prove to be inadequate to slow carbon emissions sufficiently to mitigate climate change effects. However, it had a number of important characteristics in regard to technology transfer that are relevant to the current situation. These include that it required developed countries to lead the carbon emissions reduction efforts and directed funds to developing countries in order to allow them to improve their climate change actions. Perhaps more importantly, the Convention specifically mandated that developed countries should facilitate technology transfer

35 Keith E. Maskus & Ruth L. Okediji, Intellectual Property Rights and International Technology Transfer to Address Climate Change: Risks, Opportunities and Policy Options, http://www.ictsd.org/downloads/2011/12/intellectual-property-rights-and-international-technology-transfer-to-adress-climate-change.pdf.

36 *Ibid.*

37 *Ibid.*

38 *Ibid.*

to developing countries for technologies that would help implement the Convention's provisions (specified under Article 4.5 of the UNFCCC). In order to meet this responsibility, the UNFCCC's signatories have established a Technology Mechanism designed to facilitate transfer of technologies, as well as a Technology Transfer Framework agreement. The *Poznan Strategic Framework on Technology Transfer* is another agreement that acts to facilitate technology transfer between developed and developing countries. In summary, the UNFCCC, though it would eventually be updated in light of new conditions and demands, provided the framework for technology transfer for CO_2 reduction. It did so by first establishing that facilitating this technology transfer was a responsibility of developed nations, and second by providing frameworks that would allow the transfer to take place.[39]

B. ***Kyoto protocol (1997)*:** The second stage in the evolution of technology transfer in reducing CO_2 emissions was the passage of the Kyoto protocol (1997), which updated the requirements of the UNFCCC in order to account for changes in environmental conditions. The Kyoto protocol was an advance on the original UNFCCC, because it required signatories to commit to emissions targets. However, developing nations were still not required to commit to emissions reductions, a situation that has made the Convention increasingly difficult following the increasing industrialization of countries like China and India. The Kyoto protocol did not enter into force until 2005, which explains the long gap between its passage and further developments in this area. Technology transfer through the Kyoto protocol is positioned as a cooperative process, with the Joint Implementation (JI) mechanism allowing for cooperative technology development between developed nations and the Clean Development Mechanism (CDM) providing the main means of technology transfer from developed to developing countries. There are eligibility requirements for participating in these programs, including in brief: protocol ratification, calculation of assigned emissions, establishment of a national system for estimating emissions, maintaining a national registry to track traded emissions units, and agreeing to report annually to the secretariat about emissions and removals. The CDM is the program that is of the most interest in this case. While technology transfers are still managed under the terms of the UNFCCC, the CDM provides an incentive for developed countries to transfer technology by allowing them to fulfill

[39] Thitiporn Watthanachai, Technology transfer for reducing CO_2: A critical review of intellectual property laws and trade laws in Thailand and Japan, www.diva-portal.org/smash/get/diva2:663813/FULLTEXT01.pdf (last visited Dec 23, 2016).

part of their emissions reduction requirements by implementing emissions reduction programs in developing countries. As previously discussed, this is useful for developed countries because there are often easier emissions reductions to be found in developing countries. Thus, developed countries can more easily meet their obligations, while having a greater impact on the environment.

C. ***The Bali Road Map (2007):*** The Bali Road Map agreement resulted from the 2007 Bali Climate Change Conference, which was also undertaken under the UNFCCC. The Bali Road Map is described as "a number of forward-looking decisions that represent the various tracks that are essential to reaching a secure climate change future," and includes the *Bali Action Plan,* which was intended to be operable by 2009. There were at least two Decisions from the Conference of the Parties in the *Bali Action Plan* that directly addressed technology transfer, including Decision 3 and Decision 4. Decision 3 resolved to improve the technology transfer framework of the Convention by establishing an Expert Group on Technology Transfer to specifically develop mechanisms for measuring and reporting technology transfer as well as to improve technology transfer financing. Decision 4 offered specific recommendations to improve the implementation of the UNFCCC Article 4.5 (the original article requiring technology transfer), in areas including technology needs assessments, technology innovation, enabling environments, capacity building, and technology transfer mechanisms. The agreement also specified a term of Reference for the Expert Group on Technology Transfer. This agreement is very important because it was the first to really deal with the enormous technical challenge of limiting climate change, as well as the first to spell out specific requirements for technology and measurement. The Bali meeting also advanced informal relationships between countries, improving opportunities for technology transfer partnerships.[40]

D. ***The Cancun Agreements (2010):*** The Cancun Agreements were a series of agreements for short-term action passed at the 2010 *United Nations Climate Change Conference in Cancun,* Mexico. One of the main objectives of the agreement is once again focused on improving technology transfer globally, this time seeking to "get it to the right place at the right time and for the right affords." This is a much more targeted goal than previous technology transfer requirements, which were much more open and less specific about the use of technology transfer or its targets. Particularly noteworthy in the outcomes of the Cancun meeting is that it resulted in

40 *Ibid.*

improved funding for capacity development on the part of developing nations. Provisions that were targeted to this area included fast-start funding for technology programs in developing countries (funded through 2012), improvements in log-term funding, establishment of a Technology Mechanism to improvetechnology development and transfer to developing countries, and a capacity building program. This agreement is important because absorption capacity, or the extent to which the receiving company or country is prepared to make use of the transferred technology, is a major factor in how successful technology transfer is at achieving its goals. This is one of the first acknowledgements that developing countries need assistance not just with technology itself, but also in developing the ability to use it effectively.[41]

E. ***Durban Outcomes (2011):*** The outcome of the 2011 round of negotiations in Durban, South Africa was the first time since the *Kyoto Protocol* (1997) that a significant revision of the UNFCCC was undertaken. This revision of the Convention is a long-term convention, with actions lasting to 2020 and beyond. There were a number of CMP decisions taken in regard to technology transfer and its previous firms, including Decision 8 (Further guidance related to the CDM), Decision 9 (Materiality standard under the CDM), and Decision 15 (Capacity-building). Decision 8 is particularly relevant since it specifies requirements for improved baseline and monitoring of the program, provision for a central registration and certification process, and recommendations for improving distribution and capacity building. This is particularly important since, the CDM programs enacted to date have been strongly focused on China and India, and some regions (especially Africa) have had a noticeable lack of involvement. Technology transfer has also been part of the policymaking activity following the Durban round; for example, several countries in the EU are now focusing on improving their technology transfer programs as a result of the agreement. This suggests that the Durban outcomes could be particularly important in facilitating technology transfer, although given the provisions are not yet fully in place it is difficult to tell at this time.[42]

---

[41] Thitiporn Watthanachai, Technology transfer for reducing CO_2: a critical review of intellectual property laws and trade laws in Thailand and Japan, www.diva-portal.org/smash/get/diva2:663813/FULLTEXT01.pdf (last visited Dec 23, 2016).

[42] Thitiporn Watthanachai, Technology transfer for reducing CO_2: a critical review of intellectual property laws and trade laws in Thailand and JAPAN, www.diva-portal.org/smash/get/diva2:663813/FULLTEXT01.pdf (last visited Dec 23, 2016).

F. ***Doha Climate Gateway (2012):*** The most recent evolution in technology transfer provisions for CO_2 reduction is the Doha climate gateway (2012). This gateway emerged from the 2012 Doha Climate Change Conference, which was intended to consolidate and assess the rapid changes made in Bali, Cancun, and Durban. Technology was one of the main focuses of the Doha conference. However, this agreement does not represent a major transformation of the technology transfer mechanisms of the underlying UNFCCC. Instead, it focuses on implementation concerns and procedures for existing procedures. In particular, the Technology Mechanism and Technology Executive Committee were implemented in the Bali round (2007) as a means of formalizing the technology development and transfer process. However, these agreements had limited implementation periods and an informal organization. The Climate Technology Center was established as a means of implementing the UNFCCC Technology Mechanism in the upcoming period, in order to improve technology development and transfer for developing countries. This is an incremental change that will offer more centralized support for development of metrics and channels for technology transfer, but it is not a major revision of the UNFCCC framework. This may be attributable to reluctance on the part of developed countries to commit further to financing for technology transfer programs and capacity building programs. Without this support, technology transfer for CO_2 emissions reduction may founder in future negotiation rounds.[43]

IV. NEED FOR CLIMATE-CHANGE-RELATED TECHNOLOGY

While most of the world fixates on how to reduce the amount of carbon dioxide (CO_2) and other greenhouse gases we emit into the atmosphere, scientists and engineers around the world are busy working on various "geo-engineering" technologies to mitigate global warming and its effects. Many scientists oppose using new technology to fix problems created by old technology, but others view it as a quick and relatively inexpensive way to solve humankind's most vexing environmental problem.[44] Many experts believe seeking innovative solutions is key to making a dent in carbon emissions and ensuring that Earth doesn't eventually warm to catastrophic levels, commonly considered anything beyond the threshold of 2 degrees Celsius above

[43] *Ibid.*

[44] Technological "Solutions" to Climate Change, Scientific American (2009), https://www.scientificamerican.com/article/geoengineering-solutions/ (last visited Dec 28, 2016).

the average temperature from before the Industrial Revolution.[45] Here are six technologies which might stem the worrisome warming trend:

A. ***Solar Geo-Engineering*****:** Solar geo-engineering is sort of the Hail-Mary pass when attempts to cut carbon emissions don't go far enough. It includes blasting sulfate aerosols into the stratosphere to reflect sunlight away from Earth or spraying fine sea salt into the sky to whiten clouds."They all act very fast. They are all cheap enough that money is not the issue and they are all inherently imperfect," says Keith, author of the 2013 book *A Case for Climate Engineering.* "The thing we most need to do is talk about it," he says, adding more research is needed on the effects and efficacy."One powerful country could do it by itself," if desperate enough for a quick but temporary fix," says climate scientist Ken Caldeira of the Carnegie Institution for Science. He notes how Mount Pinatubo's 1991 eruption in the Philippines, which fired sulfur particles high into the air, cooled global temperatures nearly one degree Fahrenheit in 1992 and 1993.[46]

Solar and wind-harnessed power sources have been growing in popularity over the past few years, and the cost of producing solar power has come way down. As the push for solar has grown, researchers have been looking for ways to more widely distribute the technology. For instance, scientists at the University of California, Berkeley, developed a material with a nanostructure that absorbs as much light as the standard solar cells currently, but uses less semiconductor material. This could lead to lower-cost, more accessible solar cells.[47]

B. ***Carbon Capture*****:** Carbon capture, which traps emissions from power plants and removes them the atmosphere, might obviate the need for such a drastic step.Because of its current high cost, no commercial, coal-fired facility has yet to employ this technique. In May, the first effort is slated to debut in Kemper County, Miss; it's designed to capture 65% of carbon emissions. Earlier this year, MIT developed a simpler scrubbing system that it says can be added relatively easy to existing facilities.

---

[45] Brian Mastroianni, Technology that could disrupt the course of climate change CBS News (2015), http://www.cbsnews.com/news/technology-that-could-change-the-course-of-climate-change/ (last visited Dec 25, 2016).

[46] Wendy Koch, How technology can halt climate change USA Today (2013), http://www.usatoday.com/story/news/nation/2013/12/30/climate-change-technologies/4041931/ (last visited Dec 25, 2016).

[47] Brian Mastroianni, Technology that could disrupt the course of climate change CBS News (2015), http://www.cbsnews.com/news/technology-that-could-change-the-course-of-climate-change/ (last visited Dec 25, 2016).

The U.S. Department of Energy is funding research on how to capture industrial emissions and either store them underground or use them to make products such as fuel, plastics, cement and fertilizer. Without federal funds, Mark Herrema founded Newlight Technologies, a California-based company that captures methane emissions from dairy farms and uses them to make plastic. Klaus Lackner, a Columbia University geophysicist, is working on synthetic trees that absorb carbon dioxide about a thousand times faster than natural trees. Keith's Calgary-based start-up, Carbon Engineering, funded partly by Bill Gates, is developing industrial-scale technologies to capture carbon from the atmosphere and use it to produce low-carbon transportation fuels.[48] This kind of technology separates carbon dioxide from the other gases produced from electricity generation, and then funnels that carbon through a pipeline or transports it by way of a ship and deposits it miles below the planet's surface in rock formations.[49]

C. *Artificial Photosynthesis:* Artificial photosynthesis could yield an entirely new, emissions-free energy source. In 2011, Nocera unveiled his "artificial leaf" – a credit-card-sized silicon solar wafer that, when placed in a glass of tap water and exposed to sunlight, generates hydrogen and oxygen bubbles that can be stored and – when needed – recombined in a fuel cell to generate electricity."We already know how to do this," Nocera says. The problem: His water-splitting device generates hydrogen fuel, but there's no network yet of hydrogen filling stations in the United States. So his start-up, Sun Catalytix, launched to develop the device, is now focusing instead on grid-scale flow batteries.DOE is funding related research at the Joint Center for Artificial Photosynthesis, led by the California Institute of Technology. "The goal is to produce a chemical liquid fuel" that can replace gasoline, says spokesman William Royea, adding it will likely take a decade or so to reduce costs enough to make it commercially viable.[50]

D. *Solar and Wind Power:* Solar and wind power have surged in recent years, and research is finding new applications. MIT and Sandia National Laboratories have developed ultra light, atom-thin solar cells that can be embedded in flexible products like drapes or harder structures like a tablet's outer shell to produce power. Similarly, they are developing transparent cells that can be placed on windows. Companies such as

---

48 *Supra* 47.

49 *Supra* 48.

50 Wendy Koch, How technology can halt climate change USA Today (2013), http://www.usatoday.com/story/news/nation/2013/12/30/climate-change-technologies/4041931/ (last visited Dec 25, 2016).

California-based Makani, acquired this year by Google, are trying to harness power from high-altitude wind, which is faster and steadier. Their challenge: tethering airborne turbines hundreds of feet off the ground without interfering with aircraft. MIT researchers are looking at far-offshore wind turbines and, to store their power and anchor them, huge concrete spheres that sit on the seafloor."Storage will be the game changer" for solar and wind, because their power is intermittent but electric grids need consistency, says Bob Armstrong, director of the MIT Energy Initiative. So, universities, start-ups and major companies are working to boost battery performance. Some advances debuted this year, including a battery by General Electric that's paired with a Texas wind farm to provide continuous power.[51]

E. ***Nuclear Power:*** Nuclear power, disliked by many environmentalists because of safety and waste disposal concerns, is welcomed by climate scientists including James Hansen as a major energy source that does not emit carbon.DOE has offered $8.3 billion in loan guarantees to help build a nuclear power plant in Georgia and is funding efforts by two companies—North Carolina-based Babcock & Wilcox and Oregon-based NuScale Power—to develop small modular reactors. These school bus-size versions of current light water reactors could be made in U.S. factories and moved from site to site. DOE says it expects commercial operation around 2025.TerraPower, a start-up in Bellevue, Wash., that's partly funded by Bill Gates, is developing a larger, 500-megawatt, "traveling wave" reactor that runs on nuclear waste and can go 40 years without refueling. Last year, Gates said the company is looking to build a demonstration plant and "China is one possible place." This month, DOE posted a proposed agreement between an unnamed U.S. company and the Chinese government to develop such a reactor.[52]

Efficiency is often seen as the invisible energy source, because it's energy not used. Though basic technology, its potential is huge. Long, who's studying California's efforts, estimates efficiency upgrades could halve the state's energy demand by 2050. Building practices such as superior insulation and air sealing have proven to slash a home's energy use up to 90%. "This is the best way to get at climate mitigation," says David Gottfried, co-founder of the U.S. Green Building Council, a private non-profit group. Noting that residential and commercial buildings account for nearly 40% of total U.S. energy use, he says ultra-efficient

---

51 *Ibid.*
52 *Ibid.*

buildings can essentially become "our power plants of the future."IBM is working with cities, utilities and the federal government to boost efficiency by using sensors, meters and digital controls to monitor and automate how energy is used. The Obama administration is requiring new cars and light trucks to nearly double their fuel efficiency by 2025.[53]

V. TECHNOLOGY TRANSFER & CLIMATE CHANGE

Technology transfer plays a critical role in the effective global response to the climate change challenge. Since technology is a source of greenhouse gas (GHG) emissions, achieving global reduction of GHGs requires innovation to make current technologies cleaner and climate-resilient. While there are many definitions of technology transfer, the GEF has adopted the concept of technology transfer as defined by the Intergovernmental Panel on Climate Change (IPCC) in Methodological and Technological Issues in Technology Transfer, IPCC 2000, and embodied in the UNFCCC technology transfer framework. Technology transfer is defined as: *"...a broad set of processes covering the flows of know-how, experience and equipment for mitigating and adapting to climate change amongst different stakeholders such as governments, private sector entities, financial institutions, non-governmental organizations (NGOs) and research/education institutions..."*[54]

In the academic sector, the process of commercialization – or of bringing *technologies* to the marketplace – is known as "*technology transfer.*" *Technology transfer* is now part of the government mandate for institutions receiving federal funding for research. The Council on Government Relations (COGR) defines technology transfer as "the handing off of intellectual property rights from the university to the for-profit sector for purposes of commercialization."[55]

Technology transfer has been defined by UNCTAD as *"the transfer of systematic knowledge for the manufacture of a product, for the application of a process or for the rendering of a service and does not extend to the transactions involving the mere sale or mere lease of goods."* The roles of transfer of technology in reducing CO_2 are immense. One of the ways that developing economies may be inefficient is that, using outdated production techniques and equipment, there may be higher rates of CO_2 emissions from

---

[53] *Ibid.*

[54] Technology Transfer, Global Environment Facility (2016), https://www.thegef.org/topics/technology-transfer (last visited Dec 26, 2016).

[55] What is Technology Transfer?, UR Ventures, http://www.rochester.edu/ventures/about/what-is-technology-transfer/ (last visited Dec 23, 2016).

production. However, in recent years, the increasing standard of living, especially in higher-income developing countries like India and China, has also resulted in an increasing rate of consumption-related emissions from electricity usage and cars. The Kyoto Protocol does not place any requirements on developing countries for CO_2 reductions. Technology transfer is one route to CO_2 reduction in developing countries. Low-carbon development is a significantly improved development approach for poor countries, since it avoids the use of costly inputs like fossil fuels and instead encourages long-term investments in renewable energy. However, this requires the development and transfer of low-carbon technologies that developing countries can take advantage of, which has been neglected.[56]

There has been an evolution in the international positioning of climate change, CO_2 reduction, and technology transfer as a means of reducing CO_2 emissions in developing countries over the past 20 years. In this section, a brief summary of key points in this international discussion is provided, beginning with the United Nations Framework Convention on Climate Change (UNFCCC) (1992) and closing with the Doha outcome gateway (2012). This will show the evolution of ideas surrounding this area as well as its current importance.[57]

VI. INTELLECTUAL PROPERTY & TECHNOLOGY TRANSFER

Technology transfer directly relates to trade laws and regulations passed in developing and advanced countries, since these laws govern issues like production requirements and transfer of technologies. These laws implement the provisions of the UNFCCC, which only hold force because of national-level laws passed by member states. Intellectual property laws (IPL), including laws related to copyright, trademark or registration mark, patent, and other aspects of IP, also are related to technology transfer.[58]

Once an innovation has been created, its non-rival character suggests that its benefits will be maximized if its use is free to all at marginal cost. Although this availability to all will yield benefits in the short run, it will also severely damage the incentive for further innovation. But, excessive IPR protection is likely to lead to an inadequate dissemination of new

---

[56] Thitiporn Watthanachai, Technology transfer for reducing CO_2: A critical review of intellectual property laws and trade laws in Thailand and Japan, www.diva-portal.org/smash/get/diva2:663813/FULLTEXT01.pdf (last visited Dec 23, 2016).

[57] *Ibid.*

[58] *Ibid.*

knowledge, which in itself could slow growth to the extent that access to existing technology is necessary to induce further innovation. Weak IPR protection has actually stimulated R&D activity in many countries by encouraging knowledge spillovers from transnational corporations (TNCs) and other domestic firms. Giving innovators too much protection may also lead to permanent monopoly. Entry by rivals may be impeded, and successful innovators may have reduced incentives for developing and exploiting subsequent innovations. Choice of IPR policy then reflects a balancing of these considerations. The awarding of a temporary monopoly, although second best, is intended to restore the incentive to innovate, which in turn should encourage long-run growth and improved product quality.[59]

Often technology transfer is seen as a "forced process" where the owner is reluctant to make it available to others in need of such knowledge because it constitutes "competitive advantage". This view is not entirely accurate as many large firms and several research institutions in developed and developing countries are establishing technology transfer offices primarily to manage and transfer their technology assets to interested parties at a profit. Similarly, it is not accurate to presuppose that all technology owners are willing to transfer all, some or any of their technologies to some or any interested party.[60]

A. ***Trade laws and Regulations:*** The main benefit claimed for strong IPR protection is that by allowing innovators to appropriate a share of the benefits of their creative activities, R&D is encouraged, which leads to innovation and higher long-run growth. The impact of IPR protection on domestic innovation is likely to vary with a country's level of development and its factor endowments. More generally, we may expect IPRs to impact on domestic innovation differently in countries with significant innovative capacity as opposed to those with few resources available for domestic innovation. The evidence summarized suggests that stronger IPR protection can encourage domestic innovation in countries that have significant domestic capacity for innovation, but that

59 Rod Falvey & Neil Foster, The Role of Intellectual Property Rights in Technology Transfer and Economic Growth: Theory and Evidence, http://www.unido.org/fileadmin/user_media/Publications/Pub_free/Role_of_intellectual_property_rights_in_ technology_transfer_and_economic_growth (last visited Dec 23, 2016).

60 The Role of Intellectual Property Rights in Technology Transfer in the Context of the Convention on Biological Diversity A Technical Study, https://www.cbd.int/doc/meetings/ttc/egttstc-02/other/egttstc-02-oth-techstudy-en.pdf (last visited Dec 23, 2016).

it has little impact on innovation in countries with a small innovative capacity.[61]

The impact of stronger IPR protection on technology diffusion is ambiguous in theory and depends on a country's circumstances. On the one hand, stronger IPR protection could restrict the diffusion of technology, with patents preventing others from using proprietary knowledge and the increased market power of IPR holders potentially reducing the dissemination of knowledge due to lower output and higher prices. On the other hand, IPRs could play a positive role in knowledge diffusion, since the information available in patent claims is available to other potential inventors. Moreover, strong IPR protection may encourage technology transfer through increased trade in goods and services, FDI, technology licensing and joint ventures. Despite this theoretical ambiguity, the diffusion of technology from countries at the technological frontier to other countries is considered the main potential benefit of the TRIPS Agreement, particularly for developing countries that tend not to innovate significantly. The evidence suggests that stronger IPR protection can encourage technology transfer through a number of channels, though once again its impact has been found to depend upon other factors related to a country's imitative ability and level of development.[62]

B. *Trips Agreement:* The preamble to GATT notes the need for "allowing for the optimal use of the world's resources in accordance with the objective of sustainable development, seeking both to protect and preserve the environment and to enhance the means for doing so in a manner consistent with their respective needs and concerns at different levels of economic development". Within TRIPS Art.7 requires that "the protection and enforcement of intellectual property rights should contribute to the promotion of technological innovation and to the transfer and dissemination of technology, *to the mutual advantage of producers and users of technological knowledge* and in a manner conducive to social and economic welfare, and to a balance of rights and obligations."

In WTO symposium with *NGOs on Trade, Environment and Sustainable Development* (May 20-21, 1997, Geneva) the relationship between TRIPS and environment was examined. Some participants viewed it as a positive relationship in which TRIPS Agreement was seen,"as an instrument for

---

61 Rod Falvey & Neil Foster, The Role of Intellectual Property Rights in Technology Transfer and Economic Growth: Theory and Evidence, http://www.unido.org/fileadmin/user_media/Publications/Pub_free/Role_of_intellectual_property_rights_in_ technology_transfer_and_economic_growth (last visited Dec 23, 2016).

62 *Ibid.*

promoting the development of environmentally sound technologies. Some noted that intellectual property rights (IPRs) provided time-limited exclusivity which fostered creativity in the development of new technologies, including environmentally sound technologies".

In a WTO symposium of non-governmental organization on *Trade, Environment and Sustainable Development* (March 17-18, 1998). The WTO position was that if a problem was environmental, the effort should be to develop an environmental rather than trade policy solutions. The UNCTAD representative felt that trade and environment were complimentary although the constituencies representing these interests were often in conflict. The UN Executive Director addressing WTO first time felt that the questions regarding new property rights, and also about the responsibility must be addressed as soon as possible. The need for transparency in public policy, he added, had to go hand in hand with public accountability. The discussion on TRIPS and environment was inconclusive and the general refrain was that clear relationship between TRIPS and technology transfer was weak even when such technologies had strong environmental implications.[63]

VII. ENVIRONMENT FRIENDLY TRADE & TECHNOLOGY TRANSFER

The Committee on Trade and Environment (CTE) discussed the interaction between environment and TRIPS comprehensively in June 1995. The Committee took note of the fact that only Art.27.2, as mentioned above, makes an explicit reference to the environment. The CTE (1995) made a very thorough review of various issues that arise in the interface between IPRs and environment and identified five key issues[64]

A. ***Promotion of Environmentally-Sound Technologies***: CTE (1995) noted that a fundamental feature of IPR systems and of the TRIPS Agreement, particularly in the area of patents, is to provide incentives for the generation of new technology, by giving the inventor an exclusive right (subject to certain exceptions) over the use of his invention for a finite period of time. Art 39 of TRIPS deals with the protection of undisclosed information. It requires Members to give natural or legal persons the possibility of preventing information lawfully within their control from being disclosed to, acquired by, or used by others without

---

[63] Anil K Gupta, Environmental Implications of Intellectual Property Protection (IPP): Can individual and community conservation ethic and creativity be rewarded through IPP, http://anilg.sristi.org/wp-content/Papers/Environmental%20 Implications% 20of%20IP,%20UNEP%20Paper.doc.

[64] *Ibid.*

their consent in a manner contrary to honest commercial practices. To be eligible for such protection under the TRIPS Agreement, the information in question must be secret, have commercial value because it is secret and have been subject to reasonable steps to keep it secret. CTE noted that provision of TRIPS on the protection of the layout-designs (topographies) of integrated circuits (Articles 35 to 38) could also be relevant to the promotion of technological innovation which can be of benefit to the environment.[65]

B. ***Access to and Transfer of Technology:*** An important objective of the TRIPS Agreement is to promote not only technological innovation, but also "the transfer and dissemination of technology, to the mutual advantage of producers and users of technological knowledge in a manner conducive to social and economic welfare, and to a balance of rights and obligations". It was believed that stronger IPR protection in technology receiving countries will help in transfer of technology from other countries. However, critics have argued that the level of research and manufacturing infrastructure in a developing country, and its capacity to absorb new technologies seem to matter more than just the stronger IPR regime in a technology receiving country. CTE (1995) noted that,"in the event that there is tension between the objectives of promoting technological innovation and the transfer of technology, and with the aim of securing the objectives of Article 7, the TRIPS Agreement contains a number of provisions, in particular on compulsory licensing and control of anti-competitive practices, to establish an appropriate balance between these two objectives, and thus between the interests of producers and users of technological knowledge, conducive to social and economic welfare".

VIII. TRIPS MANDATE & ENVIRONMENTAL SAFEGUARD

Five essential elements of TRIPS were found to have direct implication for environment such as: (i) disclosure, (ii) Experimental use, (iii) Incentives to transfer of technology, (iv) Compulsory licenses, and (v) Anti-competitive practices.[66] The fact that every patent has limited life and the knowledge protected by it comes under public domain after expiry of duration of its protection was cited as an example of how IPRs helped in dissemination of technology. In the absence of intellectual property rights

---

65 *Ibid.*

66 Anil K Gupta, Environmental Implications of Intellectual Property Protection (IPP): Can individual and community conservation ethic and creativity be rewarded through IPP, http://anilg.sristi.org/wp-content/Papers/Environmental%20 Implications% 20of%20IP,%20UNEP%20Paper.doc.

(Art 29 which requires disclosure of invention by every patent applicant), it was feared that much more knowledge will remain protected by trade secrets and thus not available for improvement by others for utilization by others after a given period. Article 30 allows Members to make "limited exceptions" to the rights conferred by a patent, subject of course to certain conditions. Drafting history of this provision suggested that one of the "limited exceptions" that was intended to be covered was acts done for experimental purposes. This type of provision is to be found in most, if not all, patent laws. The combination of this provision with the disclosure requirement was supposed to reflect an underlying objective of the patent system, CTE (1995) observed, "to promote, and not be an impediment to, the further advance of science and technology". Article 66.2 of the *TRIPS Agreement* requires developed country Members to "provide incentives to enterprises and institutions in their territories for the purpose of promoting and encouraging technology transfer to least-developed country Members in order to enable them to create a sound and viable technological base". This it was hoped would help in transfer of Environmentally Sound Technologies (ESTs). The provision in TRIPS for compulsory licenses (i.e. a license granted without the agreement of the patent owner) to be granted to an applicant to use a patented invention where the right holder has not been willing to grant a voluntary license on reasonable commercial terms and conditions within a reasonable period of time, subject to a number of conditions aimed at protecting the legitimate interest of the patent owner, also may be of help in this regard. The relevant provisions of the TRIPS Agreement are Article 31, the last sentence of Article 27.1 and Article 5A of the *Paris Convention* (incorporated by virtue of Article 2.1 of the *TRIPS Agreement).* Anti-competitive practices when come in the way of transfer of ESTs, member countries can use Article 8.2 of the TRIPS Agreement which requires that[67]:

> "Appropriate measures, provided that they are consistent with the provisions of this Agreement, may be needed to prevent the abuse of intellectual property rights by right holders or the resort to practices which unreasonably restrain trade or adversely affect the international transfer of technology."

The TRIPS Agreement contains a Section (Section 8 of Part II) which provides for international cooperation in the control of anti-competitive

---

[67] Anil K Gupta, Environmental Implications of Intellectual Property Protection (IPP): Can individual and community conservation ethic and creativity be rewarded through IPP, http://anilg.sristi.org/wp-content/Papers/Environmental%20 Implications% 20of%20IP,%20UNEP%20Paper.doc.

practices in contractual licenses besides Art 40.1 and Art 40.2 recognize the right of Members to "adopt, consistently with other provisions of the Agreement, appropriate measures to prevent or control such practices".[68]

A. ***Technology that May Adversely Affect The Environment:*** CTE brings in another very interesting provision of TRIPS to possibly control the use of environmentally-prejudicial technology, that is Article 39.3 dealing with "the protection of undisclosed test or other data submitted in order to obtain marketing approval for pharmaceutical and agricultural chemical products which utilize new chemical entities". The argument is that this provision helps firms or inventors protect their data available to public agencies for testing say, environmental aspects of a technology which requires enormous cost and thus maintain their competitiveness. However, the public agencies are not prevented from disclosure if such sharing of information is in public interest.[69]

B. ***Patentability of Genetic Material&Life Forms:*** Article 27.1 of the TRIPS Agreement establishes the basic criteria for patentability "...patents shall be available for any inventions, whether products or processes, in all fields of technology, provided that they are new, involve an inventive step and are capable of industrial application."

C. ***Contribution of Countries& Communities' Sources of Genetic Material:*** There are several ways in which IP regime can influence the environmental conditions in developed and developing countries[70]:

i) Lack of transfer of proprietary patented technologies from north to south which can substitute environmental unfriendly practices, generate environment friendly and efficient alternatives and remedy the negative environmental externalities of various ongoing industrial processes (such as hazardous wastes).

ii) Restriction of access to technologies which if widely used, could improve the environmental conditions considerably, particularly when substitution of technologies is mandated by MAEs.

iii) Introduction of technologies with higher production potential but of which sufficient public scrutiny may not have taken place except by the usual certification agencies (some of the transgenic crops).

---

68 *Ibid.*

69 *Ibid.*

70 *Ibid.*

iv) Incentives for private investment in technologies which will generate a public good through a system of incentives or licensing by national governments or international organizations for wider access, and

v) Access to global markets for grassroots green innovations that may provide incentives for international venture funds to invest in green innovations from one country to generate enterprises there or in another country. The linkage between green innovations, investment and enterprise is likely to become stronger in the presence of stronger IP regime.

IX. TECHNOLOGY SHARING MODELS

A. ***Compulsory Licensing:*** In some countries, a 'license of right' system provides for a reduction in official fees for patent holders who agree to make their patented technology available to anyone requesting a license, subject to terms that can be negotiated or determined by the authorities. The UK Patent Office, for instance, maintains a database of patented technology that is endorsed as available for a license of right - this includes alternative fuel technologies patented by major automotive companies.[71]

B. ***Patent Pooling:*** Patent pools are voluntary agreements between two or more patent holders to license one or more of their patents to one another or third parties based on a predetermined formula.[72] Generally broader in scope, patent commons allow technology holders to pledge their patented technologies for widespread use for no royalty payment - usually subject to certain general conditions (for instance, agreement not to enforce rights over technologies resulting from access to the commons). A recent initiative, the Eco-Patent Commons, includes patents on environmentally beneficial technologies. The participating companies legally pledge or covenant not to assert their patent rights against those implementing the technology to produce environmental benefits. These benefits include reduced/eliminated natural resource consumption, or reduced/eliminated waste generation or pollution.[73]

---

[71] Antony Taubman, Sharing technology to meet a common challenge, http://www.wipo.int/wipo_magazine/en/2009/02/article_0002.html.

[72] The Role of Intellerctual Property Rights in Technology Transfer in the Context of the Convention on Biological Diversity A Technical Study, https://www.cbd.int/doc/meetings/ttc/egttstc-02/other/egttstc-02-oth-techstudy-en.pdf (last visited Dec 23, 2016).

[73] Antony Taubman, Sharing technology to meet a common challenge, http://www.wipo. int/wipo_magazine/en/2009/02/article_0002.html.

C. ***Humanitarian or Preferential Licensing:*** This type of licensing technology policy provides highly favorable or free terms to certain beneficiaries, for example, developing country recipients, social marketing programs, or public sector and philanthropic initiatives.[74]

X. INTERNATIONAL INITIATIVES

A. ***Wipo Green***: Addressing climate change is dependent on economic growth that works with, rather than against the environment. Innovative green technology solutions can help by allowing us to do more with less - be it alternative energy production, energy saving, or greener forms of transportation, agriculture and forestry. The challenge is to enhance the environment for innovation, while enabling speedier diffusion of these green technologies to all parts of the world.[75]

- WIPO Green, an interactive marketplace that connects technology and service providers with those seeking innovative solutions, was established by the World Intellectual Property Organization (WIPO) in 2013[76].
- WIPO Green consists of an online database and network that brings together a wide range of players in the green technology innovation value chain, and connects owners of new technologies with individuals or companies who might be looking to commercialize, license or otherwise distribute a green technology[77].
- In this way, we help not only to accelerate innovation and diffusion of green technologies, but also contribute to the efforts of developing countries in addressing climate change[78]

B. ***United Nations:*** From the latest technical developments in renewable energy to innovative cropping techniques, the role of technology and research in tackling climate change in developing countries is the focus of a new facility launched by the United Nations today. Following a decision at the 2012 *UN Climate Change Conference in Doha,* governments meeting this week in Nairobi at the Governing Council of the *United*

---

74 *Ibid.*

75 Climate Change and IP, Climate Change and IP, http://www.wipo.int/policy/en/climate_change/ (last visited Dec 28, 2016).

76 WIPO GREEN, WIPO GREEN, https://www3.wipo.int/wipogreen-database/(last visited Dec 28, 2016).

77 *Ibid.*

78 *Ibid.*

Nations Environment Programme (UNEP) confirmed a UNEP-led consortium as the hosts of the Climate Technology Centre. The consortium includes the *UN Industrial Development Organization (UNIDO)* and 11 other international research and development bodies. The *Climate Technology Centre and Network (CTCN)* aims to speed up the transfer of climate-related technology and expertise to developing countries in order to reduce greenhouse gas emissions, and improve resilience to changing weather patterns, drought, soil erosion, and other impacts of climate change. At the 2010 *UN Climate Change Conference in Cancun,* countries agreed on a new Technology Mechanism to improve the transfer of climate-related technology, encompassing energy efficiency, renewable energy, early-warning systems, and other fields. Mobilizing necessary funds and eliminating policy and technical barriers to deploying such technologies have traditionally proven difficult. The CTCN will work to reduce the risks and barriers that hinder acquisition of mitigation technologies by developing countries, and support efforts to implement mitigation and adaptation actions that can reduce emissions and ensure progress towards sustainable development goals. "Innovation is the engine of development, and replacing current technologies with cleaner, low carbon alternatives is a vital part of tackling the causes and effects of global climate change," said UN Under-Secretary-General and UNEP Executive Director Achim Steiner. "Under UNEP's leadership, the Climate Technology Centre and Network will work to accelerate the use of new technologies in improving the lives and livelihoods of millions of people in developing countries who are dealing with the impacts of climate change on a daily basis," he added. "The consortium partners are already engaged in some 1500 activities related to climate technologies in over 150 countries. Together, this expertise and global reach can deliver scaled-up action on mitigation and adaptation, and support the transition to an inclusive, low-carbon green economy," said Mr. Steiner. Through nationally-designated authorities, developing countries will be able to call on the services of the centre and its wider network for technical support and advice. "The world needs to urgently accelerate climate action across all three central pillars of action - this means international, national and business action. Technology is essential to enable developing countries to pursue sustainable development and to grow their economies in a low carbon, high resilient manner," said Christiana Figueres, Executive Secretary of the *United Nations Framework Convention on Climate Change* (UNFCCC). "UNEP is well suited to be the host of the Climate Technology Centre and to lead its supporting consortium of world-class organizations. The completion of the Technology Mechanism and its related network is on track and will soon help boost efforts across all three pillars of climate action, which is essential if we are to stay within the internationally agreed limit of a 2 degrees' Celsius temperature rise," added Ms. Figueres. "The *Climate Technology Centre and Network* will reduce the risks and costs of technology transfer, and help developing countries make informed choices about mitigation and adaptation technologies," said Kandeh K. Yumkella, Director General of UNIDO. The CTCN will establish an information platform for improved sharing of knowledge related to climate technologies. This will provide data, reports, and other resources to address the specific needs of developing countries. In terms of capacity building, the centre will conduct regional and national workshops on priority issues, entrepreneurship, and the development of policies and programmes to attract foreign direct investment. The CTNC will also work to expand international partnerships to accelerate the diffusion of environmentally sound technologies, particularly among communities in developing countries. Such efforts will include 'twinnings' of organizations and centres to promote North-South and South-South partnerships, and to encourage cooperative research and development. The centre will become the implementing arm of the Technology Mechanism of the *UN Framework Convention on Climate Change (UNFCCC)*, which was backed by UN member states in Cancun in 2010. The Technology Mechanism is expected to facilitate accelerated action on technology development and transfer, in order to support action on climate change mitigation and adaptation. Earlier this week, the climate and economic benefits of deploying solar LED lighting technology were showcased at the UNEP Governing Council. Some 74 million tons of carbon emissions are produced annually by kerosene lamps and other fuel-based lighting, mainly in communities in developing countries living off the electricity grid. The UNEP studies show that in Nigeria, for example, replacing fuel-based lighting with solar-powered LED units would save the country US$ 1.4 billion in fuel and other costs, and deliver carbon savings equivalent to taking 1.6 million cars off the road. The initial costs would be repaid in only 14 months.[79]

C. ***Global Environment Facility:*** Since its inception in 1991, the GEF has been facilitating technology transfer to help developing countries address the global climate change challenge. The GEF has a mandate from the UNFCCC to finance the transfer of Environmentally Sound Technologies, and has evolved into the largest public-sector funding source in this area. These technologies, compared to others, have the potential for significantly improved environmental performance. They include know-how, goods and services, and equipment, as well as organizational

[79] UN Launches New Centre to Accelerate Use of Technology in Tackling Climate Change, http://www.unep.org/newscentre/Default.aspx?DocumentID=2704 & Article ID=9418 & l=en.

and managerial procedures. The GEF-6 Climate Change Mitigation Strategy supports innovation and technology transfer at key early and middle stages, focusing on the demonstration and early deployment of innovative options. The GEF support aims at addressing elevated risks associated with innovation, mitigating the barriers of technology transfer, and piloting promising approaches. During the first year of GEF-6 (July 2014 - June 2015), 14 projects with technology transfer objectives were approved with $221.4 million of GEF funding and $2.5 billion of co-financing. They include the Sustainable Cities IAP and projects addressing the transition from fossil fuel to renewable energy in SIDS. Under the GEF-6 Program, the GEF will support projects in the following categories:

1. Technologies with transformational potential;
2. Acceleration of low emission technology innovation and uptake through demonstration, deployment, and transfer using policies and mechanisms;
3. Collaborative initiatives with stakeholders, including the private sector, to adapt technologies to user needs.[80]

XI. CARBON EMISSIONS & IPR ISSUES

Sustainable Development, as defined by the Brundtland Commission in 1987, *'is development that meets the needs of the present without compromising the ability of future generations to meet their own needs'*. Economic growth and development have to be guided by the compulsion of sustainability, because no one has the luxury, any longer, of ignoring the economic as well as the environmental threat, that a fast-deteriorating ecosystem poses to the fragile planet.[81] No one is immune to the reality of climate change, ecological degradation, depletion of the ozone layer and contamination of our freshwater.

Globally, environment has emerged as a major area of governance—bringing the scientific, socioeconomic and political dimensions in a single crucible. Sustainability of economic development itself crucially hinges on the protection of environment. For India, challenges of arresting the pace of degradation of environment are formidable due to the imperatives of maintaining high economic growth, increasing trends of urbanization, population growth, industrialization, unmet basic needs, life style changes and biotic pressures. While these challenges are formidable, there are

80 Technology Transfer, Global Environment Facility (2016), https://www.thegef.org/topics/technology-transfer (last visited Dec 28, 2016).

81 http://planningcommission.gov.in/plans/planrel/12thplan/pdf/12fyp_vol1.pdf

also positive factors such as our strong base in science and technology, our institutional infrastructure that can drive the new paradigms and a holistic approach demanded by the environmental governance today. Impacts on environment are an amalgam of the roles of multiple stakeholders such as government, industries and citizens. To respond to a diverse range of dynamic challenges, environmental governance should now be founded on adaptive and agile systems that optimize and strengthen the roles of all stakeholders.

India has been actively involved in international fora relating to environmental protection, and has been part of 94 Multilaterals Environmental Agreements such as the *Ramsar Convention on Wetlands, Convention on International Trade in Endangered Species of Fauna and Flora (CITES), Convention on Biological Diversity (CBD),* among many others. India has also signed the *United Nations Framework Convention on Climate Change,* and has acceded to the *Kyoto Protocol* in 2002. Despite not having binding mitigation commitments as per the *United Nations Framework Convention on Climate Change* (UNFCCC), India has communicated its voluntary mitigation goal of reducing the emissions intensity of its Gross Domestic Product (GDP) by 20-25 per cent, over 2005 levels, by 2020.

Twelve Focus Areas for the Twelfth Plan (2012-2017)[82]

1.	Advanced Coal Technologies
2.	National Wind Energy Mission
3.	National Solar Mission
4.	Technology Improvement in Iron and Steel Industry
5.	Technology Improvement in Cement Industry
6.	Energy Efficiency Programmes in the Industry
7.	Vehicle Fuel Efficiency Programme
8.	Improving the Efficiency of Freight Transport
9.	Better Urban Public and Non-Motorized Transport
10.	Lighting, Labelling and Super-Efficient Equipment Programme
11.	Faster Adoption of Green Building Codes
12.	Improving the Stock of Forest and Tree Cover

Cap-and-trade programmes are often designed to achieve greater reductions over time, so the cap may be lowered in subsequent years to

82 *Ibid.*

enable market participants achieve emission reductions gradually. To achieve compliance with the capped emission level, market participants are allocated allowances to emit (1 tonne per allowance) with the total number of allowances summing to the level of the cap. Market participants can purchase allowances from other participants to cover excess emissions, or sell allowances, if they reduce emissions below their allocation. Such trading increases economic efficiency.

A carbon tax is an alternative to a cap-and trade. It can be given other names like cess, surcharge and levy among others. Although both policies generate a carbon price signal, there is a fundamental difference in the way in which the level of carbon price signal is determined under the two regimes. A carbon tax fixes the price of carbon and allows the quantity of emissions to adjust in response to the level of tax. In contrast, a cap-and-trade system fixes the quantity of aggregate emissions, and allows the price of CO_2 emissions to adjust to ensure the emissions cap is met.

India is experimenting with both cap-and-trade in the form of the PAT scheme and a carbon tax in the form of a cess on coal (INR 50 per tonne). Both are in early stages of implementation. While the cap-and-trade mechanisms have a greater certainty in emissions reduction, as a tool for financing they face greater uncertainty. Carbon tax mechanisms, on the other hand, can provide greater certainty as a source of financing, while uncertainty on emissions reduction can be brought down by using energy or emission intensity benchmarks.

XII. INTELLECTUAL PROPERTY & TECHNOLOGY TRANSFER LAW

Every technology engagement requires strong and predictable IPR protection as a pre-requisite to invest in low carbon and energy efficient technology innovation and diffusion. In addition, patent protection, specifically, supports the dissemination and advancement of Energy Sector Environmental Innovation - World Energy Council and technology itself, by providing notice of new technology solutions and assets through which to exchange expertise and giving innovators and companies the confidence they need to invest in, trade and share their technological knowhow with business partners, customers and others. Technology Sharing takes many forms, with varied approaches generally tailored to the parties and their particular circumstances. There are three principal avenues for technology sharing: trade, cooperative agreements, and assignments of rights.[83]

---

83 https://www.worldenergy.org/wp-content/uploads/2012/10/wec_rules_of_trade__ipp_paper.pdf

One of the most basic means for sharing technology is through trade, *e.g.*, a product sale, where the purchaser acquires an embodiment of the innovation. The sale gives the purchaser the right to use the technology. And the purchaser gains an understanding of how the technology functions, by operating the equipment.[84] Often, parties engage in transactions specifically designed to transfer or generate technology. For example, cooperative agreements such as joint ventures or equivalent partnerships enable parties to obtain complementary skills or resources. In such transactions, knowledge is shared between partners to develop new products or services.[85]

Licensing or actual sales of a patent are typically considered the quintessential example of technology transfer. These assignments of rights however, absent provisions to the contrary, involve little, if any, transfer of knowledge. The transaction simply provides the licensee or owner the right to practice the technology. Typically, the patent's publication is a matter of public record prior to any transaction. An additional transfer of know-how may be negotiated, but the sharing of knowledge that is likely protected as a trade secret does not occur as a matter of right.

Patents provide a mechanism to share technology advances on a global basis. By requiring and incentivizing the publication of key research results and scientific data through the patent system, IPR regimes support further innovation and development of new, derived products and technologies. Frequently, the discovery of one inventor's solution can drive other inventors to find new and more efficient ways to solve the same problem.*Patents also help convert innovation into "tradable economic assets"*.[86] When patent applications are published, they serve as a window to new solutions and a catalyst to generate technology transactions. Patents can also help secure funding for start-up firms and define what technologies different parties can bring to a venture. Meaningful trade secret protection also supports innovation, by allowing more open sharing between parties. And with the free flow of information comes new ideas and technology advances.

IPR not only provides a means to disseminate technology, but it also enables faster technology development and diffusion through partnerships. In a partnership, parties generally provide each other access to both the relevant patents and related know-how. Such communication can be critical when it comes to clean energy technology. Clean energy

---

84 *Ibid.*

85 *Ibid.*

86 *Ibid.*

technology often presents itself in the form of complex machinery, where a single technology might require hundreds of patents to be useful. Many parties may have the right to use the related patents based on licenses, a lack of local patent protection, or because the basic technology is already off patent. However, the right to practice the technology does not provide the ability to use it.

Technology transfer directly relates to trade laws and regulations passed in developing and advanced countries, since these laws govern issues like production requirements and transfer of technologies. These laws implement the provisions of the UNFCCC, which only hold force because of national-level laws passed by member states. Intellectual property laws (IPL), including laws related to copyright, trademark or registration mark, patent, and other aspects of IP, also are related to technology transfer. The focus of this research is on international trade laws and regulations related to technology transfer for CO_2 reduction. Trade laws can be defined as laws passed at the national level that address the implementation of international agreements in regard to trade between countries. These laws address a number of different issues, including the terms and conditions of trade, tariffs and duties, non-tariff barriers to trade, and areas where imports or exports of goods are forbidden or curtailed as well as international shipping rules and contractual agreements. The evidence for the use of trade laws as a means of increasing technology transfer for sustainability concerns in general, and carbon emissions overall, is very limited.

However, these agreements are often flawed in their ability to encourage technology transfer, because they are non-specific in nature and under-funded (or may even not be funded at all). Additionally, EU products are likely to be the main target of technology transfer, which is most likely to benefit the companies that produce it. This means that although these bilateral trade agreements do include provisions for technology transfer related to sustainability, they do not necessarily make a significant impact on actual technology transfer.

The main international agreement relevant to intellectual property is the *WTO TRIPS Agreement*. The TRIPS Agreement was put into place in 1995 with the establishment of the WTO, though it has since undergone revisions. The agreement covers categories including copyright, trademark, geographical indications, industrial designs, patents, and trade secrets data. The WTO describes the *TRIPS Agreement* as a set of minimum standards, which integrate the WIPO, Paris Convention, and Berne Convention. This functionally cements the pre-existing, technology creator-dominated intellectual property stage. The most relevant provisions to technology transfer are likely to be industrial designs and patents, which cover inventions and designs related to technology or consumer goods.

Patent law occurs at the national level and is important because it acts as a mechanism to force technology transfer. Compulsory licensing, where patents issued to license holders may be forcibly distributed to other manufacturers so that the underlying product can be produced. The patent holder is then recompensed at a statutory rate set by the government for the use of its patents Compulsory licensing is allowed by TRIPS, though the international agreement also requires 20-year patents for pharmaceutical products (far longer than previously required). Compulsory licensing is not routinely used even in developing countries, as it is preferred that Western companies either lower the prices of essential drugs so they are affordable or distribute the patent for the drugs for production. However, it does serve as a mechanism to ensure that developing countries do have access to life-saving medicines while still compensating the patent holder. However, this mechanism may not remain viable for developing countries, because of the imposition of later trade agreements that force abandonment of the compulsory licensing strategy. Its use has also so far been limited to a specific class of technology (pharmaceutical drugs) considered essential, rather than for more general viability that would allow its use in CO_2 reduction. Nonetheless, this does serve as an important international legal precedent for allowing developing countries to access established technologies despite the international IP regime, which privileges the rights of technology developing countries.

Whether or not IPL serves as a barrier or promoter of technology transfer is one of the core disagreements at the heart of this argument. Notably, producer countries (especially the USA) feel that IP laws are required to ensure technology transfer by allowing companies to feel comfortable transferring their products. Developing countries, including India, have rejected this argument, instead noting that loosening IP laws encourages domestic production of carbon reduction technologies. This is clearly a fundamental conflict of interest that cannot necessarily be easily resolved, since it relies on different perspectives on technology transfer and its goals, and without it technology transfer is unlikely to be successful overall.

XIII. INDIA'S EMISSIONS AND ENERGY POLICY

India is the fastest-growing major economy in the world. It is the fourth largest greenhouse gas (GHG) emitter, accounting for 5.8 percent of global emissions. India's emissions increased by 67.1 percent between 1990 and 2012, and are projected to grow 85 percent by 2030 under a business-as-usual scenario.

By other measures, India's emissions are relatively low compared to those of other major economies. India accounts for only 4 percent of global cumulative energy-related emissions since 1850, compared to 16 percent and 15 percent for the United States and China. India produces about 2 tons of CO_2 per capita, versus 20 tons and 8 tons, respectively, in the United States and China.

Coal accounted for 43.5 percent of the total energy supply in 2011, followed by biofuels and waste (24.7 percent), petroleum (22.1 percent), natural gas (6.7 percent), hydropower (1.5 percent) and nuclear (1.2 percent). India is working to meet growing energy demand by securing affordable supplies and attracting infrastructure investment in. By 2022, it aims to provide electricity to the 25 percent of the population (more than 300 million people) who don't have it.

India pledged under the Copenhagen Accord to reduce its CO_2 intensity (emissions per GDP) by 20 to 25 percent by 2020 compared to 2005 levels. India appears on track to achieve its voluntary pledge, though emissions are not projected to peak until around 2050 or later. On October 1, 2015, India formally submitted its intended nationally determined contribution (INDC) to the climate agreement due in December 2015 in Paris. Among its key elements:

1. To reduce the emissions intensity of its GDP by 33 to 35 percent by 2030 from 2005 level.
2. To achieve about 40 percent cumulative electric power installed capacity from non-fossil fuel based energy resources by 2030, with the help of transfer of technology and low cost international finance including from Green Climate Fund (GCF).
3. To create an additional carbon sink of 2.5 to 3 billion tonnes of CO_2 equivalent through additional forest and tree cover by 2030.

XIV. PUBLIC POLICIES & CLIMATE MITIGATION

India has a number of policies that contribute to climate mitigation by reducing or avoiding GHG emissions. In June 2008, the Prime Minister released India's first National Action Plan on Climate Change, which identified eight core "national missions" running through 2017.

India's current Five-Year Plan (2012-2017), which guides overall economic policy, includes goals to:

- Achieve average 8 percent annual GDP growth;
- Reduce emissions intensity in line with India's Copenhagen pledge; and
- Add 300,000 MW of renewable energy capacity.

Since taking office in May 2014, Prime Minister Narendra Modi has taken steps to scale up clean energy production and has initiated a shift in India's stance in international climate negotiations. One of his first acts was to rename the environment ministry the Ministry of Environment, Forests and Climate Change. In January, the newly reconstituted Prime Minister's Council on Climate Change launched new initiatives on wind energy, coastal zone management, health and waste-to-energy.

Renewable energy : At the federal level, India has implemented two major renewable energy-related policies: The Strategic Plan for New and Renewable Energy,which provides a broad framework, and the National Solar Mission, which sets capacity targets for renewables. The original Solar Mission includes the following targets for 2017: 27.3 GW wind, 4 GW solar, 5 GW biomass and 5 GW other renewables. For 2022, these targets increase to: 20 GW solar, 7.3 GW biomass and 6.6 GW other renewables.

A. ***Solar:*** In November 2014, the Indian government announced that it would increase the solar ambition of its National Solar Mission to 100 GW installed capacity by 2022, a five-time increase and over 30 times more solar than it currently has installed. To this end, the government also announced its intention to bring solar power to every home by 2019 and invested in 25 solar parks, which have the potential to increase India's total installed solar capacity almost tenfold.

B. *Wind:* The Twelfth Five Year Plan proposes a National Wind Energy Mission, similar to the National Solar Mission, and the Indian government recently announced plans to boost wind energy production to 50,000 to 60,000 MW by 2022. It is also planning to promote an offshore wind energy market.

C. *Coal:* A tax on coal has raised $2.85 billion for India's clean energy fund. The tax rose in July 2014 from Rs. 50 ($.80) to Rs. 100 ($1.60) per ton, and doubled again in March 2015 to Rs 200 ($3.20) per ton. The Indian coal-power sector has numerous.

D. *Energy Efficiency and Conservation:* India's *National Mission for Enhanced Energy Efficiency implements the Perform, Achieve and Trade (PAT) Mechanism,* covering the country's largest industrial and power generation facilities. PAT covers more than 50 percent of fossil fuel use and set a target to reduce energy consumption at participating facilities 4-5 percent in 2015 compared to 2010 levels.

E. *Transportation:* In early 2014, India announced new vehicle fuel-economy standards (Indian Corporate Average Fuel Consumption standard) of 4.8 liters per 100 kilometers (49 MPG) by 2021-2022, a 15 percent improvement. Biofuel legislation has set a target of 20 percent blending of ethanol and biodiesel in 2017.

F. *Smart Cities:* Prime Minister Modi has launched an initiative to create 100 "smart cities" with better transport systems, utilities, and energy networks to address the challenges of urban growth. India's National Mission on Sustainable Habitat also includes initiatives such as the Energy Conservation Building Code, mandated for commercial buildings in eight states, and actions to support recycling, waste management, and improved urban planning.

XV. CONCLUSION

The *TRIPS Agreement* and World Trade Organization was nominally constructed with more attention to the IP requirements of developing countries and with participation from major developing countries including India and Brazil. However, this agreement was also largely constructed with an eye to IP protection of advanced countries rather than the technology needs of developing countries, resulting in a non-representative and largely one-sided agreement. Thus, till date intellectual property law at the international level does not represent the needs or position of developing countries, but instead focuses on advanced country requirements.

Currently, developing countries do not have a responsibility to reduce their emissions to a specific level under the *UNFCCC and Kyoto Protocol,* while developed (Annex 1) countries do have this responsibility. Countries do, however, have the responsibility to participate in technology transfer activities that are intended to ensure that developing countries have access to (and the capability to use) low-carbon or zero-carbon technologies for power generation, industrial production, and other needs. The *Clean Development Mechanism (CDM)* is the current mechanism through which this technology transfer takes place, although there are still some improvements that could be made in terms of its implementation. Additionally, it was found that there are also bilateral agreements and regional agreements that could influence the development and use of technologies for carbon emissions, which also needed to be taken into account.

5

Law and Practice of Neighbouring Rights Under Copyright Law

Gurusharan Varandani

I. MANDATE OF COPYRIGHT LAW

The importance of intellectual property rights has arisen in recent years to a great extent. The law of copyrights protects original forms of expression *i.e.* Novels, Movies, Musical compositions and computer software etc. Earlier it was mainly confined to the -published Work and owner of it could prevent others from getting it published in the form of books or articles in order to get benefit in terms of money or goodwill or reputation. In case of such undue enrichment, the owner had a valid cause of action. The owner of the copyright has a valid cause of action against the violator. At present even in case of its adoption and translation or abridgement, it is obligatory to have consent of author. The main purpose and object of copyright law is to protect the expression in any other form from unauthorized use. Since 1847, the copyrights law is in developing stage so, many legislations has been enacted.[1] With the changing of times, the meaning of expression also changes and the style of exhibit the things also changed. The right of author who gives expression in any form is protected from unauthorized use.

II. PROTECTION OF THE AUTHOR

The *Berne Convention*, 1988 is the oldest one on copyright laws, which has undergone many revisions. The Berne Convention, 1988 is the basic or the fundamental treaty that provides protection to copyrights. The *TRIPS Agreement* which is contained in Annexure I-C of the WTO Agreement clearly mentions that the law mentioned in Article 1 to 21 of the *Berne Convention*, 1888 is still a very basic part of the copyright law.[2]

---

1 P. Narayanna, *Intellectual Property Law*, Second Edition (1997).

2 *Copinger and Skone James on Copyright*, 13" Edition, (1991).

Section 14 (e) (iii) of the *Copyright Act*, 1957 covers communication to the public. Section 2 (ff) lays down the meaning of the term "communication to public" as:

> Means making any work available being seen or heard or otherwise enjoyed by the public directly or by any means of display or diffusion other than by issuing copies of such work regardless of whether any member of public actually sees, hears or otherwise enjoys the work so made available.

The Explanation says that for the purpose of this clause, communication through satellite or cable or any other means of simultaneous communication to more than one household or place of residence including residential rooms or any hotel or hostel shall be deemed to be communication to the public. Broadcast is one such expression which in its definition subsumes the whole expression *communication to public.* Broadcast means communication to the public by wireless or diffusion by any means, whether in any one or more of the forms of signs, sounds or usual images by wire and also includes the Re-Broadcast. In case of films or sound recording, communicating to the public is an important right of the owner of the copyright of such Work. The expression more than one household shows that communication to a single household or place of residence is exempted and does not constitute; infringement of copyright.[3]

III. WIPO PERFORMANCES AND PHONOGRAMS TREATY

Article 14 of the *WIPO Performances and Phonograms Treaty (WPPT)*, 1996 grants the right to "communication to the public" in a manner that phenomenon of Internet is squarely covered under Article 14, which states that producers of phonograms shall enjoy the exclusive right of authorizing the making of work available to the public of the phonograms, by wire or wireless means, in such a way that members of the public may access them from a place and time individual chosen by them. Article 15 guarantees to producers of phonograms (copyright owners in sound recording in India) the right to equitable remuneration for commercial broadcast or communication to the public of their phonograms. According to section 37 of *the Copyright Act* 1957, the broadcaster has a duty to obtain the necessary licenses and permission from the copyright owner from who can legally broadcast a sound recording. But once that is done, he is entitled to some rights, which are termed "Broadcast a Reproduction

3 Nandan Kamath, *Law Relating to computers Internet & E-commerce*, Second Edition (2000)

Right" recognized under section 37 of the Act. There are some exceptions also under section 39 (a) states that no broadcast reproduction or performers rights shall be deemed to be infringed by the making of any sound recording or visual recording for the private use of the person making such recording, or for the purposes of bonafide teaching and research.

In this context another related aspect would be the distinction, which has to be maintained between public and private performance more significantly when the performer gives live performance before a group of persons and the number of the audience is quite limited. More so when the performer gives performance at the residence of some person either due to personal relations between the parties or on the occasion of ceremonial function and the gathering is very much limited. In such situation distinction between public and domestic performance becomes quite thin rather blurred in such a case protection of interest of performer is very essential. When the basic issue relates to the protection of right of the performer then it is equally important to ensure that the interest of the performer may be protected in all respects. For that purpose it is necessary to ensure that his work or performance may not be pirated in an unauthorized manner thereby causing loss to the performer in terms of money or goodwill. In this regard the nexus between the performer and the audience will be the basic test and secondly the nature of the performance will also be a relevant factor.

IV. VIOLATION & LIABILTY CLAUSE

The liability against the party causing the violation will before the public performance and not the private performance. Domestic or quasi-domestic performance will be considered as private performance. In case of *Duck* v. *Bate,*[4] it was rightly held that when the audience mainly composed of nurses of the hospital who were more or less living in one room, consequently, they were regarded as forming a domestic circle and dramatic performance given before them and their guests was regarded as private performance. It was different from musical entertainment given to the residents of the hotel to which any respectable member of public could obtain admission mere by payment as held in *Jenning* v. *Slephens.*[5] (Similarly in the case of *Performing Rights Society Ltd.* V. *Harlequin*[6], it was held that the playing of records over loudspeaker in

[4] 13 QBD 843 at 847.

[5] 1936 1 All. Ell 409.

[6] 1943 1 All. BIL 228.

records shop before an audience of prospective purchaser of records was with the object of promoting sale of the records or in other words increase of profit of the shopkeeper was considered to be public performance. Similarly performance of the music for motivating the audience to become member of the club by paying subscription, was held as public entertainment rather than domestic or quasi-domestic performance in case of *Harms Inc. Ltd.* v. *Marlans Club Ltd.*[7] The distinction between public and private performance the privy council in case of *Meller* v. *Australian Broadcasting Commission*[8] observed that the sale right of the owner of the musical work is to perform it in the public and that the any one could perform it in the private. The original performance in the studio might be private. Generally, the broadcast of the performance at the receiving end to all the persons including other places of entertainment or refreshment would be public performance. The aforesaid cases enable us to draw out a inference that the performers rights could not be presumed to have been infringed till that performance is being given him or her before few persons or group of persons in their private capacity and more, specifically when that gathering is purely private and the moment it is given in a club, hotel and restaurant where the motive constitutes an essential element it is immediately converted into public performance. Accordingly the original performance in the studio may be private and broadcast of that performance would result in infringement of the copyright.[9]

V. NATURE OF NEIGHBOURING RIGHTS

The term "neighbouring rights" covers three kinds of rights: the rights of performing artists in their performances, the rights of producers of phonograms in their phonograms, and the rights of broadcasting organization in their radio and television programmes. Protection of those who assist intellectual creators in the message of the author or creator of a work and help to disseminate works intended by their creators and authors to be conveyed to, and enjoyed by, the public at large, is sought to be provided by what are known as neighbouring rights or rights neighbouring on copyright. The reason for protecting neighbouring rights is that since works of human intellect are created in order to be disseminated among as large a clientele as possible and this cannot always be done by the author himself, for it often requires intermediaries whose professional capability gives to the works those forms of presentation

7 1927 1 Ch. 526

8 1927 1 KB. 553

9 David I. Bainbridge, *An Introduction To Copyright*,(1992)

that are appropriate to make them accessible to a wide public, all persons, therefore, who make use of library, artistic, dramatic, or musical works in order to make them publicly accessible to others require their own protection against the illegal use of their contributions in the process of communicating the work to the public. These persons, as discussed above, are generally performing artists, record producers and broadcasters.

The rights of these person are referred to as neighbouring rights because they have developed in parallel with copyright, and the exercise of these rights is very often linked with the exercise of copyright The development of technology resulted in the need not only to ensure protection of literary, dramatic, musical and artistic works by means of copyright, but also to establish effective protection for the various intermediaries associated with the dissemination and broadcasting of works. Neighbouring Rights are primarily a result of technological development[10] The Performances of Performers disappeared at the moment they were seen or heard by the public at large afier seeing the performance; nothing was left in any form except the impression created in the memory of the Public. Thus, every time the Public wanted to appreciate the Performers Performance. The Invention of new technological devices *i.e.* Television, Cinema and Radio and their spread in the 20th Century revolutionized the ways in which a work could be publicized. These means of communications had direct impact mainly on the Income of the Performers. The term "Neighbouring Rights"[11] includes the Rights of Performing (Actors, Singers, and Musicians etc.). The Rights granted to the categories of performers mentioned above are similar to Authors of Literary and Artistic Works.

VI. INTERNATIONAL PROTECTION TO NEIGHBOURING RIGHTS

The international protection to neighbouring rights is covered under numerous conventions most notably *Berne Convention For The Protection Of Literary & Artistic Works*, 1971, *Rome Convention For The Protection Of Performers, Producers of Phonograms & Broadcasting Organization*, 1961, *Convention for the Protection of producers of Phonograms Against Unauthorised Duplication of Their Phonograms*, 1971, *WIPO Copyright Treaty*, 1996, and *WIPO performance and Phonogram Treaty*, 1996. In the TRIPS Agreement, the expression "Related Rights" is used to refer to "Neighbouring Rights". The purpose of Neighbouring Rights is to protect the legal interests of

[10] Neighboring Rights - Presented by Mr. Sanjay Tandon (Director General, LPRS.) at National Seminar on copyright.

[11] A person who is not the creator of work but only performs work.

certain persons and legal entities who either contribute to making works available to the public or produce subject matter, which will not qualify as "Works" under Copyright systems. After the compliance of *TRIPS Agreement,* 1995 Section 2(q)[12] of *Copyright Right Act* of 1957 was amended. At the international level, the first proposals concerning *Protection of Producers of Phonograms and Performers* took form at the 1928 *Rome Diplomatic Conference of the WIPO* to revise the *Berne Convention.*[13] Further discussions took place at the *Brussels Revision Conference* in 1948. Although there was also support for development of an International Instrument providing adequate protection. In 1960, a Committee of Experts convened jointly by WIPO, UNESCO and the International Labour Office, met at Hague and drew up the Draft Convention, which served as the basis for the deliberations in Rome, where a Diplomatic Conference agreed upon the final text of the *Rome Convention* on 26th October 1961. The *Rome Convention* came into force on 18th May 1964.

Thus, the first organized international response to the need for legal protection to the 3 categories of *Neighboring Rights Beneficiaries* was the conclusion of the Rome Convention Indeed, the Laws of many Countries exceed the minimum levels of protection of copyright established by the Convention. While there is a widespread view that the Rome Convention is out-of-date in respect of its implementation and is in need of revision or replacement by a new set of International norms in the field of Neighbouring Rights. The Rights granted to the three beneficiaries of Neighbouring Rights under the Rome Convention are (1) Performers, (2) Producers of Phonograms, (3) Broadcasting Organizations. There are 2 other Conventions in the field of Neighbouring Rights *viz; Convention for the Protection of Producers of Phonograms Against Unauthorized Duplication of their Phonograms (The Phonograms Convention)* and *Convention Relating to the Distribution of Programme- Carrying Signals Transmitted by Satellite (The Satellites Convention).*[14]

VII. EXPLOITATION OF PERFORMERS

Performers are generally, covered under the category of Artists, more so, when their live performance is recorded in professional manner. In this context, emphasis has to be given to singers as well as to solo folk dancers like Daler Mehandi, Gurdas Mann, Harbhajan Mann, Pawati

12 After the Amendment of I994 in Copyright Act of 1957, the deûnition of performer has been mark quite exhaustive.

13 This convention provides the basis guidelines for the protection of Copyrights.

14 W. Calkoen, *Harmonization of law and the Internet, International Business Lawyer,* (1998).

Khan, Anoop Jalota, Pankaj Udhas etc. who are undoubtedly professional artists after getting publicity and popularity but at the budding stage it will not be wrong to say that they are mere performers. At the initial stage they lack professional knowledge and experience and their exploitation during that period by the producers is a common phenomenon. Same is the of problem of other performers like classical dancers, folk singers and dancers, sitar, violin and other instrumental players,[15] who are prone to exploitation at the budding stage when their extraordinary talent is noticed by the professional producers and they pay them only nominal amount and such artists or so called performers feel highly obliged instead of feeling exploited and cheated. Subsequently even if they show the reality they feel helpless as they feel themselves like a small fish before a whale fish.

Another important factor for protecting the interest of the performer relates to recording the performance of the performer without his consent more specifically, while he is giving performance at the public functions being organised casually either in some universities, school or any ceremonial function in some rural or urban area and unauthorized recording of the programme of such performer by some producer or other professional could not be ruled out. At the same time video piracy of the recorded programme or piracy of the live performance of the performer at the television is also a common phenomenon. For the purpose of protecting interest of such performers it is imperative that some provision should be incorporated in the *Copyright Act*, 1957 of India.[16] In this context another related aspect will be the distinction which has to be maintained between public and private performance 'more significantly when the performer gives live performance before a group of persons and the number of the audience is quite limited. More so when the performer gives performance at the residence of some person either due to personal relations between the parties or on the occasion of ceremonial function and the gathering is very much limited. In such situation distinction between public and domestic performance becomes quite thin rather blurred, in such a case protection of interest of performer is very essential.

VIII. JUDICIAL PROTECTION TO PERFORMERS

When the basic issue relates to the protection of right of the performer then it is equally important to ensure that the interest of the performer may be protected in all respects. For that purpose it is necessary to ensure

---

15 Categories of the persons excluded from the deûnition of Section 2 qq of Copyright Act of 1957.

16 Suresh T. Vishwanathan, *Indian Cyber Law*,First Edition (2000).

that his work or performance may not be pirated in an unauthorized manner thereby causing loss to the performer in terms of money or goodwill. In this regard the nexus between the performer and the audience will be the basic test and secondly the nature of the performance will also be a relevant factor. The liability against the party causing the violation will be for the public performance and not the private performance. Domestic or quasi-domestic performance will be considered as private performance. In case of *Duck* v. *Bates,*[17] It was rightly held that when the audience mainly composed of nurses of the hospital who were more or less living in one room, consequently, they were regarded as forming a domestic circle and dramatic performance given before them and their guests was regarded as private performance. It was different from musical entertainment given to the residents of the hotel to which any respectable member of public could obtain admission mere by payment as held in *Jennings* v. *Stephens.*[18] Similarly in the case of *Performing Rights Society Ltd.* v. *Harlequin*[19], it was held that the playing of records over loudspeaker in records shop before an audience of prospective purchaser of records was with the object of promoting sale of the records or in other words to increase profit of the shopkeeper was considered to be public performance.

Similarly performance of the music for motivating the audience to become member of the club by paying subscription, was held as public entertainment rather than domestic or quasi-domestic performance in case of *Harms Inc. Ltd.* v. *Marlins Club Ltd.*[20] While making the distinction between public and private performance the Privy Council in case of *Mellor* v. *Australian Broadcasting Commission*[21] observed that the sole right of the owner of the musical work is to perform it in the public and that the any one could perform it in the private. The original performance in the studio might be private. Generally, the broadcast of the performance at the receiving end to all the persons including other places of entertainment or refreshment would be public performance. The aforesaid cases enable us to draw an inference that the performers rights could not be presumed to have been infringed till that performance is being given by him or her before few persons or group of persons in their private capacity and more, specifically when that gathering is purely private. The moment it is given in a club, hotel and restaurant where the motive

---

[17] 13 QBD 843 at 847.

[18] (1936) 1 All. ER. 409.

[19] (1943) 1 All. ER. 228 on appeal 413.

[20] (1927) 1 Ch 526.

[21] (1927) IKB. 553.

constitutes an essential element is it immediately converted into public performance. Accordingly the original performance in the studio may be private and broadcast of that performance would result in infringement of the copyright. In this context the Supreme Court of India in the case of *R. G. Anand* v. *Deluxe Films*[22] could quite appropriately observe that there could be no copyright in an idea, subject matter or theme or historical or legendary facts and violation of the copyright in such cases is confined to the form, manner and arrangement and expression of the idea by the author of the copyright work. In case the same idea is being developed in a different manner, it is manifest that the source being common; the similarities are bound to occur. In order that it may amount as infringement of copyright it is necessary that the copy must be substantial and violation of copyright of a stage play by a producer or a director of film, it is manifestly material one which may immediately lead to conclusion that the wronged over should be held liable for the Act of piracy. In case the theme is same but the subsequent work is presented and treated differently so that subsequent work becomes a completely new work in such a situation there could be no question of violation of copyright.[23]

In order that a violation of copyright amounts to an act of piracy. It must be proved by clear and cogent evidence. If the basic issue pertains to the question of art that a film has a much broader perspective as compared to a stage play and by introducing variety incidents the producer or director of the film could introduce a variety of incidents and give color and complexion to the film quite different from the stage play so far as the copyright work may present a story idea. But in spite of all these factors if the audience carry an impression that the film is by and large a copy of original play, an inference could be drawn that the violation of copyright has been proved. This test would certainly enable the performer if in case he is a storywriter of a drama already staged in a theatre to protect his interest more specifically, if the producer or a director of film has produced a film with the same story. Accordingly the Supreme Court in the case of *R. G. Anand* v. *Deluxe Film*[24] held that on a close and careful comparison of the stage and cinematograph film it was not possible to conclude that the film was by and large violation of copyright.[25]

---

22 AIR 1978 SC 1613.

23 Katsh, *Electronic Media & Transformation of Law*, (1989).

24 AIR 1978 SC 1613.

25 See for details: Gurusharan Varandani, 'Inclusion of International Law of Copyright in The Copyright Act, 1957 of India & Its Implementation With Special Reference to Protection of Rights of Performer', A.K.Koul & V.K.Ahuja, *Law of Copyright: From Gunterberg's Invention to Internet*, 144 (2000).

IX. ANALYSIS AND ASSESSMENT

Such categories of performers mainly include male and female dancers for different Deities. Who on account of repeated performance before their deities, achieve perfection which in turn is recorded by the professional producers, who on account of their professional connections even in foreign countries like America, England and other European Countries fetch huge income without paying any substantial part of it to such performers, who are exploited in this manner. In the case of folk dancers in tribal and other rural areas who in groups give attractive performance and the producers record such performance earn huge profits at the cost of the performance given by the real performers, as discussed above. It is imperative to protect the interest of such artist or performer by incorporating such category of performers within the parameters of the above said Amended section.[26] Prior to 1994 the word performer includes only artistic and literary works. After the amendment of 1994 in the *copyright Act* of 1957, the word performer also includes, actors musicians and other performers who performs the work In the developing world, it is imperative goo our legislators to think about other performers who perform artistic work but they are not included in the definition of performer. So looking into the present scenario, it is the need of time to amend the Section (qq) of *Copyright Act,* 1957 again.

[26] Section 2 qq *Copyright Act,* 1957.

6

Poverty, Human Rights and Intellectual Property Regime: An Appraisal of Farmer's Rights and Right to Food

Zafar Mahfooz Nomani

I. INTRODUCTORY OUTLINE

The post-Vienna legal phase is remarkably known for revolutionary changes across the global wherein the third generation of human rights became the hallmark for the comity of nations and a liberational instrument to come out of nightmarish experiences of poverty and hunger.[1] On the other hand the post-GATTised legal ordering is known for much publicized and debatable conclusion of Trade Related Aspect of Intellectual Property Rights (TRIPs) and creation of World Trade Organisation (WTO).[2] This new jurisprudential polemics soon evoked fierce scrutiny from the stand point of human right and poverty among third world countries.[3] At home, it is dubbed as 'bleeding operation with the dubious promise of benign global competition', '*de facto* nullity of constitutional goal of social welfare' and 'contra- constitutional coup.[4] Since India has become a member of WTO it indulged into massive rehabilitation and fundamental mutation of IPR regime. Despite the fact that it has a stark distinction of being a grain- surplus and food and livelihood insecure country. An inventory of over forty five million tonnes

---

1 See: Nomani, Zafar Mahfooz., 'The Human Right to Environment in India: Legal Precepts and Judicial Doctrines in Critical Perspective; V *The Asia Paciûc Journal of Environmental Law*, I13-34 (2000).

2 Christopher Arup, *The New World Trade Organization Agreements: Globalizing Law Through Services and Intellectual Properly*, 27 (2000).

3 See: A. Wood, North-South Trade and Inequality (1994). See also : M.R. Agosin *et al.*, "Developing Countries and the Uruguay Round : An Evaluation and Issues for the Future" in United Nations Conference on Trade and Development Report (I995); T. Banuri, *Economic Liberalization: No Panacea* (I991).

4 V.R. Krishna Iyer, "GATT, TRIPs and Patent Izaw — I, "*The Hindu Daily*, New Delhi Edition, Sept. 1, 2000 at p. 10.2.

of wheat and rice in granaries remains ready for consumption. On the other hand over two hundred fifty million people generally go to bed partially hungry every day. There is a near consensus on the need to banish hunger but the realities on the ground remain that even at the risk of raising hopes the goal of food security may not be realized for generations.[5] At home under the cover of food security the government is keeping millions of tonnes of food out of reach of the poor people.[6] In fact India's record breaking 200 plus million tonnes harvest is the result of steep fall in purchasing power of poor. The myth of surplus is based on sending hundreds of millions of human being hungry to their beds.[7] Taken to its logical end we have abundance of food, surplus of hunger and *scarcity of vision* under the garb of food security.[8]

There is scant realization of the fact that if our agriculture goes wrong nothing else in our economy and social fabric will have a chance to go right. Further a society deprived right to dignified life and human rights may generate serious disorder to the rule of law and human governance. That is why presently the ecological degradation, unsustainable manaevouring of biological productivity and inequitable regime of intellectual property right (IPR) are shaking the foundations of human governance. The monopolization of agriculture under WTO, TRIPS and Exclusive Marketing Right (EMR) resulted in an unequal treatment to Indian sovereignty over agriculture resources.[9] The promises of Blue Box (direct payment to farmer under production limiting programmes) and Green Box (benefits to agriculture and rural community, stockholding for food security, domestic food and investment. Subsidies agricultural input subsidies for low income resource poor families) social safety clauses for developing countries under WTO agreement have also proved short lived euphoria.[10] The paper takes a legal stance on the impact of IPR regime on poverty and consequent denial of human right to food livelihood and hunger free life.

---

5 *See* generally Sir Arthur C. Clarkes, 2001: *A Space Odyssey* (2001) & *Proûles of the Future,* (1962) 1999 Rev. Ed.

6 Jean Dreze, Starving the Poor-I, *The Hindu Daily*: New Delhi Edition, Feb. 26, 2001 p.10.

7 P. Sainth, Will The Real National Calamity Please Stand UP'? *The Hindu Daily: Sunday Magazines,* Feb. 22, 2001 p.I.

8 P. Sainath, 'Rajasthan's Drought : Abundance of Food, Scarcity of Vision, *The Hindu Sunday Magazines,* March I8, 2001 p.l.

9 Nomani, Zafar Mahfooz., 'Environment Agriculture and Challenges of Bio-Piracy 1 A Blue Print of Indian Sui Generis Legal Order' 1 (2) *Indian Journal of Environmental Law,* 3 (2000).

10 M.S. Swaminathan, 'For A Livelihood Box', Convocation Address at Kerala. Agricultural University, Trissure Dec. 29, 2000; *See* also: 18(3) *The Frontline.* 115 (2001).

II. DOCTRINAL FLAWS OF POVERTY

The right to be free from the crushing burden of poverty is among the most fundamental of human rights. The United Nations Development Programme (UNDP) has been engaged in poverty eradication for many years. The *UNDP Human Development Report* and *World Development Report* by introducing the concept of human poverty have made poverty eradication as a dominant theme of development, agenda multilateral cooperation and bilateral relationship among the member states. In March 1998, the *Administrative Committee on Coordination,* comprised of executive heads of all UN agencies including the *Bretton Woods institutions,* assembled to chart out a common approach to poverty eradication and paradigm shift.[11] The scaling of poverty on human indicators inspite of numerous merits masks many assumptions such as 'deprivation poverty' and 'income poverty'. The *Human Development Report,* 1997 documented that correlation between income poverty (using the U.S $1 a day standard) and human deprivations are not always one and the same. Income is not only a partial translation of these deprivations; it is not cause of these deprivations, but also remained heavily flawed and reflected deeper roots of human misery (See Table 1).

Table 1. Indicators of Human Development for Some

	Asian Countries — 1997		
Country	**Life Expectancy At Birth (Year)**	**Infant Mortality Rate (Per Thousand Births)**	**Adult Literacy Rate (Per cent)**
India	62.4	71	62
Kerala State (India)	72.0	12	93
Bangladesh	58.1	81	39
China	69.8	38	83
Indonesia	65.1	45	85
Korea, Republic	72.4	6	97
Malaysia	72.0	10	86
Pakistan	64.0	95	41
Philippines	68.3	32	95
Thailand	68.8	31	95

Source: UNDP — Human Development Report, 1998. For India, estimates are from Office of the Registrar General of India (SRS) and NSSO Surveys.

[11] James Gustave Speth, 'Poverty : A Denial of Human Rights' 52 (1) *Journal of International Affairs*, 278 (1998).

This becomes very important as countries increasingly move to develop anti-poverty strategies. There is need to focus on symptoms. and genesis as well as.[12] The World Social Summit in Copenhagen in 1995, therefore agreed to develop anti-poverty strategies to eliminate the worst aspects of poverty in their countries on a time bound basis. Part of this strategy is by poverty mapping, poor people's location, numbers and characteristics (*i.e.,* urban or rural backgrounds, ethnic identity and minority status). The Summit also underlined the fallacies of a single indicator, and income poverty and implored on the adoption of indicators to reflect complexity of live.[13] To come out of this doctrinaire impasse and to supplement traditional income-measures of poverty, the *Human Development Report* proposed a new composite measure of the *Human Poverty Index (HPI).* The HPI bring together, in a composite index, different features of deprivation in order to determine an aggregate judgment on the extent of poverty in a community. These measures of deprivation are combined to reach the HPI:

1. Deprivation of life, which is measured by the percentage of people expected to die before the age of 40;
2. Deprivation of knowledge, which is measured by the percentage of adults who are illiterate; and
3. Deprivation in living standards, which is measured as a composite of three variables, the percentage of people without access to health services, the percentage without access to safe water and the percentage of malnourished children under five.[14]

In the 1998 *Human Development Report,* the index is refined to capture the depth of human poverty in industrialized countries. But even a refined HPI does not capture the full extent of human poverty. Critical dimensions of human poverty excluded from the HPI are lack of political freedom, inability to participate in decision making and community life lack of personal security and threats to environmental sustainability. These variables are difficult to measure a sufficiently large number of countries.

---

[12] *Id* at 280.

[13] The text of the "Copenhagen Declaration and Programme of Action" can be found in United Nations, *Copenhagen Declaration and Programme of Action: World Summit for Social Development* (New York: United Nations, 1995): See also UNDP. UNDP Series on Sustainable Human Development, Country Strategies for Social Development (New York: UNDP, 1995) for examples of national implementation of the Copenhagen Declaration and Programme of Action.

[14] *See* : Jean Drez & Amartya Sen, *India Economic Development and Social Opportunity,* (1995).

Hence, the HPl is not a perfect measure. However, it has provided us with an interesting insight on human poverty, which income measures had failed to capture.[15]

III. IMPERATIVES OF HUMAN RIGHTS

The right to be free from the crushing burden of poverty is among the most fundamentals of human rights. Perhaps the most basic human right challenged by human poverty is the right to food and dignified existence life. Nearly one-third of the people in the least developed countries cannot expect to live beyond the age of 40. Another mark of poverty, adult illiteracy, means that the poor are severely restricted in their access to knowledge, to information and to the press as well as in their ability to exercise connected rights such as political participation.[16] *Universal Declaration of Human Rights*, 1948 long back adopted an unmistakably pro-poor stance and right to development by stating:

> Everyone is entitled to the realization ....of ....economic, social, cultural rights indispensable for his dignity[17]... Everyone has the right to work[18]... Everyone has the right to a standard of living adequate for the health and well-being of himself and of his family, including food, clothing, housing and medical care, and necessary social services, and the right to security in the event of unemployment, sickness, disability...or other lack of livehood[19]... Evelyone has the right to education.[20]

The right to live a life of dignity was reaffirmed in subsequent instruments of *international law, including the International Convention of Economic, Social and Cultural Rights," Convention on the Elimination of All*

---

15 *Id* at 281.

16 UNDP, *Human Development Report*, 5 (1997). See also 1 UNDP, "Ending Poverty and Building Peace through Sustainable Human Development", *Annual Report* I 996/I 997 (New York: UNDP, 1997b) p.6 "Women do 60 percent of the world's work but receive only-tenth of its income. They own less than l percent of the land, have limited access to educational and ûnancial resources and have less say than men in decisions affecting their future. Most of the household and community work done by women worldwide is unpaid and therefore ignored by household surveys and national censuses. *The Human Development Report* for 1995 estimates of the value of women's invisible contribution to global economic output at U.S.$l l -trillion ofthe total U.S.$23 trillion, "*Ibid* p. l0.

17 Article 22, *Universal Declaration ofHuman Rights*, 1948.

18 *Id* Article 23.

19 *Id* Article 25.

20 *Id* Article 26.

Forms of Discrimination Against Women; Convention on the Elimination of All Forms of Racial Discrimination, and Convention on the Rights of the Child.[21]

World Conference on Human Rights (known as Vienna Declaration), 1993 dovetailed the correlation of the right to development with different categories of human rights, namely economic, social, cultural and civil as a universal and inalienable right.[22] It also reaffirmed the solemn commitment of all States to fulfill their obligations to promote universal respect for, and observance and protection of all human rights and fundamental freedoms for all in accordance with Charter of the United Nations, prominent instruments of human rights and international law. The universal nature of these rights and freedom is beyond question. In this framework, enhancement of international cooperation in the field of human rights is essential for the full achievement of the purposes of the United Nation.[23] Thus human rights and fundamental freedoms from the crushing to burden of poverty are the birth right of all human beings and; their protection and promotion is the solemn constitutional responsibility of Governments. The Conference further reaffirm the right to development, as established in the *Declaration on the Right to Development*, 1986 as a universal and inalienable right and an integral part of fundamental human rights. As stated in the *Declaration on the Right to Development*, the human person is the central subject of development. While development facilitates the enjoyment of all human rights, the lack of development may not be invoked to justify the abridgement of internationally recognized human rights. States should cooperate with each other in ensuring development and eliminating obstacles to development. The international community should promote and effective international cooperation for the realization of the right to development and the elimination of obstacles to development. Lasting progress towards the implementation of the right to development requires effective development policies at the national level, as well as equitable economic relations and a favourable economic environment at the international level.[24] Of significance is the declaration that the existence of widespread extreme poverty inhibits the full and effective enjoyment of human rights; its immediate alleviation and eventual elimination must remain a high priority for the international community.[25]

---

21 For a compilation of human rights instruments of the United Nations, as well as the text of the major instruments, see United Nations. *The United Nations Human Rights*, Blue Book Series (New York: United Nations, 1996).

22 Para 5, *The Vienna Declaration & Programme of Action : World Conference on Human Right*, 1993.

23 *Id* Para 4.

24 *Id* Para 10.

25 *Id* Para 14.

The right to development was linked in Vienna to the collective obligation of the international community. The *Vienna Declaration* further stated that the least developed countries, in particular, deserve the support of the international community. This seminal document in the rights based approach to development called for equitable economic relations among states, and favourable economic environment at the international level.[26] To achieve these objectives, the *Vienna Declaration* stressed that the external debt burden must be alleviated, and that widespread poverty and illiteracy in various countries must be combated.[27] Moreover, the *Vienna Declaration* called on industrialized countries to refrain from causing injury to populations of other countries by exporting environmental hazards.[28] This is a powerful statement on the right to development and on the duty of states in the international community to promote this right. The responsibility is not solely that of the international community. The *Vienna Declaration* put the onus for achieving the right to development firmly on individual countries themselves, in part by calling for long-term work to put in place the infrastructure of a society capable of guaranteeing democracy and the rule of law.[29]

IV. HUMAN RIGHT BASED APPROACH

The human rights approach to the eradication of poverty was forcefully restated by Secretary General Kofi Annan, in his report to the General Assembly by emphasizing the links between democracy, development and human rights.[30] As a practical application of this principle, human rights are represented in all aspects of the work of the United Nations, such as peace and security, humanitarian affairs, economic and social affairs and development operations. Despite the international mandate for a human rights approach to poverty eradication, such an approach has been largely neglected in most alleviation programs. The eradication of poverty has been seen in two ways. One approach tends to look at the eradication of poverty as international charity. This view has lost salience in recent years, but it still emerges from time to time. There is nothing wrong with charity.[31] This sense of charity is one of the important means by which valuable resources are collected and allocated

26 *Id* Para 9.

27 *Id* Para 12.

28 *Id* Para ll.

29 *Id* Para 8.

30 General Assembly Report, *Renewing The United Nation: A Programme For Refom'* [No 51/950/1997].

31 *Supra note* l l at 286.

to development cooperation. As strong as charitable impulses may be, they are not easily translated into the predictable and growing resources which are increasingly necessary. Funds for development cooperation are declining in a world where 1.3 billion persons live on less than U.S. $1 a day, and where debt service in sub-Saharan Africa is equivalent to four times the expenditure on health.[32] The second approach is to view the eradication of poverty in purely functional terms. The rationale behind this approach holds the eradication of poverty as perhaps good in itself, but more important, as prevention against the rise of confiicts, social disruption and many other social ills such as drugs, disease and terrorism. In this view, the eradication of poverty is an instrument in the search for peace and security. The events of the Great Lakes region of Africa, for instance, are telling in the terrible levels of poverty and hopelessness which accompanied the genocidal wars of the 1990s. Recent concerns with advance warning for civil conflict are laudable, but we have ample advance warning from the lives of millions living without jobs and without hope, who are at the margins of society. The desperation of the poor is never quite for long.[33]

The link between economic and social development and peace is also quite strong. In country after country, failures of development can be seen as contributing to instability and the eruption of conflict. Experience demonstrates that penury, hopelessness, inequity and marginalization are often among the root causes of devastating conflict. In crisis situations, and in societies emerging from confiict, human rights are often violated. International support for governance mechanisms leading to the restoration of the rule of law is important for the protection of human rights. Indeed, it is significant that some of the most important actions in terms of peace-building in post-confiict situations have been projects that seek to promote greater employment opportunities for the demobilized and the disadvantaged, and programs to rebuild national capacity for good governance.[34]

The human rights approach to poverty eradication is motivated by duty. Even if we, as human beings, do not feel particularly charitable, even if we believe we can wall ourselves off from the consequences of poverty, we must respect the rights of others, including the right to be free from poverty. Poor people around the world, and the organizations that represent them, see poverty as an injustice, a denial of freedom

---

[32] UNDP. Human Development Report Office. *Poverty and Human Development: the sub-Saharan African Perspective* (New York: UNDP; May, 1997) p.5.

[33] Supra note 31.

[34] *Id* at 286-7.

from want. By following a human rights-based approach to the eradication of poverty, a variety of human rights goals can be achieved within the same set of policies. For example, enacting and implementing equal opportunity laws will help empower men and women to gain more equitable access to productive resources. liberation individual initiative and creating economic opportunities.[35] A human rights-based approach to the eradication of poverty enables international development agencies to provide the essential bridge between two of the main pillars on which the United Nations rests: respect for human rights and the promotion of social progress enshrined in Article One of the *Charter of the United Nations.*

V. INTELLECTUAL PROPERTY RIGHTS REGIME

In order to locate the poverty, food security and human rights within the framework of intellectual property rights regime it is necessary to underline the broader implications of Post-TRIPS era on Indian law and policy.[36] After the assumption of original membership of WTO India is already on the threshold of revamping her IPR laws.[37] Some of the important radical changes effectuated to fulfill the TRIPs Agreement mandate include:

a) A system for filing and handling product patents applications for pharmaceutical and agriculture chemical products and the granting of exclusive marketing rights (EMRs) to be implemented as of 1 January 1995; adopted in march 1999);

b) The elimination of any restriction on the grant of product patents (as of 1 January 2000) except for product patents on pharmaceutical and agricultural chemical products (where restriction can remain until 1 January 2005);

c) The elimination of restrictions on patentable subject matter such as the current exclusion of methods of agriculture or horticulture (as of 1 January 2005);[38]

---

35 *Id* at 287.

36 Nomani, Zafar Mahfooz., 'WTO, TRIPS Agreement and Protection of Plant Variety : Imperative and Implication For Indian Intellectual Property Regime' in A.K. Koul & V.K. Ahuja (Ed.) *The Law of Intellectual Property Right : Prospect and Retrospect.* 118 (2001).

37 Jayanti Bagchi, *World Trade Organization:' An Indian Perspective,* (2000). See also, Surendra Bhandari, *World Trade Organization and Developing Countries,* (1998).

38 Phillipe Cullet, "Revision of the TRIPs Agreement Concerning the Protection of Plant Varieties : Lessons from India Concerning the Development of a Sui Generis System", 2(4). *The Journal of World Intellectual Properly* 625, (1999).

d) The lengthening of patent duration to twenty years, from the current fourteen years, and seven years for food and pharmaceuticals (as of 1 January 2000);

e) Restrictions and modifications concerning compulsory licensing licences of right and the right of revocation (as of 1 January 2000); and

f) The adoption of a legal regime for the protection of plant varieties (as of 1 January 2000). This probably takes the form of a *Plant Variety Protection Act.*[39]

The operational strategy has been devised into two phases. The first phase of reform which encompassed provisions for filing product patent and grant of exclusive marketing right is already over. The second phase reform subsumes implications on the overall growth of pharmaceutical industry, share of foreign and domestic investment, research and development and international trade mechanism.[40] Unlike the general perception, the *TRIPS Agreement* provides considerable manoeuvring to make it developing country friendly. A perusal of some of provisions of TRIPs Agreement supports this view. Any developing country Member which is in the process of transformation from a centrally planned into a market – free enterprise economy and which is undertaking structural reform of intellectual property system and facing special problems in preparation and implementation intellectual property laws, may benefit or entitled for delay.[41] In view of special needs and requirement in least developed countries. Their need for fiexibility to create a viable technological base. Such member shall not be required to apply to the provisions of this Agreement, other than Articles 3, 4 and 5 for a period of ten year.[42] A further latitude is granted under the TRIPSAgreement which is an armoury in hands of municipal legislature to safeguard the national interests. It runs as under:

> Member States may exclude from patentability inventions, the prevention within their territory of the commercial exploitation of which is necessary to protect public order or morality, including to protect human, animal or plant life or health or to avoid serious prejudice to the environment. Provided that such exclusion is not made merely because the exploitation is prohibited by domestic.[43]

---

39 *Id* at 625.

40 M.D. Nair, "Amendment to Patents Act : Option Under TRIPs", *The Hindu Daily,* March 8, 2000 at p. BS-3.

41 Article 65, *TRIPs Agreement,* 1995.

42 *Id* Article 66(1).

43 *1d* Aiticle 27 (2).

Member States may also exclude from patentability the diagnostic, therapeutic and surgical methods for the treatment of humans and animals *vis-a-vis* plants and animals other than micro-organism and essentially biological processes for the production of plants or animals other than non-biological and micro-biological processes. However, the Member shall provide for the protection of plant varieties either by the patent or by an effective sui generis system or by any combination thereof.[44]

This constitutes one of the few areas where India is conferred some margin of appreciation in devising protective *sui generis* system. Some countries in the South American region and South African IPR laws have made use of these provisions to bring in restrictions on patentability in their national patent laws. As far as India is concerned, in order to combat the menace of hunger and poverty,[45] Article 27(3) (a) can be interpreted to include the human right to food, farmers right to conserve, cultivate and breed.[46]

Recently *Sub-commission of UN Commission on Human Rights* in their 52nd Session resolved that the intellectual property rights in the TRIPs Agreement constitutes contravention of international human rights law. It also noted that actual or potential confiicts exist between the implementation of *TRIPs Agreement* and the realization of economic, social and cultural rights. The Resolution further requests all Governments to integrate into their national and local legislations and policies, provisions in accordance with international human rights obligation and principles, which protect the social function of the intellectual property.[47] It is important that in the context of these introductory remarks and view of the Sub-commission on *TRIPs Agreement* that the amendments to the existing patents system in India in the Patents Act 1970 should be considered.[48]

Article 7[49] and Article 8[50] explicitly provide for sufficient scope for safeguarding the national interest and the role of the domestic industry

---

44 *Id.* Article 27 (3). 45 *Supra* note 9 at 11. 46 *Id* at 12.

47 B.K. Keayla. 'TRIPs Patent System: Issues for Patent (Second Amendment) Bill, 1999 in *Supra* note 36 at 78.

48 *Id* at 79.

49 Article 7 of TRIPS reads: The protection and enforcement of intellectual property rights should contribute to the promotion of technological innovation and to the transfer and dissemination of technology, to the mutual advantage of producers and users of technological knowledge and in a manner conducive to social and economic welfare, and to a balance or rights and obligations.

50 Article 8 of TRIPS reads : Member may, in formulating or amending their national laws and regulations, adopt measures necessary to protect public health and

by providing balancing of rights and obligations conducive to social and economic welfare. Even the preamble of the *TRIPs Agreement* recognizes "the underlying public policy objectives of national systems for the protection of intellectual property, including developmental and technological objectives". This stipulation has direct relationship, with our public policy objectives in the constitutional obligation of 'right to life' (including right to health) as guaranteed through the Fundamental Rights in the Indian Constitution. The following suggestions are based on the above introductory remarks. International human rights law and provisions in Articles 7 and 8 and the preamble of the *TRIPs Agreement.* Section 83 of the *Patents Act,* 1970 should be enlarged by adding a Sub-section (c). In this new Sub-section (c) the entire Article 7 of the TRIPs agreement should be reproduced.[51] This will strengthen the general principles applicable to the working of patented inventions through the domestic enterprises and to the accomplishing of the TRIPs objectives.

VI. FARMERS AND BREEDERS' RIGHT

Under this back drop one finds Indian agriculture in throes of transition.[52] Liberalization, globalization, privatization, structural adjustment programmes and skewed policy approaches are hitting hard the Indian farming sector.[53] Reduction of public non-price support and opening up of the sector to international trade has further added to the uncertainties and chaos.[54] The regulatory hegemony and intrusive powers over national and agricultural resources by WTO has become a central focus for livelihood anxieties of Indian breeders and consumers alike. The simmering discontentment among the leading lights of law and constitution, environmental activist organizations and framers are now echoed far and wide. The Punjab Legislative Assembly at a recent sitting resolved that the impact of the WTO regime on agriculture had been

---

nutrition, and to promote the public interest in sectors of vital importance to their socio- economic and technological development, provided that such measures are consistent with the provisions of this Agreement. Appropriate measures, provided that they are consistent with the provisions of this Agreement, may be needed to prevent the abuse of intellectual property rights by right holders or the resort to practices which unreasonably restrain trade or adversely affect the international transfer of technology.

51 Section 83 of Patent Act, 1970 runs as under.

52 *Supra* note 9 at 6.

53 Sukumar Muralidharan, 'The Farming Crisis', 18(2) *The Frontline* 4 (2001). *See* also : S.K. Batra, *Indian Agriculture And New Economic Policy .' Impact of Agro-Industry* (1995).

54 Abhijit Sen. 'A Whole Crop of Uncertainties'. 18(2) *Frontline'* 8 (2001).

uniformly adverse. The Karnataka Chief Minister S.M. Krishna has lent his voice to the chorus of demands for a radical review of international trade arrangements. Also adding to their pleas have been Chief Ministers of Haryana, Andhra Pradesh and Bihar.[55] The West Bengal Government along with three other states has decided to move to Supreme Court on the Centres Agreement with the World Trade Organization on Agriculture because agriculture is a 'state subject' and the centre cannot arbitrarily enter into an agreement with the WTO without the consent of State Governments.[56] There is no denying of the fact that the WTO has the potential to bite deep into the material well-being of Indian agricultural sector as it agreed early last year to phase out all quantitative restrictions (QRs) on import on an accelerated schedule. Part of this agreement was implemented and complete phase out of QRs has taken place in 2001.[57]

The farm sector is presently reeling under the fear of loss of all protection against import except through tariff. Once the QRs are finally lifted the government will be called upon to make a series of decisions on the appropriate tariffs levels.[58] The explicit assurance by the government is the retention of sufficient fiexibility by way of tariffs to offset any unsettling surge in imports. These tariff are governed by binding commitments of WTO regime. Broadly three levels of binding commitments have been given to WTO, all of which seem to endow India with a great measure of autonomy in determining tariffs. On raw commodities, India has commitment to limit the import tariff to 100 percent.[59]

On processed agro-commodities, the specified level is I50 percent. On edible oils (with exception of soya oil) the tariff offered is 300 percent. On the other hand India is obliged under WTO rule to reduce agricultural subsidies which are deemed 'trade distortions'. On this count it maintains that the agriculture sector is far from enjoying my positive subsidies rather a negative protection by the administered price regime.[60] This means effectively that the global market continues to be awash in developing countries with-potentially destablising consequences. And

---

55 Sukumar Muralidharan, 'On The World Trade Front', 18(2) *The Frontline*, ll (2001).

56 Bengal Leftist To Move Supreme Court Against WTO Agreement 'The *Hindu Daily* : *New Delhi Edition*, August, 2001 p.9.

57 CRR & VSS, 'What Are Indians Importing After the QR Era? *The Hindu Daily* 3 *New Delhi Edition*, Feb. 22, 2001: BS 1.

58 *Supra* note 17.

59 *Ibid.*

60 *ld* at 12.

the tough minded trade negotiations at the WTO have been indicating that they will vigorously challenge any country that seeks to replace QRs with high tariffs walls as an equivalent method of protection. With the continuing inclemency of the global economic environment and the imminent end of the protectionist measures India's farming sector could soon be directly encountering all the damaging consequences of WTO regime.[61]

VII. NORMATIVE AGENDA AND VISION

The protection of plant variety, farmers and breeders rights derives its life breath and sustenance from *union International Pour Law Proteution Des Obtentions Vegetables* or International Union for the Protection of New Varieties of Plants or *UPOV Convention.* The Convention was signed in Paris in 1961 and enforced in 1968. It was put to revision in 1972, 1978 and 1991. It ensures protection to plant variety and grant exclusive property right on DUS criteria i.e., distinct, uniform and stable.[62] For three decades (1961-1991), UPOV Convention has been granting privileges of breeder exemptions, which allowed the breeders to use the protected varieties for research purposes and for breeding new varieties; and farmers' privilege, which allowed the farmers to use their own harvested material of the protected variety for sowing the next crop on their own farm.[63] It further provides a non-exhaustive list of examples of acts that may result in the essential derivation, including the selection of a natural or induced mutant, or of a somaclonal variant, the selection of a variant individual from plants of an initial variety, back-crossing or transformation by genetic engineering. The *UPOV Convention* constitutes the ultimate ground norm for normative innovation in Member States in relation to protection of plant variety, breeders and farmers right.[64]

It is significant to note that the Convention was developed specifically to suit the conditions and needs of European agriculture, which differ markedly from those of a majority of the developing countries where agriculture constitutes the central economic activity.[65] Since *TRIPs Agreement* leaves Member States to choose their own system

---

61 *Ibid.*

62 *Supra* note 36 at 120.

63 See D. Leskien and M. Flitner, "Intellectual Property Rights and Plant Genetic Resources : Option for *Sui Generis System* V1 *Issues in Plant Gentic Resources,* 1997.

64 *Supra* note 36 at 121.

65 Phillippe Cullet, 'Farmers' Rights in Peril', *The Frontline Magazine,* April 4, 2000 at p. 71.

of plant varieties protection, it is evident that countries such as India where agriculture provides employment to at least two thirds of the working population should adopt a system adapted to their own needs and requirements.[66] The introduction of plant varieties protection thus constitutes significant departure from the existing regime. Intellectual property rights in agriculture has historically been denied as is reflected in the *Patents Act* of 1970 on the twin rationales of food security and basic need of life whose fulfilment should not be governed by private commercial interests and free accesses and sharing of information in agricultural managements.[67] Under this backdrop, Indian Government drafted a *Plant Variety Protection Bill* (PVP Bill), 1993 to protect the interest of the farmers as well as the private seed industry. The draft for PVP Bill could not be approved by the Parliament, although it was passed earlier by the Ministries of Commerce. Law, Environment, Industry and Agriculture.[68] The new draft Bill of I999 mainly focuses on the definition of formal plant breeder's rights and follows closely on the model of the UPOV Convention and strives to achieve the following objectives:

i) Stimulation of investment for research and development in public and private sectors for the development of new plant varieties by ensuring returns on such investments;

ii) Promotion and growth of the seed industry through domestic and foreign investment;

iii) Recognition of the role of farmers as cultivators, conservators;

iv) The contributions of traditional rural and tribal communities to the country's agro-bio-diversity; and

v) Benefit sharing and protection of the traditional rights of the farmers and breeders.[69]

To achieve these objectives, the Protection of Plant Varieties and Farmers Right Authority will perform the functions which *inter alia* include:

i) Promotion and development of new varieties of plant and rights of farmers and breeders;

ii) Registration of new plant varieties;

---

66 *Ibid.*

67 *Supra* note 7.

68 *Id* at 125.

69 Section 5, *The Protection of Plant Varieties and Farmers' Right Bill*, 1999.

iii) Characterization and documentation of varieties;

iv) Compulsory licensing of protected varieties; and

v) Collection, compilation and publication of plant varieties, seeds and germ plasm.[70]

Though the title suggests that the Bill provides for farmers' right in reality it focuses more on plant breeders' right, which are inherently incapable of recognizing farmers as breeders. A perusal of protection of *Plant Varieties Act*, 2001 reveals that while the basics framework of the law does not go anywhere near devising an indigenous system the includes a number of provision which do not arise out of the *UPOV model.*[71] On a closer scrutiny one finds that specific content of these rights are so weak that their complete absence from the text would possibly be more appropriate. Indeed, the Act does no more than protect the rights of farmers to save, use, exchange, share or sell their produce of a protected variety. In other words, the Act only seeks to grant farmers rights over the crops they have grown. This right is so basic that there should be no need to restate it. It also sidelines the seeds which should be central in this piece of legislation.[72]

VIII. RIGHT TO FOOD SECURITY

The food security debate has been mooted since last five decades still the prognosis seems to be far from the satisfactory. In the historical context right from heart shaking famine of Bengal to starvation deaths in Kalahandi, Bolangir, Korapat and Kashipur in Orissa in contemporary India right to food security is blatantly set at naught by the governmental apparatus. In 1942, more than three million people died in Bengal and Orissa due to starvation. Famine has returned to Orissa, Madhya Pradesh, Maharashtra, Gujarat and Andhra Pradesh. Between July 27 and August 28, twenty deaths were reported from Kashipur district, Orissa. Eleven children were reported dead in Udaipur, Rajasthan, over a week. Earlier, 800 of tribal children had died of starvation. The Bengal famine forced intervention by the Government to ensure the supply of food. A rationing system was introduced. The *First Food Grains Policy Committee,* appointed in 1913, recommended procurement of food grains from surplus areas rationing for equitable distribution and statutory price control for checking

---

70 *Id* Section, 7.

71 Phillippe Cullet, "Intellectual Property Rights : For An Alternative Patent Regime" XVI (21) *The Front Line*. 1999 at p. 91.

72 *Supra* note 36 at 127.

the price rise. Food Corporation of India (FC1) Agriculture Prices Commission (APC). The Constitution guarantees the right to life and the right to food is at the heart of the right to life. The State has a related duty to ensure that no one goes hungry. Food for work programmes, the Public Distribution System (PDS), price regulation and anti-hoarding measures have been diverse policy components of ensuring that people's food entitlements are protected.[73]

All elements of India's food security policy are today being dismantled under pressure from the World Bank and the WTO. Starvation is the inevitable result of policies promoting a sudden withdrawal of the role of the State and reckless dependence on markets to bring food to the poor. In 1991, the World Bank, that had designed the centralized system called for its dismantling through its Structural Adjustment Programmes (SAP) of the PDS system the removal of *Essential commodities Act,* 1955 and price and inventory control and a total deregulation of agricultural trade. The revamped PDS (RPDS) was supposed to better target vulnerable regions and reduce public expenditure. However, all it did was created more hunger while increasing Government expenditure. In I995 at preparatory exercise for the World Food summit, civil society in India had drafted a *People's Charter for Food Security* in and anticipated starvation deaths and suicides by farmers. In 1997, the PRDS was replaced by the Targeted PDS (TPDS) which provided 10 kg of wheat or rice per month to families below the Poverty Line (BPL) at highly subsidized prices, and withdrawal of all subsidies from families above the poverty line (ALP). As a result, food prices increased, off take decreased, and stocks grew. There were major problems with the TPDS system.[74] First, the BPL/APL categories were arbitrary and the BPL beneficiaries who were to be targeted were artificially reduced.

The whole exercise of targeting the BPL families was exposed as a farce when 12 States informed the Supreme Court in public interest litigation in *Kashipur Starvation Death* Case that they could not identify people in the BPL category. Instead of targeting the poor, the World Bank driven policies made the poor end their food entitlements. The TPDS has artificially divided the population into those below the poverty line (BPL) and those above the poverty line (APL). It is common knowledge that those access food from fair price shops are those who cannot buy it from the market. Those above the poverty line have been defined earning

[73] Vandana Shiva, 'At the Mercy of Globalisation' *The Hindu Sunday Magazine.* September 23, 2001. P.II

[74] Ruddar Dutt, 'Effectiveness of Public Distribution System As A Provider of Food Security' 42(3) *The Indian Journal of Labour Economics,* 403 (1999).

above Rs. 1,500 a month. Those in the APL category also have to bear I00 per cent of the procurement and distribution costs, which places the food grains far above their reach. In fact the Government committee formulating the long-term grain policy has demanded that the price of gain tor those APL be slashed by 25 per cent. Further the quantum of allotment of 10 kg per family at best meets only 12 per cent of the nutritional requirement, forcing the poor to depend on high markets for 88 per cent of their requirements and eat less, thus reducing off take from the PDS.[75]

The hunger and starvation death is the inevitable result of sudden withdrawal of role of state under the pressure of WTO and World Bank policies. The food security of this new class of "dispensable" people with neither food entitlements nor purchasing power will be totally denied by an agri-business dominated agriculture. This trade liberalization will result in the creation of a class of "redundant" humans, comprising mainly displaced landless rural agro-related communities, including artisans and fisher folk, who will be doubly hit by the less of their traditional markets and linkages with the agro-sector as well by loss of food entitlements.[76]

The pauperization of Adivasi of Kalahandi - Bolangir - Korapat (KBK) region is a case in point. The Adivasis have no rights in forest lands that used to provide them food and shelter in times of distress. Adivasi oral traditions from many areas in eastern and central India recount how leaves from mahua tree or ripe fruits, seeds and leaves from other plants were an essential dietary supplement, especially in times of famine. The denial of rights in the colonial and subsequently post-colonial period was motivated not only by the needs to maximize revenues from forest timber, but also to harness forest produce for industrial purposes. Of these, *mahua* and mango kernel were some of the most valuable species in the KBK area and were therefore appropriated by traders and the state. The Adivasis were only included in the system as a labourers who had no rights over the produce and would be paid less than the minimum wage for the collection of *mahua* seed or the *mango* kernel. Given this desperate situation, it is not surprising that the only food the local Adivasis can have access to at the time scarcity is poisonous mango kernels and

---

75 Rajeev Malhotra, Incidence of Poverty In India : Towards A Consensus on Estimating Poor' 40(1) *The Indian Journal of Labour Economics*, 68 (1997).

76 S. Mahendra Dev, Social Security for Indian Workers 1 Performance & Issues 39(4) *The Indian Journal of Labour Economic*, 889 (1996).

77 CRR & VSS, Limited Growth In Post-QR Imports, *The Hindu Business & Science Magazine*, March 8, 2001.

roots (Kanda).[77] The dumping of imported, subsidized commodities and the removal of import restrictions (Quantitative Restrictions) is another dimension of the erosion of entitlements of agricultural producers in India.[78]

The destruction of food entitlements by dumping is an unfair trade practice which is totally legal in the asymmetric and unbalanced W.T.O. rules. For example, U.S. soybeans are cheap not because of cheap production but because of subsidies. This government support is not really a farmer subsidy; it is an indirect corporate subsidy. As heavily subsidized soybeans fiooded India's domestic market, prices crashed India's domestic market, prices crashed by more than two-thirds. The dumping of subsidized soya, wheat, rice, sugar on Indian markets is called competitiveness have suggested that Indian farmers should be allowed to be destroyed by opening markets because they are not competitive. The *Prime Minister's Committee on W.T.O. and Agriculture* has actually recommended that the Government to implement an EXIT policy for peasants and farmers. It is this mindset of our elite which sees the rural poor as dispensable and disposable which is causing starvation deaths, even as grain rots in our godowns.

IX. IPR STRATEGY AND PLAN

The second generation reform of IPR regime generally reflect the trend towards the appropriation by states and private actors of multiplicity of property rights, the gradual dismissal of common property rights (CPR) regimes and the denial of the principle of free exchange of resources and knowledge as the basic premises for managing genetic resource. The sovereign rights over biological resources are relatively week and it is likely that main beneficiaries of this regime will be the private sector, local industry and multinational companies. Exclusion of patent in natural and agricultural resources have been traditionally premised on elements of public morality the need to foster innovation at all levels from the smallest farmer to MNCs and need to restrict the commercialization of sectors dealing with the most basic needs of human kind such as food, health and environment. The *PPV Act*, 2001 is closely modelled on *UPOV Convention*, 1978 and recognizes plant breeders' rights which are, like patents, monopoly rights meant to foster the involvement of the private sector in the seed industry. Bio-diversity, Patent Amendment and Geographical Indication laws are some of the other extremely interesting

[78] Archana Prashad, Food Security: Hunger and Democracy, 18(20) *The Frontline* 56 (2001 Sept. – Oct. 12).

proposals but do not necessarily contribute to the development of an alternative.

An alternative regime should be premised on the mixed bags of legal and communal system of IPR. First it should provide for the establishment of property right for all actors involved in agricultural management and seed improvement. To this end, it should aim at protecting not only the interests of corporate bio-technology firms and seed companies but also the interests of farmers and seed producers in India. Secondly, the system should provide for non-monopoly rights implying that no single entity derives all the benefits associated with a given invention and that various inventors may have concurrent rights. The mandates of TRIPS agreement to the effect that the alternative system should be an effective *sui generis* system or by any combination thereof logically implicates India's international obligations be construed in the broader framework of *U.N. Declaration on Human Right*, 1948 *Right To Development*, 1986, *Vienna Declaration 1993, Convention of Bio- diversity*, 1992 *UNESCO and WIPO municipal legal models on the Protection of Expression of Folkore, Draft Declaration on Indigenous Rights and U.N. Commission On Human Rights Fifty Second Resolution*, 2000. India should utilize the *TRIPS Agreement* in devising an *effective sui generis, protectectionist* alternative socio-legal model for fighting against poverty and heralding a human right friendly IPR regime in for a hunger-free India.

Section-III

Patent, Health & Public Policy

7

Remedies Relief & Recompense Under Patent Infringement: A Critical Analysis

Sajid Zaheer Amani

I. INTRODUCTION

Procedural remedies for the infringement of one's right are not enough by themselves unless they result in some reliefs of substantive nature whereby it can reasonably be said that these reliefs, temporary or permanent, as the case may be, are enough in the circumstance to make good or, say, compensate the genuine loss of the aggrieved party to an infringement suit. The substantive remedies available to a successful plaintiff at any stage in any suit for patent infringement could, however, be derived from the express as well as by necessary implication of the provisions of the Patents Act, 1970 dealing with the "Reliefs in suit for infringement". Its Sec. 108 declares in terms quoted below:

> [1]*[(1)] The relief which a court may grant in any suit for infringement include an injunction (subject to such terms, if any as the courts thinks fit) and, at the option of the plaintiff, eitherdamages or an account of profits.*
>
> [2]*[(2) The court may also order that the goods, which are found to be infringing and materials and implements, the predominant use of which is in the creation of infringing goods shall be seized, forfeited or destroyed, as the court deems fit under the circumstances of the case without payment of any compensation.]*

Taken as such Sec.108 specified reliefs, which a court may grant in a suit for patent infringement, are:

- Injunction (subject to such terms, if any, as the court thinks fit);
- Either 'damages' or 'an account of profits' (at the option of the plaintiff);

---

1 Section 108 re-numbered as sub-section (1) thereof by Act 38 of 2002, sec. 45 (w.e.f. 20. 5. 2003).

2 Instituted by Act 38 of 2002, sec. 45 (w.e.f. 20. 5. 2003).

- seizure, forfeiture or destruction of the infringing goods, and the materials and implements used for such goods (as the court deems fit) but without payment of any compensation.

The said section is, thus, clear on the point that it provides substantive remedies of civil nature only and does not command for the criminal remedies of any sort. The reliefs provided under Sec.108 of the *Patent Act,* 1970, however, could not be demanded by a successful plaintiff as a matter of right, but can be granted on the discretion of the court as is obvious from the word 'may' used in the language of the said section. Even the defendant's consenting to the grant of relief or reliefs, prayed for by the plaintiff, would not mean that the court will automatically grant them as a matter of course; rather the court must always be satisfied that the facts justify their grant.[3] The discretionary power of the court in granting the reliefs does not mean the whimsical power or, say, arbitrary power to refuse or not to refuse even if justice does not demand. The discretionary power of the court is subject to the requirement of justice. It has been judicially observed:

> *"While exercising its discretionary power the court. . . . should exercise the discretion only if the end of justice requires, for justice is an object that cannot be administered in vacuum."* [4]

The law, therefore, requires that the court's discretion in granting such reliefs had always to be in conformity to such limitations as are prescribed by the laws in force apart from the well settled principles of justice and fair play. It may be pointed out here that Sec.108 specified reliefs are governed according to the general principles and rules as contained in the *Code of Civil Procedure,* 1908, *Specific Relief Act,* 1963 and other relevant laws save in respect to those aspects of such reliefs which have been specifically dealt by the *Patents Act,* 1970. Sec.108, however, is not exhaustive of the reliefs that a court may grant. The court can also grant reliefs, other than those specified in Sec.108. So is clear from the use of the expression:

> *"The reliefs . . . . include an injunction . . . . . and . . . . either damages or an account of profits."*

In other words, the specified reliefs are not the only reliefs but some instances of various reliefs, which the court is equally empowered to grant in its discretion under the relevant laws of the land. The substantial

---

3 *See Critchley Brothers v. Englemaun and Buckham* (1971) RPC 346.

4 *Executive Committee of Vaishya Degree College, Shamli v. Laxmi Narayan,* AIR 1976 SC 888, p. 894.

reliefs as drawn from express as well as by necessary implication of the provision of Sec.108 can conveniently be classified, from the viewpoint of the object of the relief, into the following three classes:

1. Remedy by way of regulating the behaviour of the party addressed by the court, such as reliefs in the forms of 'injunction'(interlocutory as well as final), *'anton piller order', 'mareva injunction'* etc.;
2. Remedy by way of payment of money as recompense for patent infringement, such as 'damages', 'accounts of profits' etc., and
3. Remedy by way of dealing with the disputed property or infringing goods, such as 'delivery up', 'seizure', 'forfeiture', 'destruction' or 'disposal' of infringing goods as well as of the materials or implements used in the creation of infringing goods.

However, from the view point of measure of reliefs, the remedies may be put into the following two classes:

1. Remedy by provisional measures, such as temporary or, say, interlocutory injunction, *anton piller order, mareva injunction* etc., and
2. Remedy by permanent measures, such as permanent injunction, damages, accounts of profits, and other remedies such as seizure, forfeiture, destruction etc. of infringing goods, and of the materials and implements used for the creation of such goods.

A patent infringement is treated as tortuous invasion of the patent rights. It is, therefore, common in such cases for the plaintiff -the patent owner, while filing an infringement suit, to allege that the defendant - the infringer complained of, is liable for damage or, say, injury sustained due to the said infringement. To fix or, say, determine the 'liability', even in appeal, is the task of the court. It is only after liability of the infringer is fixed that the stages of determining the permanent reliefs are set in motion. The determination of liability, in patent infringement suit, raises binary questions having clear alternatives: Is the patent valid or not? Is the patent unauthorized resorted to by the person complained of? If the patent is valid and firmly ensconced in infringing activity or product, that the liabilities are treated as finally fixed or determined and thereupon the reliefs, such as final injunction, damages, account of profits, seizure, forfeiture and destruction of infringing goods etc. become due in favour of the patentee. It is during the period of determination of the liabilities that the request for provisional measures, such as interlocutory injunction, including *Anton Piller Order, Mareva Injunction* etc., can be made and may well be ordered by the court in its discretion. The present paper is designed to have an understanding of the civil remedies of the kind of recompense of two kinds 'damages' and 'account of profits', and see their relative importance with the marked difference amongst them.

II. REMEDIES BY MONEY RECOMPENSE-PERMANENT RELIEF

The two types of remedies, specially specified in Sec.108 of our Patents Act, 1970 in patent infringement cases, namely, 'damages' and 'account of profits', have each one object: to recompense economically or, say, monetarily for patent infringement, though the principles of such recompense in each case differ from one another as discussed in the subsequent headings and sub-headings. It is, however, important to note that these two remedies are alternatives to each other, that is, plaintiff is to opt out either one of them and not to resort to both or one after another. This is clear from the language of the very section which says: *"The reliefs which the court may grant . . . . include. . . , at the option of the plaintiff, either damages or an account of profits"*. This is based on the principle that in respect of any one infringement the plaintiff should not be entitled to be both reimbursed and compensated as that would be a double remedy for the same infringement which is not just and equitable.

Although remedy by way of 'account of profits' is not so much concern with the damage or loss, yet it can be said that there is no claim for an 'account of profits' if there is no damage. For, if there is no damage there is no remedy by way of damages and, hence, no question of exercising of an option between it and account of profits arises at all. To exercise option existence of both is inevitable and if there is no remedy by way of damages in the absence of any damage, there could be no remedy by way of account of profits either. It can, therefore, be aptly said that there is no remedy by way of account of profits if there is no damage or to put in one's words: "an account is not available in cases where there is no right to damages."[5]

It is to every law-knowing man that, as a matter of general principle, the end of every award of damages is to recompense the plaintiff for the economic or, say, monetary loss or damage occasioned to him by injury. Damages cannot be awarded if there is no proof of the amount of loss or, say, damage, so that any award would be purely speculative[6], yet the plaintiff may be entitled to nominal damages, that is, damages awarded only for the name sake just to establish plaintiff right to decree and that the defendant did really infringe the plaintiff's right. These are only general principles.

In the context of patent infringement, which is a tortuous invasion of the patent rights, it is common for the plaintiff-patent owner, while

---

5 Hilary Pearson & Clifford Miller, *Commercial Exploitation of Intellectual Property*, (Universal Law Publishing Co. Pvt. Ltd., Delhi, 2nd Indian Reprint 1997), p. 233.

6 Ibid.

filing an infringement suit to allege that the defendant -the infringer complained of, is liable for damages, that is, to compensate for monetary loss or, say, damage, if not for restoration in species (kind) being almost a non-feasibility in patent infringement. The damages generally aims to put the right-holder back to his position of 'no lost profit' he was in before the tort and so, subject to exclusion of the losses that are unforeseeably remote, he may recover profits that he would have made in the absence of such tort. However, "when lost profits cannot be proven, or aren't considered appropriate, damages are often measured by a reasonable royalty."[7] In other words, nominal damages theory in case of 'no lost profits' to the patent holder for infringement of his patent is of little importance. Such is clear from the following observation of the British Court of Appeal:

> *Where there is no doubt that the patentee has suffered substantial damage, the difficulty and impossibility of stating the precise ground for assessing it at any particular figure does not seem to be a sufficient reason for giving only a nominal sum. Where the damages are such that they cannot be calculated by figures, they are problematical damages, and has to be guessed at, that is, not a mere guess, as if one were tossing up for the thing, but it must come to mere question of what in the mind of the person who has to estimate them was a fair sum.*[8]

What the common law courts provide as to the award of patent damage in case of difficulty of calculating actual loss; that is, of awarding of a 'fair sum' to the patentee instead of nominal damages, the *United States Code* (1970) seems to give a statutory recognition to such provision. To wit, Title 35 of its Section 284 states that:

> *Upon finding for the claimant the court shall award the claimant damages adequate to compensate for the infringement, but in no event less than a reasonable royalty for the use of the invention by the infringer, together with interest and costs as fixed by the court.*

In other words, even if there comes such a situation that despite the patent infringement no loss was occasioned to the plaintiff and, therefore, the nominal damages become inevitable to meet the justice, the same, in US, must in no event be less than a reasonable royalty for the use of the invention by the infringer and, in common law countries, no less than a

---

7 Russell L. Parr, *Intellectual Property Infringement Damages – A Litigation Support Handbook, 2nd* Ed. (1999), p. 17.

8 *Ungar v. Sugg* (1892) 9 RPC 113, p. 117 (CA) as referred to in P. Narayanan, P. Narayanan, *Patent Law,* (Eastern Law House Pvt. Ltd New Delhi, 1998, 3rd Ed.), pp.502-503.

'fair sum'. It is suggested that Indian law-makers must strive to equate the common law 'fair sum' with the American approach of 'reasonable royalty', which, followed on licence analogy, stands for the minimum damages the right holder has suffered.

Whether the patent damages is measured in the forms of 'Lost-Profits' or common law 'fair sum' or U.S. 'Reasonable Royalty' what is necessary to a claim for damages is that some economic loss must have occasioned to the patentee due to patent infringement, it being immaterial with the loss or gain of the infringer. The profits made, or loss suffered by the infringer is a matter of no consequence. "However large he gains, he is only liable to nominal damages so long as his illegal sales do not injure the trade of the patentee; and however great his loss, he cannot escape from liability to make full compensation for the injury which his competition may have occasioned."[9]

Any arriving at the measure of damages for loss or, say, damage is always guided by two policy considerations, which sometimes seem to contradict each other: On the one hand, damages should be assessed in a way to compensate as far as possible for the financial losses the plaintiff suffered, that is, damages should be commensurate to economic loss. This forbids double or, say, excess recovery for the same damage. On the other hand, while so assessing no advantage be left to the infringer; for, "it is necessary for the law to show that it cannot be broken with impunity"[10]. It means that in cases where the defendant's conduct has been calculated by him to make a profit for himself which may well exceed the compensation awarded to the plaintiff, then, neither the defendant, on the analogy of 'right must not be invaded with impunity', be allowed to retain the excess profit earned by him, nor the plaintiff, on the analogy of 'damages must be commensurate to the economic loss' or 'damages should not be awarded to punish the infringer', be entitled to that profit, for doing so would be awarding exemplary damages of twice or thrice more than the actual damages and hence be as if punishing the infringer, which is uncommon in Indian legal system as well in England, though common in the United States of America.[11]

Such being the conflicting policy considerations in the matter of award of damages, the theory of damages for infringement seems impracticable to deal with the cases of infringer's excess profits over the awarded compensation to be paid by him to the plaintiff. Suggestions are, therefore,

---

9 *United Horse Shoe v. Stewart* (1888) 5 RPC 260, p. 266 (HL).

10 Per Lord Devlin in *Rookes v. Barnard* (1964) A.C. 1129, pp. 1220-1231.

11 See Title 35, Sections 284, 289 of the United States Code (1970).

coming for preferring another remedy-action for unjust enrichment, which, strictly speaking, does not fall under the heading 'Damages', but is closely related to it. According to this action a person has to deliver up the (monetary) advantage, which he has gained unjustly at the cost of another. The observation of Dr. Joachim Bornkamm as regards action for unjust enrichment is worth quoting below:

> *The action for unjust enrichment may be preferable for two reasons: Firstly, no negligence has to be shown (unlike claim for damages where damages can't be awarded for innocent infringement), and, secondly, the statutory limitation is 30 years instead of three years limitation applying to action for damages. On the other hand, the claim does not reach as far as the claim for damages. It will only cover a reasonable royalty for making use of the patent, trademark or copyrighted work. The actual loss of the right holder cannot be recovered in this way nor can the defendant be forced to turn out his profits on a claim for unjust enrichment.*[12]

The above observation is a general remark showing the merits and demerits of the theory of unjust enrichment action and not favouring it over action for damages.

In the context of the Indian legal system, it is still an open question whether action for unjust enrichment as a remedy against patent infringement is acceptable or not while in copyright infringement cases it has always been accepted that a claim for unjust enrichment can be raised. It is submitted that the above observation of Dr. Joachim is worth considering and it is open to the Indian courts to entertain, under its inherent power, action for unjust enrichment in the matter of patent infringement cases particularly in the light of Indian Civil Procedure Code, 1908.

It is simple to make an order for damages as it depends on the finality of the liability. This liability, however, should be the result of the infringer acting at least negligently or, say, in ignorance of the infringed right. The real problem is faced when it comes to the measure or, say, assessment of damages. An answer to this problem could be found in Title 35 Section 284 of the *United States Code* (1970), which, regarding 'patent infringement damages' reads:

---

[12] Dr. Joachim Bornkamm of Germany, "Action and Remedies for Infringement of Intellectual Property Rights", *WIPO Pub.No.726 (E)*, p. 96. Bracket supplied.

"Damages.

Upon finding for the claimant the court shall award the claimant damages adequate to compensate for the infringement, but in no event less than a reasonable royalty for the use of the invention by the infringer, together with interest and costs as fixed by the court."

It is, therefore, found that normally measure or, say, assessment of damages, in patent infringement cases, can possibly be made either in terms of 'Lost Profits' or 'Reasonable Royalty' calculations. So is clear from the following observation of Russell L. Parr:

Each type of intellectual property has its own closely aligned definition of damages. Lost profits of the infringed are usually at the top of the list. When lost profits cannot be proven, or aren't considered appropriate, damages are often measured by a reasonable royalty.[13]

Determining the amount of patent damages by either ways is a very complex subject not germane to the present study, which is being focused on "patent infringement and legal remedies" rather than "patent infringement damages". Yet a short account of both for measuring patent damages given below is of necessity oversimplified. A detail account of the twin methods of measuring patent damages can be found in Russell L. Parr's work: *Intellectual Property Infringement Damages–A Litigation Support Handbook,* 2nd Ed. 1999.

III. PATENT DAMAGES IN THE FORM OF "LOST PROFITS"

By 'lost profits' in infringement cases means the plaintiff's profits that he failed or, say, lost to have made due to infringement and the damages that is awarded to him for such lost profits is referred to as 'lost profits damages'. Lost-profit calculations are the functions of *sales volume (i.e. amount, that is, units of sale), sales price,* and *sales cost.* It is, therefore, by determining the lost sales volume, the price at which those lost sale would have been made, and the characterization of the costs i.e. whether fixed costs or variable costs, necessary to make the lost sales that the lost-profits can be determined. These being the fundamental principles in the calculation of the 'lost-profits damages', the lost-profits by themselves have a different connotationin patent damages from those of the trademarks and copyright damages.

In patent damages 'lost-profits' connote the profits which the patentee failed or, say, lost to earn due to patent infringement. A patent

---

[13] Supra note 7, p. 17.

damages is different from the trademark damages and, for that matter, copyright damages in the sense that in the latter two cases the plaintiff can receive the profits earned by the defendant (the infringer) from his infringing activities. The plaintiffs in a patent case are limited to recovering only the profits that he would have earned absent the infringement. In patent damages case, the patent holder can show that absent the infringement, he would have made the sales made by the infringer, while in trademarks and copyrights damages' cases the plaintiff is required to prove the defendant's sale only. In patent damages case, it does not mean that whatever profits the infringer had made is the only profits lost to the plaintiff-patentee but is only an indication and available to calculate the profits what the plaintiff patentee in all reasonable probability would have earned from the sales made by himself had it not been made by the infringer. As regards the patent damages measured by the owner's lost profit, Russell L. Parr observes as:

> *The focus of the damages in the form of lost profits in a patent infringement matter is the lost profits of the plaintiff (the patent holder) and not on the defendant (the infringer). In some cases, the profits of the infringer are considered as an indication of the profits that the patent holder would have earned had there been no infringement. It should be noted that the profits of the defendant are available as a measure of damages for the infringement of design patents.*[14]

And observes United States Court of Appeals for the Federal Circuit:

> *"If in all reasonable profitability, the patent owner would have made the sales which the infringer has made, what the patent owner in reasonable probability would have netted from the sales denied to him is the measure of his loss, and the infringer is liable for that."* [15]

Once the patentee proves in patent damages case that absent the infringement, he would have made the sales made by the infringer by showing, for example, that the demand existed for the infringed product, that the acceptable non-infringing substitute products were not available to satisfy the demand, that the patent owner possessed the manufacturing and marketing capacity to exploit the demand etc. etc. that the next question that obviously comes on the surface is the one posed by Justice Brennan, *"Had the Infringer not infringed, what would Patent Holder. . . . have made?"* [16] Or by paraphrase: *But for the infringement by the defendant,*

---

14 Id p. 50.

15 *Livesay Window Co. v. Livesay Industries, Inc.,* 251 F.2d 469, 471-72: 116 USPQ 167, 168-70 (5th Cir. 1958).

16 *Aro Manufacturing Co. v. Convertible Top Replacement Co.,* 141 USPQ 681, 694 (1964).

how much more would the plaintiff have made? "The question may be answered", says Russell L. Parr, "by identifying and then quantifying the amount of sales that were lost due to infringement, and the amount of profits that the patent holder would have made on those lost sales."[17]

This identifying and then quantifying of the two amounts is by itself a very delicate and complex exercise. The starting point to ask is whether the patentee and the infringer are in actual competition or not. If they are in actual competition, the court will look to the patentee's lost profits through the defendant's competition after getting needful information as to what the infringer has exactly done, how many infringing articles were produced at which cost, how many articles were sold, when were they sold and to whom at which price. Always provided that at least one act of infringement is proved, the infringer is obliged to give this information on a petition for rendering account. Many of this information are delicate business secrets. In order to give the defendant as much secrecy as possible, he will be allowed to give the names and addresses of his clients to an auditor. The auditor will then answer on the specific request of the plaintiff whether or not a particular client of his has been supplied by the defendant with the infringing product. Thus, it can be found out to what extent patentee-plaintiff's own business connections were jeopardized. It is only where the plaintiff's and defendant's anticipated profits are the same in the same market that the defendant's gain or, say, profits will be plaintiff's loss.[18] Where they are not so, for reason that, even if the plaintiff is provided with all the necessary information, it will be extremely difficult to show that plaintiff's sale figures have suffered to a particular extent. The defendant, having undercut the prices of the right holder, will submit that his success was only due to the lower prices, to his excellent business connections and to the special reputation he enjoyed among his customers. In such a situation, although the courts are empowered to make a rough estimate of the plaintiff's lost profits when assessing damages, based on reasonable probability of his reasonable profitability, the foundation for such assessment, *i.e.* the lost-profits calculation, will often be too narrow or, say, be considered inappropriate, so much so that a 'reasonable royalty', on licence analogy, becomes another option as a form of damages for patent infringement.

---

[17] Supra note 7, p. 49.

[18] Cornish, W.R.: *Intellectual Property: Patents, Copyright, Trade Marks And Allied Rights,* (Sweet & Maxwell Ltd., U.K. 3rd Edition, 1966, reprinted as Second Indian Reprint, 2003, Universal Law Publishing Co. Pvt. Ltd., Delhi), p. 62.

IV. PATENT DAMAGES IN THE FORM OF REASONABLE ROYALTY

Where the 'lost profits' cannot be proved as a form of patent damages or is considered too inappropriate or when there is a non-competitive infringement; for example, because the patentee had insufficient manufacturing capacity to meet the demand, or the infringer activities were in the market or area where the patentee did not operate, the courts have generally held that a reasonable royalty could be awarded as a form of damages for patent infringement. Speaking on the royalty as a basis of patent damages, Lord Shaw observation, in *Watson Laidlaw v. Pott, Cassels & Williamson*, is worth quoting below:

> *If with regard to the general trade which was done, or would have been done by the respondents within their ordinary range of trade, damages be assessed, these ought, of course, to enter the account and to stand. But in addition there remains that class of business which the respondents would not have done; and in such cases it appears to me that the correct and full measure is only reached by adding that a patentee is also entitled, on the principle of price or hire, to a royalty for the unauthorized sale or use of every one of the infringing machines in a market which the infringer, if left to himself, might not have reached. Otherwise, that property which consists in the monopoly of the patented articles granted to the patentee has been invaded, and indeed abstracted, and the law, when appealed to, would be standing by and allowing the invader or abstractor to go free. In such cases a royalty is an excellent key to unlock the difficulty .... Each of the infringements was an actionable wrong, although it may have been committed in a range of business or of territory that the patentee might not have reached, he is entitled to hire or to royalty in respect of each unauthorized use of his property. Otherwise remedy might fall unjustly of the short of the wrong.* [19]

The quoted observation in simple language means that if there is no unauthorized use or sale of the patented invention and any breach of any other right or rights occur, for example, breach of a contract, then damages as generally assessed becomes due to the aggrieved party; but where there is the unauthorized use or sale of the patented invention, damages ought not be assessed as generally assessed but rather best way of rewarding damages is to reward it in the form of royalty; for, in such cases general way of assessing damages would not do complete justice because of some deadlock difficulty in such assessment.

The amount of royalty should, however, be that amount which adequately compensate for the infringement.[20] Royalties usually relate

---

[19] (1914) 31 RPC 104, p.120 (HL).

[20] See *Stickle v. Heublein, Inc.*, 716 F. 2d 1550, p. 1562: 219 USPQ 2d 377, p. 386 (Fed.Cir.1983).

to the profits and where there is no profit the royalty stands at zero. However, in patent damages case establishing reasonable royalties is often accomplished by applying licence analogy, that is, by looking at the royalty terms specified in licences involving similar patents. In other words, the patentee can ask for a reasonable royalty from the infringer which he could have asked on the basis of royalty terms as specified in any licensing agreement under his patent or as drawn from a fictitious or, say, hypothetical licence agreement involving such patent. It shall be granted whether the patentee had actually granted a licence or not. It, however, does not mean that where there is evidence of the licensing practice, the court will be prevented from taking other more general considerations or, say, factors to reach a reasonable royalty for patent damages.[21] Because, naturally, the views of the parties differ substantially when it comes to calculating the reasonable royalty by applying licence analogy: the plaintiff, for one example, will claim that a high percentage of the selling price, for instance 20%, would be adequate while the defendant may try to show that in other licence agreements 2 or 3% are common. "The ultimate process is one of judicial estimation of the available indications."[22]

The true principle which cover both cases when there have been licence, and those where there have not, remains that stated by Fletcher Moulton, L.J. in the *Meters Ltd. v. Metropolitan Gas Meters Ltd* case as quoted below:

> *There is one case in which I think the manner of assessing damages in the case of sales of infringing articles has almost become a rule of law, and that is where the patentee grants permission to make the infringing article at a fixed price -in other words, where he grants licences at a certain figure. Every one of the infringing articles might then have been rendered a non-infringing article by applying for and setting that permission. The court then takes the number of the infringing articles, and multiplies that by the sum that would have had to be paid in order to make the manufacture of that article lawful, and that is the measure of damage that has been done by the infringement. The existence of such a rule shows that the courts consider that every single one of the infringements was a wrong, and that it is fair -where the facts of the case allow the court to get at the damages in that way – to allow pecuniary damages in respect of every one of them. I am inclined to think that the court might in some cases, where there did not exist a quoted figure for a licence, estimate the damages in a way closely analogous to this. It is the duty of the defendant*

21 See *General Tire v. Firestone Tyre* (1976) RPC 197, p. 214 (HL).

22 *Ibid.*

> *to respect monopoly rights of the plaintiff. The reward to a patentee for his invention is that he shall have the exclusive right to use the invention, and if you want to use it your duty is to obtain his permission. I am inclined to think that it would be right for the court to consider what would have been the price which –although no price was actually quoted –could have reasonably be charged for that permission, and estimate the damage in that way. Indeed, I think that in many cases that would be the safest and best way to arrive at a sound conclusion as to the proper figure. But I am not going to say a word which will tie down future judges and prevent them from exercising their judgment, as best they can in all the circumstances of the case, so as to arrive at that which the plaintiff has lost by reason of the defendant doing certain acts wrongfully instead of either abstaining from doing them, or getting permission to do them rightfully.* [23]

Speaking on the usefulness of the above quoted observation of Fletcher Moulton, L.J., it was Lord Wilberforce in *General Tire's* case of 1976 who observed as follows:

> *A proper application of this passage, taken in its entirety, requires the judge assessing damages to take into account any licence actually granted and the rates of royalty fixed by them, to estimate their relevance and comparability, to apply them so far as he can to the bargain hypothetically to be made between the patentee and the infringer, and to the extent to which they do not provide a figure on which the damage can be measured, to consider any other evidence, according to its relevance and weight, upon which he can fix a rate of royalty which would have been agreed.* [24]

The courts in their zeal to determine a reasonable royalty for patent damages have been striving to enlist a number of factors to be reckoned with. Such an attempt is found in the 1970 case of *Georgia-Pacific Corp. v. United States Plywood Corp.*[25]. wherein the court listed fifteen factors that it considered important for deriving a reasonable royalty in the context of the patentee and infringer engaging in a hypothetical agreement for a licence of the patent alleged to be infringed. These factors are:

1. The royalties received by the patentee for the licensing of the patentin suit, proving or tending to prove an established royalty.
2. The rates paid by the licensee for the use of other patents comparable to the patent in suit.

---

[23] (1911) 28 RPC 157, p. 164-165.

[24] (1976) RPC 197, p. 214 (HL).

[25] 318 F. Supp. 1116 (S.D.N.Y. 1970), modified, 446 F.2d 295 (2d Cir.1970).

3. The nature and scope of the licence, as exclusive or non-exclusive; or as restricted or non-restricted in terms of territory or with respect to whom the manufactured product may be sold.
4. The licensor's established policy and marketing program to maintain its patent monopoly by not licensing others to use the invention or by granting licences under special conditions designed to preserve that monopoly.
5. The commercial relationship between the licensor and the licensee, such as, whether they are competitors in the same territory in the same line of business; or whether they are inventor and promoter.
6. The effect of selling the patented specialty in promoting sales of other products of the licensee; the existing value of the invention to the licensor as a generator of sales of its non-patented items; andthe extent of such derivative or convoyed sales.
7. The duration of the patent and the term of the licence.
8. The established profitability of the product made under the patent;its commercial success and its current popularity.
9. The utility and advantage of the patent property over the old modes or devices, if any, that had been used for working out similar results.
10. The nature of the patented invention; the character of the commercial embodiment of it as owned and produced by the licensor; and the benefits of those who have used the invention.
11. The extent to which the infringer has made use of the invention; and any evidence probative of the value of that use.
12. The portion of the profit or selling price that may be customary in the particular business or in comparable businesses to allow for the use of the invention or analogous inventions.
13. The portion of the realizable profit that should be credited to the invention as distinguished from the non-patented elements, the manufacturing process, business risks, or significant features or improvements added by the infringer.
14. The opinion and testimony of qualified experts.
15. The amount of the licensor (such as the patentee) and a licensee (such as the infringer) would have agreed upon (at the time the infringement began) if both had been reasonably and voluntarily trying to reach an agreement; that is, that amount which a prudent licensee -who desires, as a business proposition, to obtain a licence to manufacture and sell a particular article embodying the patented invention -would have been willing to pay as a royalty and yet be

able to make a reasonable profit and which amount would have been acceptable by a prudent patentee who was willing to grant a licence.

Russell L. Parr, commenting on the above quoted fifteen factors, concludes in the following terms:

> *The Georgia-Pacific factors provide a framework for determining a royalty rate for use in calculating damages. Not all the factors provide exact quantification of an answer but they are an excellent starting point for qualifying the value of the patent in suit.*
>
> *The Georgia- Pacific factors are fundamental to establishing a reasonable royalty rate. Other methods are useful for refining the final answer but these fifteen factors are the traditional starting point for royalty rate-based damages.* [26]

In the context of the Indian legal system, it can be pointed out that there does not exist as such any specific statutory provisions concerning the measure of patent damages. It is submitted that the principles involved and the law declared by the English courts as well as by the US courts are of immense importance for the Indian courts whenever confronted with the problem of measuring damages in a patent litigation.

On the whole it could be said that where the patentee is the manufacturer of the goods covered by the patent, there are four possible ways of measuring patent damages:

1. Loss of profits on sales lost to the infringer of goods covered by the patent.
2. Any loss of profits caused by price-cutting by the infringer on goods covered by the patent, which caused the plaintiff to cut its prices.
3. A reasonable royalty on any sales made by the infringer of the infringing goods which could not have deprived the plaintiff of a sale; for example, because he had insufficient manufacturing capacity to meet the demand, or the infringer's sales were in a market the plaintiff did not sell into.
4. A reasonable royalty on the entire defendant's sale.

The bases number 1, 2 and 3, as discussed above, are applied in the measure of patent damages in the form of 'Lost Profits', while basis number 4 is applied in the form of 'Reasonable Royalty' on licence analogy. Among the first three, the bases number 1 and 2 can always be combined, as these are two different kinds of loss. Use of basis number 3 in addition

[26] Supra note 7, p. 119.

to numbers 1 and 2 is only possible where it does not result in a double or, say, excess recovery to the plaintiff on any of the infringer's sale. The basis number 4 is indeed an alternative to the other three and could be used independent of them.[27]

V. MONETARY RELIEF ON ACCOUNT OF PROFITS

This very expression suggests that one must be provided with the relief by having an account of the profits earned by other or others and, accordingly, in the context of patent infringement it means commanding the infringer to account to the patentee for profits made by him out of such infringement. The remedy by way of 'account of profits' in patent infringement case is just reverse to the remedy by way of damages. What is necessary to a claim for 'account of profits' is that some economic gains or, say, profits, must be proved to have occasioned to the infringer of the patent right, it being immaterial with the loss or gain of the patentee due to such infringement. The profits made, or loss suffered by the patentee due to any reason is a matter of no consequence while considering relief by way of 'account of profits'. The modern approach towards an 'account of profits' is that it is restitutionary in character, aiming to put paid to an unjust enrichment to the defendant at the plaintiff's expense.[28]

By such restitutionary character, the plaintiff (the patentee) is treated as standing in the shoes of the defendant (the infringer) and condones, so to speak, his having been carrying on infringing business and gets control of the profits made there on.[29] On such assumption the infringer, being a constructive trustee, is, therefore, made liable to hand over the profits made from his business. When a patentee elects to claim an 'account of profits' from the infringer, it does not mean that he is entitled to entire profits earned by the infringer out of his business involving also the patented invention, but it is only a portion of that profits that could be attributable to the unauthorised use by him of the plaintiff's invention in the carrying of his business.[30] "It would be unreasonable to give the patentee profits which were not earned by the use of his invention.[31] " This principle, thereby, requires the court, when there is a

[27] Supra note 5, p. 232.

[28] Supra note 18, p. 64.

[29] See *Saccharin Corporation v. Chemicals and Drugs Co.* (1900) 17 RPC 612, p. 615.

[30] See *Siddle v. Vickers* (1892) 9 RPC 152 (CA).

[31] Per Lord Watson in *United Shoe and Nail Company Ltd. v. Stewart & Co.* (1888) 5 RPC 260, p. 266-267 (HL).

claim for 'account of profits', to ascertain how much of the patentee's invention was actually appropriated, in order to determine what portion of the net profits realized by the infringer was attributable to its use. Theoretically, the remedy for patent infringement by way of a claim for an 'account of profits' is open to the aggrieved patentee to opt for, yet the practical side of it is so cumbrous, laborious and expensive procedure in comparison to the plaintiff entitlement to that portion of the profits by which it was increased that this remedy is rarely invoked.

VI. LIMITATIONS ON THE GRANT OF RELIEFS

According to Section 108 of the *Patents Act*, 1970, only a court in a suit for patent infringement may grant the various reliefs, including injunction, damages as well as account of profits. It is the court which has been given discretion in the matter of grant of relief. In other words it cannot be granted as a matter of right to the aggrieved party. The discretionary power of the court to grant reliefs, however, does not go unbridled. In certain cases it has to be granted subject to certain limitations imposed by our patent statutes as discussed below.

A. ***In Suits by Exclusive Licensee:*** Section 109 of the *Patents Act*, 1970 specifically provides that in any suit for infringement of a patent instituted by the holder of an exclusive license, the court, as per sub-sec. (1) of the said Section, 'in awarding damages or an account of profits or granting any other relief in any such suit shall take into consideration any loss suffered or likely to be suffered by the exclusive licensee as such or, as the case may be, the profits earned by means of the infringement so far as it constitutes an infringement of the rights of the exclusive licensee as such'.

Thus according to the said sub-section, the restrictions imposed in the discretionary grant of the said reliefs are that before such exercise the court is to take into consideration any 'loss' suffered or likely to be suffered by the exclusive licensee or 'profits', if any, earned by the alleged infringer while the exclusive licensee is maintaining an infringement suit. This follows from the expression 'exclusive licensee as such' used in the said sub-section. Thus, while assessing any 'damages' or 'account of profits' to be awarded as reliefs to the exclusive licensee or granting 'any other relief', like injunction, delivery up etc., whatever loss occurs to the exclusive licensee or whatever profits occur to the infringer while the exclusive licensee is maintaining the infringement suit, the court accordingly would do plus and minus to the advantage of the plaintiff-exclusive licensee in computing the reliefs it decides to award him which the court is not bound to do so while the suit was being maintained by the patentee, either as plaintiff or co-plaintiff, in which case it would exercise its granting-discretion following the normal principle.

It may be pointed out that when an exclusive licensee institutes a patent infringement suit, the patentee, by virtue of Sec.109 (2), is necessarily implicated either as plaintiff or as defendant. Sec.109 (2) is, however, emphatic in saying that where the patentee has been added as defendant, he shall not be liable for any cost unless he enters an appearance and takes part in the proceedings. It has also been pointed out earlier that where a patent infringement suit is filed by a Sec. 84 compulsory licensee, the patentee, by virtue of Sec.110, is necessarily implicated as a defendant. But the said section is also emphatic in saying that where the patentee is so added as defendant, he shall not be liable for any cost unless he enters an appearance and takes part in the proceedings.

Thus, in both cases of patent infringement suits instituted by exclusive licensee or compulsory licensee, the mere fact of the patentee being implicated as a defendant will not make him liable to share in the cost, which the court may have awarded against the infringer-defendant. He will only be liable if he appears before the court as defendant and takes part in the proceeding. In other words, mere appearance is also not enough to make him liable to share in the cost unless he takes active part in defending, obviously, against the plaintiff. In case where the patentee and the exclusive licensee sue as co-plaintiffs, each plaintiff is entitled when successful to injunctive reliefs and damages and any other relief as assessed on normal principles.

B. ***In Suits Involving Innocent Infringement of Patent:*** Sub-Section (1) of Sec.111 of 1970 Act, dealing with the power of the court to grant reliefs to the plaintiff filing a patent infringement suit against the defendant-infringer, declares that "in a suit for infringement of patent, the damages or an account of profits shall not be granted against the defendant who proves that at the date of the infringement he was not aware and had no reasonable ground for believing that the patent existed." The above said sub-section embodies the concept of 'innocent infringement' which can be raised as a defence against the plaintiff's claims for damages or account of profits but not against an injunction. In other words, in any suit for infringement of patent, the plea of innocent infringement shall not prevent the court from granting an injunction against the infringer, that is, preventing him from continuing the infringing act, but the court is, of course, prevented from awarding any damages or account of profits against such an infringer.

C. ***In Suits Involving Failure to Pay Renewal Fee:*** Sub-Section (2) of Sec.111 of the 1970 Act, dealing with the powers of the court to grant reliefs to the plaintiff in case of infringement of patent committed after the failure to pay renewal fee by him but before the extension of payment period declares that "in any suit for infringement of a patent the court may, if it thinks fit, refuse to grant any damages or an account of profits in respect of any infringement committed after a failure to pay any renewal fee within the prescribed period and before any extension of that period."

Thus, in any suit for the infringement of the patent, the plea of non-payment of the renewal fee shall not, like Sec.111 (1) plea of innocent infringement, prevent the court, according to Sec.111 (4), to grant an injunction against the infringer, that is, preventing him from continuing the infringing act, but the court, of course, may refuse to award/grant the damages or account of profits, in favour of the plaintiff.

D. ***In Suits Involving Infringement Done before the Amendment of Specification:*** Sub-Section (3) of Sec.111 of the 1970 Act, dealing with the powers of the court to grant reliefs to the plaintiff in case of infringement committed before the decision of amendment but after the publication of the Specification, declares that " where an amendment of a specification by way of disclosure, correction or explanation has been allowed under this Act after the publication of the specification, no damages or account of profits shall be granted in any proceedings in respect of the use of the invention before the date of the decision allowing the amendment, unless the court is satisfied that the specification as originally established was framed in good faith and with reasonable skill and knowledge."

E. ***In Suits Involving Partially Valid Specification:*** Section 114 of the 1970 Act, dealing with the powers of the court to grant reliefs to the plaintiff in case of infringement of partially valid specification or, say thereby, partially valid patent, declares that :

1. If in proceedings for infringement of a patent it is found that any claim of the specification, being a claim in respect of which infringement is alleged, is valid, but that any other claim is invalid, the court may grant relief in respect of any valid claim which is infringed:

   Provided that the court shall not grant relief except by way of injunction save in the circumstances mentioned in sub-section (2).

2. Where the plaintiff proves that the invalid claim was framed in good faith and with reasonable skill and knowledge, the court shall grant relief in respect of any valid claim which is infringed subject to the discretion of the court as to costs and as to the date from

which damages or an account of profits should be reckoned, and in exercising such discretion the court may take into consideration the conduct of the parties in inserting such invalid claims in the specification or permitting them to remain there.

It could be said that under Sec.114 the claims of the specification need to be considered on the individual basis. For, the general rule is always in favour that the invalidity of some only of the claims does not invalidate the whole patent.[32] This principle, in turn, allows what sub-sec. (1) of the said section declares as "the court may grant relief in respect of any valid claim which is infringed".

However, the relief in the circumstances of the said sub-section shall be only in the form of 'injunction' as is clear from the Proviso to it that "the court shall not grant relief except by way of injunction". In other words, under the said sub-section the plaintiff can apply for injunction and the court will have the usual discretion with regard to the granting of the injunction but not with respect to other reliefs, like damages and account of profits etc. which shall not be granted at all in the circumstances of the said sub-section but shall be granted if, according to sub-sec. (2), the plaintiff proves that "the invalid claim was framed in good faith and with reasonable skill and knowledge", though, it is submitted, there is no decided case law to suggest a clear test of what is needed to prove this good faith and reasonable skill and knowledge.

Thus, under sub-sec (2) of Sec.114 the plaintiff, by proving that the invalid claim was drafted in good faith and with reasonable skill and knowledge, can also ask for damages or an account of profits in respect of infringed valid claim, and the court thereupon shall grant him that relief. In granting the relief of the kind other than injunction, the court is, however, empowered, according to the said sub-section to exercise discretion (i) as to cost and (ii) as to the date from which damages or an account of profits should start to run. And in exercising this discretion the court is empowered to take into consideration the conduct of the parties in inserting valid claims in the specification or permitting them to remain there, that is, for not making any effort to get the specification amended for deleting the invalid claims.

---

[31] See P. Narayanan, P. Narayanan, *Patent Law*,(Eastern Law House Pvt. Ltd New Delhi, 1998, 3rd Ed.), p. 492.

VII. CONCLUSION

So far as remedies by way of payment of money for patent infringement are concerned, two types of remedies, specially specified in Sec.108 of our *Patents Act*, 1970 in patent infringement cases, are damages' and 'account of profits'. Each has one object: to recompense economically or, say, monetarily for patent infringement, though the principles of such recompense in either case differ from one another. It is clear from the language of the said Section that these two remedies are alternatives to each other, that is, the plaintiff is to opt out either one of them and not to resort to both or one after another. Although remedy by way of 'account of profits' is not so much concern, unlike the 'damages', with the damage or loss, yet there is no claim for an account of profits if there is no damage.

In the context of patent infringement, which is a tortuous invasion of the patent rights, the damages generally aims to put the right-holder -the patentee-plaintiff, back to his position of 'no lost profit' he was in before the tort and so, subject to exclusion of the losses that are unforeseeably remote, he may recover profits that he would have made in the absence of such tort. However, when lost profits cannot be proven, or aren't considered appropriate, damages are often measured by a 'reasonable royalty'. In other words, nominal damages theory in case of 'no lost profits' to the patent holder for infringement of his patent is of little importance; for, the English courts equate this nominal damages to be no less than what in the mind of the person who has to estimate them was a 'fair sum' and the US law equate it in no event less than a 'reasonable royalty' for the use of the invention by the infringer. Suggestion is given that the Indian law-makers must strive to equate the common law 'fair sum' with the American approach of 'reasonable royalty' which, followed on licence analogy, stands for the minimum damage the right-holder has suffered.

The measure of damages is always guided by two conflicting policy considerations: one 'damages should be commensurate to economic loss' and second, 'no advantage be left to the infringer'. As such theory of damages for infringement seems impracticable to deal with the cases of infringer's excess profits over the awarded compensation. Suggestions are, therefore, coming for preferring another remedy -action for unjust enrichment, which, strictly speaking, does not fall under the heading 'Damages', but is closely related to it. According to this action a person has to deliver up a (monetary) advantage which he has gained unjustly at the cost of another. In the context of patent infringement it is still an open question whether such action is acceptable or not.

It is simple to make an order for damages but real problem is faced when it comes to measure or assess the damages. Normally in patent infringement cases it is measured either in terms of 'Lost Profits' or 'Reasonable Royalty'. In the context of the Indian legal system, it can be pointed out that there does not exist as such any specific statutory provisions concerning the measure of patent damages. As such the principles involved and the law declared by the English courts as well as the US courts is of immense importance for the Indian courts whenever confronted with the problem of measuring damages in a patent litigation.

Relief in the form of 'Account of Profits' suggests that one must be provided with the relief by having an account of the profits earned by other or others and, accordingly, in the context of patent infringement it means commanding the infringer to account, to the patentee, for profits made by him out of such infringement. The remedy by way of 'account of profits' in patent infringement case is just reverse to the remedy by way of damages. What is necessary to a claim for 'account of profits' is that some economic gains or, say, profits, must be proved to have occasioned to the infringer of the patent right, it being immaterial with the loss or gain of the patentee due to such infringement. The profits made, or loss suffered by the patentee due to any reason is a matter of no consequence while considering relief by way of 'account of profits'. Theoretically, the remedy for patent infringement by way of a claim for an 'account of profits' is open to the aggrieved patentee to opt for, yet the practical side of it is so cumbrous, laborious and expensive procedure in comparison to the plaintiff entitlement to that portion of the profits by which it was increased that this remedy is rarely invoked.

8

Rights to Health and Access to Medicines in the Context of Intellectual Property and Sustainable Development

Anis Ahmad

I. INTRODUCTION

Over the last few decades, protection of intellectual property rights (IPRs) has become a global issue. The existing international intellectual property rights regime has been governed by the Trade- Related Aspects of Intellectual Property Rights (TRIPS) Agreement.[1] Inspite of maturity of intellectual property laws in post TRIPS era it still desiderate to established coherence with human rights laws particularly right to health and maintain a distance with the socio-economic dimension of intellectual property protection. On the other hand the international human rights instruments from the very beginning appear to be considerable to make certain links with intellectual property rights.[2] The issue that is now debated that the adoption of the *TRIPS Agreement* provisions have serious impact on the realization of certain basic human rights such as the right to health because of non availability and affordability of much needed medicines for the poorer populations of the world particularly in majority of developing countries. Meanwhile TRIPS flexibilities as confirmed by the *Doha Declaration on Public Health* were adopted in 2001 by the global community to address medicines as public health issue.[3] Keeping in view the above developments the problem of right to health and the relationship between medical patents and access to medicine in the case of the HIV/ AIDS and T.B epidemics is complex challenge in the context of the *2030 Agenda for Sustainable Development Goals in 2015* adopted by

---

1 Hiroko Yamane, *Interpreting TRIPS: Globalization of Intellectual Property Rights and Access to Medicines* 03 (Hart Publishing, United Kingdom, Oxford and Portland, Oregon 2011).

2 Philippe Cullet, *Intellectual Property Protection and Sustainable Development* 385 (Lexis Nexis Butterworths: New Delhi, 2005).

3 M.D. Nair, "TRIPS and Access to Affordable Drugs", 17(4) *JIPR* 305 (2012).

Member States of the United Nations in Sep, 2015. One of the aims of the agenda is to ensure healthy lives and promote the well-being of people of ages.[4] In such a situation it is high time to revisit the existing intellectual property regime in the broader context to protect everyone who is likely to be negatively affected by intellectual property standards imposed by developed nations. Under this backdrop the present paper wishes to examine the various kinds of potential impacts of intellectual property regime on the realization of access to medicine as part of human right to health as universal entitlements amongst the most disadvantaged and marginalized peoples and communities in the broader context of sustainable development goals.

II. GLOBAL HEALTH SCENARIO

It is a well recognized fact that in the past few decades, new innovations in modern medicines has dramatically unproved the live of millions of people across the globe. According, to the recent *Report 2016 of the United Nations Secretary- General's High- Level Panel on Access to Medicines: Promoting innovation and access to Health Technologies* which review and assess the situations of health technologies and its impact on access to medicine scenario in globalised world particularly challenges exist in developing countries is an eye opener.[5] The Report said that the vaccines have significantly reduced the prevalence of diseases, ranging from polio to human papillomavirus. Antiretroviral medicines have greatly improved the lives of people living with the Human Immunodeficiency Virus (HIV). Despite this noteworthy progress, millions of people continue to suffer and die from treatable conditions because of a lack of access to health technologies and unaffordable to the majority of patients in developing countries since they constitute around 75 per cent of the world's population. It is a matter of great concern that, if the majority of the world's population access to medicines, which are patent by the pharmaceutical industry is denied. The report also mentioned the truth that:

> Investment in research and development (R&D) of health technologies does not adequately address a number of important health needs, in some cases, the cause lies in inadequate resourcing of R&D for diseases where the market does not provide sufficient return on investment.

---

4 *Sustainable Development Goals, available at*: http://www.un.org/sustainabledevelopment/sustainable-development-goals/ (Visited on October 10, 2016).

5 Report of the United Nations Secretary-General's High- Level Panel on Access to Medicines: Promoting innovation and access to heath technologies, *available at: http://www.unsgaccessmeds.org/new-page/.* 07 (Visited on October 02, 2016).

Antibiotics typically offer little pecuniary reward for years of often costly research. In these circumstances, experts warn that drug-resistant viruses, bacteria, parasites and fungi could cause 10 million deaths a year worldwide by 2050. The current model of medical innovation is ill-equipped to respond to the increasing emergence of infectious diseases, such as Ebola and Zika. Meanwhile, neglected tropical diseases (DTNs) continue to receive inadequate funding for R & D and access to health technologies, despite more than a billion people living with one or more NTD. The situation is driven by the relatively low purchasing power of people disproportionately affected by such conditions. Further, in the past decades, revolutionary treatments for cancer have been developed. But, these life-saving treatments, while under patent protection, can be financially unsustainable, particularly when the costs have to be borne by the patients themselves. Even in countries with public and/or private healthcare systems, patients are frequently saddled with unmanageable out-of pocket expenses. In the United States, prices of cancer medicines have almost doubled from a decade ago, averaging from US$ 5,000-10,000 per month. Of the 12 medicines approved by the United States Food and drug Administration (FDA) for various cancer indications in 2012, 11 were priced above US$ 100,000 per year. In rich and poor countries with public health system, government expenditures on health technologies is a significant proportion of overall government and health department expenditure, diverting resources away from other essential health services.

There are many reasons why people do not get the healthcare they need, including, inter alia, under-resourced health systems, a lack of sufficiently qualified and skilled healthcare workers, inequalities between and within countries, regulatory barriers, poor health education, unavailability of health insurance, exclusion, stigma, discrimination and exclusive marketing rights. The report also mentioned the impact of the high cost of the health technologies by citing the example of the Kingdom of the Netherlands that "Sofosbuvir is an important breakthrough in the treatment of patients with chronic hepatitis C. The problem is that a one-time treatment costs between 48,000 and 96,000 Euros. The Netherlands has an estimated 20,000 patients with this disease. The supplier defends this price in part by pointing to the great value to the patient and to those affected by the patient's illness. But such costs make healthcare unaffordable. If the Netherlands continues in this way, it will become nearly impossible to reimburse patients for these medications."[6] As a whole the report calls for human rights to place over intellectual property

6 *Ibid.*

laws and all countries must freely be able to use flexibilities granted under TRIPS to access affordable medicines. He also calls to delink drug prices from R&D costs and ensure greater transparency in drug pricing and public health.[7]

The impact this economic and political trend on global health is complex. In recent years there has been a rapid increase globally in technological and economical potential, implying a enhanced ability to overcome with the problems related to poverty and poor health. But there has also been an actual deterioration in health status in many developing countries, largely as result of HIV/AIDS and other infectious diseases. According to the recent report of *World Health Statistic,* 2016 monitoring health for Sustainable Development Goals published by the World Health Organization, it documented that in 2014, the global HIV incidence rate among adults aged 15-49 years was 0.5 per 1000 uninfected population, with 2 million people becoming infected that year. HIV incidence is highest in the WHO African Region (2.6 per 1000 uninfected population in 2014) compared to other WHO regions where incidence among adults aged 15-49 years ranges from 0.1 to 0.4 per 1000 uninfected population. Incidence rates are much higher in key populations. Forty percent of those living with HIV are receiving antiretroviral therapy, with 1.2 million dying from HIV-related causes in 2014. A little over half of the 37 million people living with HIV are aware that they are HIV positive. Sustainable Development Goals SDG Target 3.3 by 2030 also projected to end the epidemics of AIDS, tuberculosis, malaria and neglected tropical diseases and combat hepatitis, water-borne diseases and other communicable diseases. The Viral hepatitis infection kills an estimated 1.45 million people per year. Approximately 90% of deaths are due to chronic HBV and HCV infections that cause cirrhosis and hepatocellular carcinoma. The majority (85%) of viral hepatitis deaths occur in Asia, East Africa, North Africa and West Africa. Despite the high disease burden and available prevention and treatment interventions, hepatitis has not received the same attention as other diseases with a comparable burden of disease, such as HIV, TB or malaria.[8]

III. INTERNATIONAL LEGAL PERSPECTIVE

A. ***TRIPS Agreement:*** The Uruguay Round of Multilateral Trade Negotiations met at Marrakesh in 1994 signed the Final Act. It came into

---

[7] *The Hindu*, September. 16, 2016.

[8] World Health Statistic 2016, *available at: http://www.who.int/gho/publications/world_health_statistics/2016/en/* ((Visited on October 15, 2016).

[9] Christopher Arup, *The New World Trade Organization Agreements: Globalizing Law Through Services and Intellectual Property* 177 (Cambridge University Press, United Kingdom, 2000).

force by 1 January 1995.[9] The adoption of the WTO Agreement on Trade-Related Aspects of Intellectual Property Rights (TRIPS) ushered in a new and unprecedented era of global intellectual property norms and created a new standard to intellectual property protection and enforcement. It generally prescribes for the introduction of minimum standards in all areas of intellectual property rights protection in all WTO member states. Among all categories of IPR patent is most contentious it requires patentability of innovations in all fields of technological development whether it is processes or products.[10] Moreover, the introduction of medical patents in developing countries by this Agreement has significant impacts on human rights particularly right to health/access to medicines for their poor populations. It is quite pertinent to mentioned that TRIPS Agreement laid down a strict legal regime for intellectual property protection but at the same time it provides certain exceptions in TRIPS Agreement through the two general interpretative clauses of Articles 7 and 8 to take into account socio- economic goals. Article 7 is the only provision which evokes the balance between the rights granted to individual intellectual property rights holders and the broader interests of the society at large. Further, Article 8 applies more specifically to measures adopted by states to implement their TRIPS obligation. It provides that "States can adopt measures to protect public health and nutrition, as well as to promote the public interest in sectors of vital importance to socio- economic and technological development.[11]

Apart from that there are numbers of important exceptions are found in the patents section itself. First, some exceptions to the scope of patentability are allowed. Article 27.2 allows states to restrict the patentability of inventions, for instance, if they pose a threat to human life or health. Additionally, Article 30 permits states to limit the exclusive privilege granted through patent rights in the interest of third parties, such as people suffering from HIV/AIDS diseases and further supplemented by Article 31, which sets out a regulatory framework for compulsory licensing with number of conditions.[12] One of the strategies which have been debated in recent times is based on the implicit provision in the TRIPS Agreement on the issue of parallel imports or the principle of exhaustion of rights of the patent holder under Articles 6 as a means of reduced prices and increased access. However, negotiators included

---

[10] *Supra* note 2 at 56.

[11] Philippe Cullet, "Patents Bill, TRIPS & Right To Health" XXXVI *Economic & Political Weekly* 4049 (2001).

[12] T.G. Agitha, "Intellectual Property Regime and Developing Countries Health Concerns", 18(2) *JIPR* 186 (2013).

safeguards, or 'flexibilities,' within the *TRIPS Agreement* that could be used by signatories to tailor national intellectual property regimes so that countries could fulfill their human rights and public health obligations.[13]

B. ***Doha Declaration & Access to Medicines:*** The role of *TRIPS Agreement* and its implications on public health crises in developing countries was realized in its totality for the first time at the Inter-Ministerial Conference in Doha in 2001. Thereafter a declaration on access to medicines was adopted within the context of the *TRIPS Agreement.* The declaration recognizes that the existence of patent rights in health sector does not stop states from taking measures to protect the public health in particular sub-Saharan countries affected by HIV/AIDS and the medicines had become available to keep people alive. The *Doha Health Declaration* was a consequence of such a realization.[14]

Para 4 of the Doha Declaration not only confirmed the rights, but also the obligations of WTO members to interpret and implements the *TRIPS Agreement* in a manner supporting the protection of public health through access to needed drugs. In addition, it recommended the provision to export patented products to countries which lack technical strengths to utilize their compulsory licenses have been granted. A particularly interesting case would be the case of compulsory licenses for anti-HIV/AIDS drugs providing the life line to millions of patients who have no access to much needed drugs at affordable costs. While the *Doha Declaration* (Para6) of 2001, maintained that public health issues will supersede private interests protected through the patent system when it concerns life threatening diseases such as tuberculosis, malaria and HIV/AIDS; and compulsory licenses could be issued under Article 31 of TRIPS. The *Doha Declaration* reaffirmed the rights of WTO members to utilize flexibilities available under the *TRIPS Agreement* for the purpose of promoting the right to health and public health objectives. Despite these pronouncements, the sovereign right to issue compulsory licenses provided for by TRIPS has been stymied by threats of retaliation from governments and corporations against countries who have followed the prescribed process set out in TRIPS.[15]

---

13 *Supra* note 3 at 307.

14 *Supra* note 2 at 69.

15 *Supra* note 3 at 310.

IV. HUMAN RIGHTS PERSPECTIVE

The legal and normative framework of International human rights law is well established. The international human rights regime was started by the *Universal Declaration on Human Rights,*1948.[16] The place of private property rights in human rights treaties and in bill of rights has been controversial for a long times, and remain debates and discourses concerning the place of property in society. The Declaration does not explicitly recognize the intellectual property rights, it treats real property and intellectual property independently. But Article 27.2 states that "Everyone has the right to the protection of the moral and material interests resulting from any scientific, literary or artistic production of which he is the author." At the same time Article 27.1 states that everyone has "the right freely to participate in the cultural life of the community, to enjoy the arts and to share in scientific advancement and its benefits." The recognition of the interests of authors in the Declaration is complemented by the proclamation in Article 17.1 of a general right of property. This Article states that "[e]veryone has the right to own property" and 17.2 states that "[n]o one shall be arbitrarily deprived of his property". The implication of Article 17.2 is that states do have a right to regulate the property rights of individuals, but that must do so according to the rule of law.[17] Further the right to property was not included in the *International Covenant on Economic, Social and Cultural Rights (ICESCR) (1966)* while the rights recognized under Article 27 were substantially incorporated in Article 15(1) of the Covenant.[18]

From a contemporary point of view, the first general characteristic of Article 15(1) is that it recognizes a number of distinct rights that everyone's cultural rights, right to benefit from scientific and technological development and everyone's right to benefit from individual contributions they make. In other words, it provides a framework within which the development of science and culture is undertaken for the greater good of society while recognizing the need to provide specific incentives to authors for this to happen. Article 15 (1) is more specifically concerned with the balance between individual and collective rights of all individuals to take part in culture and enjoy the fruits of scientific development, as the rights of individuals and groups makings specific contributions to the development of science or culture. In this sense, Article 15 (1) focuses on society's interest in culture development of science while providing

[16] See the preamble of *Universal Declaration of Human Rights,* 1948.

[17] Peter Drahos, "Intellectual property and Human Rights" 1 PQ 358 (1999)

[18] *See*: *International Covenant on Economic, Social and Cultural Rights*, 1966.

recognition for the rights of specific individual or collective contributions to the development of a science, arts or culture.

The two provisions of Article 15 (1) that are of specific importance here are sub-sections (b) and (c). The right to enjoy the benefits of scientific progress and its applications needs to be understood in its national and international dimensions. At the national level, there is a duty for governments to ensure that has access to all technologies that contribute to the fulfillment of human rights. Given the highly skewed distribution of technology around the world, the realization of this right in most developing countries necessitates international assistance and co-operation. The realization of the right recognized at Article 15 (1) (b) therefore necessitates significant technology transfers in favor of developing countries. As far as Article 15 (1) (c) is concerned it is more narrowly drafted provision, which only talks on the interests of authors. Overall Article 15(1) left open a number of important questions. While intellectual property rights frameworks introduce rights for individual contributors, they only balance it with a general societal interest in benefitting from artistic or technological developments. Further intellectual property rights frameworks do not recognize everyone's right to enjoy the benefits of scientific progress and its applications as an individual or collective right. In fact Article 15(1) (c) is sometimes read as referring to existing intellectual property rights.[19]

Apart from these two Covenants along with the UDHR some other regional and national instruments such as European region, India, and South Africa, they recognize the right to property as a human rights. Over and above, there remains uncertainty relating to the place of intellectual contributions in human rights framework. An assertion to this effect the United Nations under his aegis, one of the bodies addressing the question of the impacts of intellectual property rights on the realization of human rights has been dealt by the *Sub-Commission* on the *Promotion and Protection of Human Rights*. The Sub-Commission strongly worded statement indicated in 2000 that:

> Since the implementation of the *TRIPS Agreement* does not adequately reflect the fundamental nature and indivisibility of the all human rights, including the right of everyone to enjoy the benefits of scientific progress and its applications, the right to health, the right to food, and the right to self-determination, there are apparent conflicts between the intellectual property rights regime embodied in the *TRIPS Agreement*, and international human rights law, on the other.

[19] Philippe Cullet, "Human Rights and Intellectual property protection in the TRIPS Era" 29 *Human Rights Quaterly* 404 (2007)

After that the Committee on Economic, Social and Cultural Rights in his report started to deliberate on the issue and to establish the links between economic, social and cultural rights and intellectual property rights in 2000. The *ESRC Committee* went further and adopted a specific statement on intellectual property rights and human rights in 2001, because the public controversy about access to drugs, medical patents and right to health in the context of the high price of HIV/ AIDS drugs in the sub-Saharan African countries which is most affected by the epidemics. In this Statement, the ESCR Committee has indicated in its authoritative interpretation of the right to health that states have an obligation to facilitate access to essential health facilities, goods and services when it required and strongly argued that intellectual property regimes should promote and protect all human rights.[20] The relationship between the intellectual property rights and human rights reaffirmed by the United Nations Human Rights Council in June 2016 adopted a resolution Access to medicines in the context of everyone to the enjoyment of the highest attainable standards of physical and mental health particularly with regard to high prices.

V. PATENTING & RIGHT TO HEALTH

Human health is one of the fundamental basic needs of all human beings. The importance of a healthy life has generally finds place in all domestic as well as in international levels. The international human rights conventions have included the component of human right to health. The *Universal Declaration on Human Rights,* 1948 is the pioneering law on the subject. It deals with the basic human right questions within the framework of health, food, housing and particularly the right to live with human decency and dignity. The importance of a healthy life finds a place in an article, which mandates that "everyone has the right to standard of living adequate for the health and well being of himself and of his family[21]......... including food, clothing, housing and medical care and necessary social services....... This global human rights further found a detailed pronouncements in the *International Covenant on Economic, Social and Cultural Rights, 1966* (ESCR) which recognizes the rights of every one to the "Enjoyment of the highest attainable standard of physical and mental health".[22] This Covenant requires member states to take steps to

[20] *Supra* note 2 at 387.

[21] Article 25 (1), *Universal Declaration of Human Rights,* 1948.

[22] Article12, *International Covenant on Economic, Social and Cultural Rights,* 1966 [hereafter ESCR Covenant], See generally, Bright C.A.Toebes, *The Right to Health as a Human Right in International Law* (1999).

the maximum of their available resources to realize the protected rights. It also exhibits that these measures should be taken by each state separately as well as through International assistance and cooperation.[23]

With the adoption of TRIPS Agreement and the introduction of pharmaceutical patents in developing countries to the development of Antiretroviral (ARV) drugs related to HIV/AIDS and other tropical diseases have become matters of great concern and posing continuous challenge. The medical patents which provides incentives to private sector pharmaceutical industry to do more research and development (R&D) in finding cures for diseases common in developing countries.[23] The pharmaceutical companies survive on the availability of patents because patents are indeed the lifeline of them. The patent protection has close relation between the incentives to private sector pharmaceutical industry and the higher prices of drugs. It is also significant to note in the context of the introduction of patents on drugs because patents have potential to improve access by providing incentives for the development of new drugs as well as restrict access because of the comparatively higher costs of patented drugs, low purchasing power or non-availability. Accessibility generally refers to the fact that health policies should foster the availability of drugs to all those who need them at affordable prices. There is a close link between the lack of access to drugs and poverty, especially in countries where a large proportion of people do not have access to medical insurance and pay for their own healthcare. The magnitude of the challenge is generally illustrated by the fact that one-third of the world's population does not have access to basic drugs. Under the existing regime which denies product patentability in the field of health, if compliance with TRIPS leads to reduced access to drugs, this might imply a substantive violation of the ESCR covenant.[24]

Around 1990, the overall pharmaceutical market in developing countries comprised less than 13 per cent of the world market. Of the total, South Africa's share was approximately 1 per cent. Since that time, the emerging pharmaceutical markets such as China, Russia, Brazil, Turkey, The Republic of Korea, Mexico and India have expanded considerably and will continue to do so in future by 13-16% in 2010. Today, the overall drug market of developing countries is estimated to be approximately 19 per cent of the world market.[25] The problem of

---

23 Nomani, Zafar Mahfooz, *Right to Health: A Socio-Legal Perspective*, 18 (Uppal Publication: New Delhi, 2004).

24 *Supra* note 1 at 261.

25 Pradeep Agrawal & P. Saibaba, "TRIPS and India Pharmaceutical Industry", 36 *Economic & Political Weekly* 3787 (2001).

purchasing power gaps in a country is usually resolved through policies taken by the government of that country, or international procurement systems through international and national organizations, but drug companies could also practice what is usually called differential pricing which could be efficient for the companies themselves. However, concerning the initial pricing of AIDS drugs, the originator companies apparently followed traditional global pricing policies for ARVs and paid little attention to patient access and affordability problems. The fact that ARV drug prices were affordable only for sufficiently insured patients in developed countries and the rich classes in developing countries was bound to open political debates and civil society groups. Markets where there were no patents on ARVs soon began to get supplies from less expensive Indian producers.

In many developing countries, high prices, together with underdeveloped state of health care system and lack of financial resources have made it difficult for most patients to get access even to old, unpatented drugs. Annual per capita public expenditures for pharmaceuticals are low in most of developing countries, and the high potential in this vast public sector market is yet to be realized. Further, the average percentage of expenditures on drugs, as a percentage of total health expenditure is relatively low and stable in developed countries 7-20 per cent in 2006. In developing countries, however, it is 24-66 per cent on average and still reasons remains unclear in this regard.[26] The originator companies in the early 1990s, by ignoring patient access and affordability problems, opened the political field to civil society groups and Indian generic producers, who soon found commercial markets in non-patented countries. The chairman and managing director of the Indian generic company Cipla, took the lead in providing inexpensive drugs to AIDS patients in African countries and established the credibility between the civil society groups and Indian drug producers.[27]

Apart from the contribution done by the pharmaceutical companies, the international organizations WHO, UNICEF, WFP, UNDP, NFPA, UNODC, ILO, UNESCO, UNHCR and the World Bank and governments of the developed countries as well were slow to respond to the urgent pharmaceutical needs arising from the HIV/AIDS pandemic.[28] In fact, access to drugs is governed by varieties of factors. There price of the

---

26 *Supra* note 1 at 273.

26 *Id* at 275

27 *Id* at 278.

28 *Id* at 279.

drugs is one of the main factors, often times depending on supply chain management including distribution. Most of the developing countries have very ineffective distribution system. Therefore, the patented drugs are nearly always more expensive with comparison to generic drugs is a relevant consideration. For a country like India which has to introduce product patents as a result of TRIPS commitments, it has been calculated that the annual welfare loss for the country as a whole would range from $ 162 million to $ 1.26 billion with an annual profit transfer to foreign from ranging between $ 10 and $ 839 million.[29] Further, between 2006 and 2010, six major Indian pharmaceutical companies have been taken over by multinational companies (MNCs). The trend of multinational companies taking over Indian pharmaceutical firms will undermine the efforts of Ministry of Health and Family Welfare Government of India at making the generic version of drugs available at affordable prices. Since 2001, when full FDI was allowed, only 10% of investment has gone to green -field ventures. But now Health Ministry wants to review in the wake of fears about the impact of takeovers on drug industry. Other factors that influence access include situations where there is only limited competition between generic producers, no sophisticated pharmaceutical industry in developing country. The impressive performance of the private pharmaceutical industry does not, however, ensure in and of itself better access to essential drugs to neediest people in the country.[30] In such scenario this is problematic where there is little public sector pharmaceutical manufacturing, no system to ensure the free availability of essential drugs to people below the poverty line and a decreasing number of drugs whose price is controlled. From the perspective of access to medicines, the challenges is to find ways to make sure that existing drugs are available at little or no cost to people who need them. On the whole, the medical patents do not necessarily conflict with the realization of human right to health.

VI. ACCESS TO MEDICINES IN INDIA

The post GATTised legal order under the aegis of the TRIPS Agreement to introduce a relatively high standards of protection of intellectual property rights protection forcing most of the developing countries to face the full consequences of intellectual property rights regimes which they had previously partly been able to avoid as a result of the principle of territoriality which ensured that high standards of patentability in developed countries were not automatically extended to developing countries. This has impacts not only for economic

[29] Supra note 2 at 386.

[30] Aarti Dhar, "FDI in Pharmaceutical Sector" *The Hindu*, September 4, 2011.

development in developing countries but also on basic human rights such as right to health of the poor people.[31] The links between intellectual property rights and the realization of human rights in developing countries exist with regard to a member of human rights. They are easily visible in the case of the rights to health and to food. With regard to the access to medicines as part of human rights to health, the link has become apparent in the relationship between medical patents and the realization of the right to health, particularly in the context of the HIV/AIDS epidemics. This is due to the fact that a member of drugs used to alleviate HIV/AIDS is protected by patents. There is a direct link between patents, the price of drugs, and access to drugs.[32]

Patents for pharmaceutical substances have been a subject matter of special interest in India. Modern pharmaceutical industry, which is popularly identified with the allopathic from of medicine, blossomed and flourished as a result the therapeutic revolution of the twentieth century. With the increase in the production and development of new drugs, the pharmaceutical industry became an industry based on R&D. Eventually dominance in the pharmaceutical industry came to be a direct consequence of the R&D efforts put in by the pharmaceutical companies. As the cost of research and development of new drugs involved exceptional professional expertise and burgeoning R&D expenditure, not all pharmaceutical companies could participate in the development and promotion of new drugs.[33]

India took advantage of the transitional period until 2005 offered under the TRIPS agreement before it had to introduce product protection on pharmaceuticals (and chemicals). Such legislation was introduced as from 1 January 2005, a fact known for more than a decade, following India's signature of the TRIPS agreement in 1994. The post-1970 patent regime and the transitional period without product patent protection permitted India to develop a thriving pharmaceutical industry, supplying pharmaceutical products domestically and globally (including low-cost active pharmaceutical ingredients). This development created conditions for some of the companies in the industry to initiate investment in R&D.

[31] Nomani, Zafar Mahfooz., WTO, TRIPS Agreement and Protection of plant Variety: Imperative and Implication for Indian Intellectual Property Rights Regime in A.K. Kaul (Ed.) *et al., The Law of Intellectual Property Rights: In Prospect and Retrospect* 116 (2001).

[32] Philippe Cullet, "*Patents and Medicines: The Relationship between TRIPS & Human Right To Health*" 79: 1139 (2003).

[33] Feroz Ali khader, *The Law of Patents with A Special Focus on Pharmaceuticals In India* 17 (Lexis Nexis Butterworths , New Delhi, 2009).

The central question concerns the impact this transitional period had on R&D and innovation in the industrial sector. The evidence suggests that industry R&D increased very modestly from 1990 to 2000, rising from just over 1% of sales to about 2% with total investment of US$ 73.6 million in 2000. Since 2000, there has been a very rapid increase in pharmaceutical R&D by 2003/2004. The combined investment of 12 of the leading companies was estimated to be US$ 230 million annually, representing nearly 8% of turnover.

Much of the impetus for this growth derives from the markets in the developed world, not the impending introduction of patent protection in India. For instance, Ranbaxy, one of India's leading companies, aims to increase the share of its revenues from the developed world from 20% in 2000 (when worldwide sales were US $ 475 million) to 70% in 2007 (when sales are projected at US $ 2 billion). Other companies have similar growth objectives, focusing on building on their strengths by launching generic versions of big-selling drugs in the United States and other developed country markets, including challenging patents where necessary. In 2003, India was granted 72 pharmaceutical patents in the United States. Although this is a small proportion of the total, it makes India the eleventh largest foreign source of United States patents in that category.[34]

VII. INDIAN PATENT LAWS

After independence, the government constituted special committees to study and suggest changes in the Patent Law to suit the needs of this country. The report submitted by Justice N Rajagopala Ayyanagar, which set the tone for the Patents Act 1970. The critical decision of not providing product patents for pharmaceuticals was suggested by the Committee which found its way into the Act.[35] The Indian Patents Act, 1970 which came into force in 1972 having several discriminatory clauses. Between 1972 and 2005, India had one of the most progressive patent laws in the world. The Act introduced a number of significant exceptions such as the patentability of life form and the patentability of methods of agriculture or horticulture, to reject the possibility of granting patents in respect of substances intended for use as food, medicine or drugs. The Act introduced a distinction between product and process patents in the fields of nutrition and health. The product patents were excluded, process patents were allowed in the Act. The Act also discriminated between

34 World health Organisation, Report: *The Commission on Intellectual Property Rights Innovation and Public Health* (2006).

35 *Supra* note 33 at 13.

different types of inventions with regard to the right conferred. The normal duration under the Act of patent rights was 14 years it was of a reduced for period of 7 years in case of processes of manufacture for substances intended for use as food, medicine or drug. The Act also included a series of measures restricting the rights of patent holders, in particular to encourage use of the invention in India. It provides the compulsory licensing regime to encourage inventions and to secure that the inventions are worked in India a commercial scale. But this license could be granted upon application if after three years it was shown that the reasonable requirements of the public that the patented invention was not available to the public at a reasonable price. Such a highly diluted patent system in India enabled better access to medicines at more affordable prices. In the absence of provisions for grant of product patents, Indian companies were free to manufacture and market product patent. Due to this India became a major supplier of active pharmaceutical intermediates (APIs) to both the developed and the developing countries. Moreover, it is pertinent to mention that the Indian *Patents Act,* 1970 provides the compulsory licences for all patents but during the 35 years of its operation no effective compulsory licences were granted by the Indian Patent Office.[36]

The above situation was changed with the adoption of *TRIPS Agreement* mandate, the Act has to undergo fundamental change of patent policy which amounts in part to a return to the pre-1970 regime. This is significant because the changes imposed by TRIPS were not the object of full policy debates at the national level. Therefore, the *Patents (Second Amendment) Bill* of 1999 generally seeks to modify the Act to allow compliance with TRIPS Agreement.[37] However, the *Patents (Amendment) Act,* 1999 introduced two main changes in the Act. Further, it was amended by passing of the *Patents (Amendment) Act,* 2002 has removed most of the elements that gave the *Patents Act,* 1970 its specificity. The most important impact of these changes is to have clearly shifted the balance between the interests of patent holders and society's interest towards the former. Some of the changes include the increase of the term of protection to a uniform 20 years thereby increasing significantly the average duration of protection and removing the discrimination put in place in the case of process patents in the fields of health and nutrition where the term was of only 7 years. At the level of the sections governing the working of patents, the amendments have removed altogether licences of right from the Act.[38] The 2002 amendments will be followed by a last

---

[36] Supra note 3 at 308.

[37] Supra note 33 at 14.

[38] *Ibid.* at 15.

set of amendments. The *Patents (Amendment) Act,* 2005, which are required to put India in compliance with its obligation to introduce product patents in drugs and food sectors as of 1 January 2005. A 10 year period was granted to developing countries like India to align their patent laws with TRIPS Agreement. This Amendment Act, 2005 omitted Ch IV A of the principal Act dealing with EMR and provided for certain transitional provisions. It also introduced certain provisions to protect the interest of the generic manufacturers who have been manufacturing certain drugs patented elsewhere.[39]

VIII. HEALTH & PUBLIC POLICY

For the first time the Government of India formulated the National *Intellectual Property Right (IPR)* Policy, 2016 by the Department of Industrial Policy and Promotion.[40] It provides the roadmap for the future of IPRs in India. The policy reinforces the strengths of IPRs to acquire both economic and social benefits on a bigger and higher scale for India. A vibrant Intellectual Property (IP) ecosystem with not only enhance the economic development of India, but also promote public welfare by protecting the rights of all its citizens. The rationale for the National Intellectual Property Right (IPR) Policy, 2016 lies in the need to create awareness about the importance of IPRs as a marketable financial asset and economic tool. The mission statement of the policy is to stimulate a dynamic, vibrant and balanced intellectual property rights system in India to:

- Foster creativity and innovation and thereby, promote entrepreneurship and enhance socioeconomic and cultural development, and
- Focus on enhancing access to healthcare, food security and environmental protection, among other sectors of vital social, economic and technological importance.

The Policy lays down seven objectives. One of the objectives to have strong and effective IPR laws, which balances the interests of rights owners with larger public interest. India has a long history of IP laws which have evolved taking into consideration national needs and international commitments. The existing laws were either enacted or revised after the *TRIPS Agreement* and are fully compliant with it. These

---

39 *Ibid.* at 16.

40 National Intellectual Property Right (IPR) Policy, 2016 *available at*: http://dipp.nic.in/English/Schemes/Intellectual Property Rights/National IPR Policy 08.08.2016.pdf (Visited on October 23, 2016).

laws along with various judicial decisions provide a stable and effective legal framework for protection and promotion of IPRs. India will continue to utilize the legislative space and flexibilities available in international treaties and the *TRIPS Agreement,* even as it continues to engage constructively in the negotiation of such international treaties and agreements. India shall remain committed to the Doha Declaration on Public Health.[41]

In the area of patent law and its impact on human right to health includes access to medicines/drugs is debatable issue before courts in India.[42] The Indian Parliament by amending the Indian *Patents Act,* 1970 to conform to the obligation set by the WTO agreement passed the *Patents (Amendment) Act,* 2005. The Indian law faces a challenge from the Swiss drug maker Novartis from 2006 the patent application for Glivec was rejected by the Indian Patent Office. It appealed to Intellectual Property Appellate Board (IPAB) in June 2009; the APAB upheld the decision of the Patent Office. Simultaneously, NOVARTIS filed two writ petitions in the Madras High Court, one challenging the decision of the patent office and the other challenging Section 3(d) of the Patent Act. The Madras High court rejected both these appeals. It pointed out that domestic courts could not be asked to give an opinion regarding international treaties and obligations and that Novartis should take its complaint to the disputes settlement mechanism in the WTO.[43] Thereafter Novartis went to Supreme Court through special leave petition in 2012. The Supreme Court merged three petitions in one popularly known as *Novartis AG Vs Union of India*[44] and observed that:

> The Court was urged to strike a balance between the need to promote research and development in science and technology and to keep private monopoly (called an 'aberration' under our Constitutional scheme) at the minimum. Arguments were made about India's obligation to faithfully comply with its commitments under international treaties and counter arguments were made to protect India's status as "the pharmacy of the world".

---

[41] Objective 3, *National Intellectual Property Right (IPR) Policy,* (2016).

[42] Anand Grover, "Analyzing the Supreme Court Judgment", XLVIII (32) *Economic & Political Weekly* 46 (2013).

[43] Amit Sengupta, "Patent to Plunder", *Frontline* May 4, 2012. *See also*: Carlos M Correa, "Is Section 3 (d) Consistent with TRIPS? XLVIII (32) *Economic & Political Weekly,* 49 (2013)

[44] (2013) 6 SCC 1.

The Court was reminded of its duty to uphold the rights granted by the statute, and the Court was also reminded that an error of judgment by it will put life-saving drugs beyond the reach of the multitude of ailing humanity not only in this country but in many developing and under-developed countries, dependent on generic drugs from India. The Indian Judiciary played a very pivotal role in enforcing the fundamental right to life and has been very much expanded to encapsulate the different unarticulated rights. The broad sweep of right to health as a part right to life and personal liberty is one of them.[45]

IX. CONCLUSION AND SUGGESTIONS

The intellectual property Protection framework generally concerned with the rights of inventors and creators and never addressed the possible impacts of the introduction of intellectual property rights standards laid down by the *TRIPS Agreement* on the realization of human rights and wider societal interests. In fact the adoption of *TRIPS Agreement* and its implementation in developing countries like India facing number of problems in the context of pharmaceutical patents, and genetic engineering in agriculture, they are hitting hard and limiting access to drugs and access to food of poor people particularly the disadvantaged and marginalized communities. This is something which would be inconsistent with norms in the *UDHR* and *ICESCR*. In such a situation a legitimate sense of urgency required to establish coherence between intellectual property rights and human rights in order to reduce the impact and improve access to affordable drugs to the poor people living in developing countries like India for realizing agenda of sustainable development goals. In that direction the following suggestions are quite important and imperative. The priority should be given to human rights over the intellectual property rights. In order to make full use the TRIPS flexibilities as approved by *Doha Declaration*, and *TRIPS- plus Provisions*, Public funded research must prioritize public health objectives. There is need to create public awareness about the economic, social and cultural benefits of IPR as visualized in recent India's *IPR Policy*, 2016.

45 Nomani, Zafar Mahfooz., *Right To Health: A Socio- Legal Perspective*,56 (Uppal Publication: New Delhi, 2004).

9

Patenting Jurisprudence in Biotechnology Law: A Comparative Perspective

Faizanur Rahman

I. INTRODUCTION

In a global, knowledge-based economy, Intellectual Property Rights (IPRs) are a key to the international competitiveness of both nations and firms. International competition in the traded goods increasingly contains a high degree of innovation. IPRs have thus; become a trade issue and a major component of the World Trade Organisation (WTO). Adequate IP protection at an international scale has become essential for appropriating global revenue streams to support investments in developing state of-the- art technology. Although the concept of intellectual property is very old, there appeared the need to harmonize laws to facilitate international trade and free flow of technology. This became very necessary because it was difficult to obtain sufficient protection in the other countries of the world, in view of the disparity in the laws in each country. As per World Intellectual Property Organisation (WIPO) definition, intellectual property refers to creations of the mind, inventions, literary and artistic works, symbols, names, images and designs used in commerce. Broadly, intellectual property is divided into two categories. The first category covers industrial property, which includes patents, industrial designs and trademarks, all of which have industrial applications. The other refers to copyright laws, which are applied to such things as literary, dramatic and artistic works; rights relating to performing artists, the production phonograms and rights of broadcasters in their radio and television programs.[1] Patented inventions have, in fact, pervaded every aspect of human life, from electric lighting and plastic, to ballpoint pens and microprocessors. During a time when the future of many industries seems uncertain, one industry in particular appears to be positioned for

---

1 Wadehra, B.L., *Law Relating To Intellectual Property* 3 (Universal Law Publishing, New Delhi, 2009).

expansion and enduring success. This is the biotechnology industry, which according to some analysts will be a major driving force behind the new economy of the 21st century.[2] This seemingly lofty prediction is based in large part on the immense promise offered by biotechnology. The innovations developed with biotechnological techniques promise to prolong and improve our lives and the world we live in by achieving advancements in health care, agriculture, food products and production, industrial processes and environmental preservation. Biotechnology is not a new science and it has existed in some form or the other for centuries. Biotechnology in one form or another has been part of human development since the dawn of agriculture. Human ingenuity has led to increased production and greater diversity and quality of livestock and varieties of crops. Today's food crops and domestic animals embody the benefits of many generations of selection and breeding. However, the advent of genetics has opened exciting opportunities in this sector, because of its numerous applications, which range from improvement of human health and food production to reduction of environmental damage. These opportunities are also coupled with controversies that not only challenge the laws within which society functions, but also our ethical and religious beliefs.

The biotechnology revolution is gaining momentum all around the world. The biotechnology sector, unlike the information technology sector is highly regulated. Intellectual property is the most valuable asset of a biotechnology company and the most important intellectual property rights relating to biotechnology companies tend to be patents. India has tremendous potential in the biotechnology sector, but one of the significant hurdles facing the industry is the current legal and regulatory framework. This includes the lengthy approval process for drugs and genetically modified organisms, import duties on raw materials for the sector, lack of protection for product patents, weak patent enforcement and the need for well trained patent examiners.[3] In order to ensure growth, cross licensing between biotechnology companies will be essential and companies will have to develop inter-dependencies. Biotech parks present a great opportunity for companies and academic institutions to collaborate for the growth of this sector. The current focus of companies is on strategies, because any future alliance they enter into will have to be in sync with their long-term strategies. Biotechnology companies have to focus on developing effective patent strategies along with business

---

2 Suresh, N., 'Today's Biotech Industry in India', 4 *Biotechnology Journal* 291-294 (2009).

3 Bhargava, P M., 'Biotechnology in India: The Beginnings', 4 *Biotechnology Journal* 313-318 (2009).

models and with the required funding for innovative research and development and strengthening of government initiatives in framing effective policies and regulations, India is poised to emerge as a force to reckon with in the global biotechnology sector.[4] This paper critically examines the Biotechnology Patent Law in United States of America, European Union and India. It guides the foray into biotechnology patenting debates by offering a brief overview of the historical and general background.

II. MEANING OF BIOTECHNOLOGY

Biotechnology is not a new science. It is based on very old traditions used since the beginning of the civilized world to improve products of the land such as agricultural products and animal farming. The origin of biotechnology can be traced back to prehistoric times, when microorganisms were already used for processes like fermentation. Beer brewing, cheese making and production of sour milk are some of the common examples which are often included in describing what is called biotechnology.[5] The term 'biotechnology' generally refers to the use of biological processes, as through the exploitation and manipulation of living organisms or biological systems, in the development or manufacture of a product or in the technological solution to a problem. As such, biotechnology is a general category that has applications in pharmacology, medicine, agriculture, and many other fields. In relation to genetic engineering, the techniques have been used to manipulate the deoxyribonucleic acid (DNA) of bacteria and other organisms to manufacture biological products such as drugs. Plants and foods with desired qualities such as prolonged shelf life or increased resistance to diseases and pests have been created through genetic engineering; that is, by inserting DNA from other organisms.[6]

In the context of the modern biotechnological revolution, plant genetic resources have become a significant source for plant breeding, crop development and enhancement. Undoubtedly, like most technology, biotechnology can be used for good or ill, but in the field of agriculture,

---

4 Drahos Peter, 'Biotechnology Patents, Market and Morality', 21(9) *European Intellectual Property Review* 441-449 (1999).

5 Chaturvedi, Sachin, 'Dynamics of Biotechnology Research and Industry in India: Statistics, perspectives and Key Policy Issues', STI Working Papers 2005/06, Directorate for Science, Technology and Industry, OECD (2006).

6 Verma, S.K., Fitting Plant Variety Protection and Biotechnological Inventions in Agriculture within the Intellectual Property Framework: Challenges for Developing Countries, *available at*: http://www.iprsonline.org/unctadictsd/dialogue/docs/Verma_2004-11-08.pdf (Last accessed on April 12, 2015).

it has the prospect of giving enormous benefits in the quality and yield of foods and the range over which they can be grown. The advent of genetic engineering has permitted the expeditious introduction of a wide range of desirable traits into plants. These include: pest control traits such as insect and virus resistance as well as herbicide tolerance; post-harvest traits such as delayed ripening of spoilage prone fruits; male and/or seed sterility for hybrid systems; and output traits such as plant colour and vitamin enrichment.[7]

Despite the fact that some people have been opposing and viewing biotechnology with caution, the remaining section of the public is attracted to the benefits of biotechnology for food, for example as evidenced by the demand for Falvr-savr tomatoes, that is a new variety of tomatoes which remain ripe far longer than normal tomatoes before they rot after their introduction in the United States. Biotechnology has taken the development of new plants and seeds into the fast lane. The world is experiencing a 'breakthrough in agricultural technology that may soon enable us to harvest crops from deserts, farm tomatoes in seawater, grow super potatoes in many new localities, and enjoy entirely new crops such as tomato. We can now isolate and manipulate the genes that constitute the hereditary materials of each species' genetic makeup.' These recent developments in biotechnology have increased the need to protect inventions and regulate commercial exploitation.[8]

A. ***Classification of Biotechnology Inventions:*** The biotechnological inventions are broadly classified into two categories, namely, biotechnological process and biotechnology product. The former includes inventions related to genetically engineered micro-organisms, plants or animals; process of isolating and incorporating genes; process of fermentation of beverages; process to clean up pollutants in the environment. The latter category includes genetically engineered microorganisms, plants or animals; isolated and purified cells, genes, DNA; proteins identified in the body of living beings and commercially produced outside the body; genetically engineered food such as *BT cotton, BT rice, BT tomato, BT potato, BT soyabean*, etc., and beverages.

B. ***Applications of Biotechnology:*** Today biotechnology is being used in different fields for better results.[9] The applications of biotechnology

---

[7] Sharma M, *et al.*, 'Agricultural Biotechnology Research in India: Status and Policies', 84(3) *Current Science* 297-302 (2003).

[8] Shiva, Vandana., *Patents, Myths and Reality* 14 (Penguin India, New Delhi, 2001).

[9] Dr. Talwar Sabanna, *'Information Technology and Biotechnology, Globalization and WTO'*, (Serials Publications, New Delhi, 2006).

are increasingly diverse. Biotechnology functions like a fruit on a tree having roots of biological sciences, microbiology, genetics, molecular biology and biochemistry and trunk of chemical engineering. So, it is indeed difficult to define the precise scope and extent of the applications of biotechnology. The introduction of biotechnology to produce new products or molecules poses various challenges, which may be technical or ethical. However, biotechnology has numerous applications, with the potential to affect every facet of our lives in positive ways. Some of the various applications of biotechnology are as follows:

a) Genetic Engineering
b) Gene Cloning
c) Gene Transfer Mechanism
d) Plant Cell & Tissue Culture
e) Animal Cell Culture
f) Agriculture
g) Industrial
h) Health Care
i) Environmental etc.

Biotechnology has been promoted as being necessary and essential for human survival and as a technology that will improve the quality of life in every country. Biotechnology presents itself as a blessing, with the potential to improve the quality of life of every person in the world and allow sustainable living. It may not be untrue if it is said that there is no field where biotechnology has got no application.[10]

III. GENESIS OF BIOTECHNOLOGY

In 1919, Karl Erkay, a Hungarian Engineer, coined the term bio-technology.[11] At that time the term biotechnology encompassed the production of desired goods from raw materials with the aid of living organisms.[12] Historically, biotechnology was an art, involved in the production of wine, beer and cheeses. In recent years innovations involving genetic engineering have had a major impact on biotechnology.

---

[10] John E. Smith, *Biotechnology*, (Cambridge University Press', London, 2006).

[11] Brain Robert Shmaefsky, *Biotechnology 101*, 1 (Pentagon Press, New Delhi, 2008).

[12] Rockman, Howard B., *Intellectual Property Law for Engineers and Scientists*, 259 (Wiley-interscience, New Jersey, 2004).

Modern biotechnology can be traced back to the eighteenth century when smallpox was cultured invoke an immune response and prevent development of more serious diseases later in life. During the eighteenth century cross-fertilization was discovered and crop rotation was practice to increase yield. The process of sterilization was also discovered during the eighteenth century. In the nineteenth century, Louis Pasteur, known as the father of biotechnology, demonstrated fermentative ability of micro-organisms.[13]The development of biotechnology can be studied when classified into three generations. They are as follow:

a) **First Generation:** This generation involves the practices which involved minimum or no technology efforts. These techniques date back to the Stone Age and involve using of biological organisms such as bacteria, yeasts, enzymes and traditional methods of fermentation to produce food and drink such as bread and wine. The benchmark achievement of this generation was the production of cheese and beer with use of micro-organisms.[14]

b) **Second Generation:** The beginning of this generation is marked by interwar period during which there were developments in fermentation technology involving the application of pure cell culture and sterile manufacture, which yielded new products. During this generation innovations such as acetone, butanol, glycerol, vitamin B_2, citric acid and lactic acid took place. This generation is earmarked with the invention of penicillin in 1928.

c) **Third Generation:** This generation, also known as modern biotechnology, is represented by three technologies namely, tissue cell culture, Hybridoma technology and recombinant DNA technology, also known as genetic engineering, developed in third generation.[15] The invention of DNA by Crick and Watson in 1953 was the milestone of this generation.[16]

IV. BIOTECHNOLOGY & PATENT LAW

The field of biotechnology has emerged in the recent past. Undoubtedly, it is one of the fields of science and technology which was unimagined and unexpected. Everyday new developments in this field

---

[13] Varaprasad Reddy, K.I., 'Biotech Regulation in India: Problems and Promises', 4 *Biotechnology Journal* 306 (2009).

[14] Bennett *et al.*, 'The Economics of Agricultural Biotechnology-An Overview', 10 *Int. J. Bio. Tech.* 109-112 (2008).

[15] Thomas L. Lemke, et.al., *Foye's Principle of Medicinal Chemistry*, 2(Lippincott Williams and Wilkins, China, 2013).

[16] Rodney Carlisle, *Inventions and Discoveries*, 422 (John Wiley and Sons, New Jersey, 2004).

are coming up.[17] Biotechnology has in one form or the other flourished since prehistoric times. When the first human beings realized that they could plant their own crops and breed their own animals, they learned to use biotechnology. One of the first forms of biotechnology applications was the use of yeast to liven bread, in 1873 when the French scientist Louis Pasteur received a US patent for a method of purifying yeast for use in making beer, for the yeast derived by that method, and for the apparatus used to purify the yeast, on the basis of the significant improvement to beer making technology that was disclosed in the patent document.[18] Since then, biotechnology has been applied in numerous instances, right from cheese, wine, beer, yogurt, medicines and genetic applications.

After thousands of years of melting, forging or burning inanimate matter to create things, we are now able to reinvent the natural world at the most fundamental level, the genetic one. Genetics and biotechnology offer a door to a new era in the history of mankind. The first genetically engineered products were medicines designed to combat human diseases. Insulin, used to treat diabetics, and blood clot-reducing enzyme for heart attack victims are now produced easily and cheaply as a result of biotechnology. In agriculture, first generation biotechnology products have traits that result in reduced pesticide use or higher yields due to reduced pest losses.[19]

Throughout human history, mankind has learned a great deal about the different organisms that our ancestors used so effectively. The marked increase in our understanding of these organisms and their cell products brought about the ability to control the many functions of various cells and organisms. In the mid-eighties and early-nineties it became possible to transform (genetically modify) plants and animals that are important for food production. 'Transgenic' Animals and plants, including cows, sheep, tomatoes, tobacco, potato and cotton have now been obtained.[20] Genes introduced may make the organism more resistant to disease, may influence the rate of fruit ripening, or may increase productivity.

---

[17] Sreenivasulu, N. S & Raju C. B., *Biotechnology and Patent Law*, 3(Manupatra Information Solutions Pvt. Ltd., Noida, 2008).

[18] Gervais, Daniel., *The TRIPS Agreement: Drafting History and Analysis* (Sweet & Maxwell, London, 2003).

[19] Ghosh, P K., 'Evolution of the Transgenic Organisms', 39 *RIS Biotechnology and Development Review* 57 (2000).

[20] Available at: http://photoscience.la.asu.edu/photosyn/courses/BIO_343/lecture/biotech.html http://dbtindia.nic.in/uniquepage.asp?id_pk=102 (Last accessed on April 12, 2015).

India has been involved in conventional biotechnology for several decades but modern biotechnology is currently in its nascent stage. Products manufactured by the use of genetic engineering, immunological techniques, cell culture methods are increasingly being used during the last five years and local research in these areas has intensified. There is little doubt that the applications of modern biotechnology will increase rapidly as the products or process hold great potential for providing much better solutions to improve the health of people or the quality of life, improve agricultural productivity significantly along with supplying more nutritious food, produce industrial bio-products at much cheaper prices and improve the quality of environment on a sustainable basis.[21]

V. COMPARATIVE LEGAL PERSPECTIVE

The credit for the birth of biotechnology goes to the Constitution of America, which strongly support the progress of science and technology. Also, it was the liberal approach of the US Courts which aided in the evolution of biotechnology patent law; and was backed by the support of US Patent Office which granted patents on biotechnological invention. Though the European Union was ahead of the US, yet it was the US Courts which gave green signal to patenting of biotechnological invention through the landmark judgment in *Chakraborty*. The European Union took no time in adopting the liberal approach of US Courts. Following the footsteps of US and European Union, many countries amended their respective laws and granted protection to biotechnological inventions. [22]

A. ***United States of America:*** In the United States (US), Thomas Jefferson drafted the first patent statue which was enacted in the year 1793. The conditions to be fulfilled for grant of patent were same as mentioned under the Venetian statute, namely, utility, novelty and non-obviousness. In all these statutes, living organisms were kept out of the purview of patentability on the ground of them being considered as 'common heritage' of human mankind and not patentable.[23]

---

21 Seuba, Xavier, and Correa, Carlos., *Biotechnology in India: Its Policy and Normative Framework*, December 2010, Available at: http://www.clustercollaboration.eu/documents/2736637/2789253/Biotechnology+in+India_+Its+Policy+and+Normative+ Framework.pdf/b07e1ec3-ce33-4efe-966e-8f64619cc731?version=1.0 (Last accessed on April 12, 2015).

22 Bhargava, P.M., 'Biotechnology in India: The Beginnings', 4 *Biotechnology Journal*, 313-318 (2009).

23 K.R.G. Nair, Ashok Kumar, *Intellectual Property Rights*, 189 (Allied Publishers, New Delhi).

The US Constitution states:[24] 'the Congress shall have the power to promote the progress of science and useful arts, by securing for limited time to authors and inventors the exclusive right to their respective writings and discoveries'. The US Patent Law does not expressly lay down any provision for the patent protection of biotechnology inventions. It merely lays down that whoever invents or discovers any new and useful process, machine manufacture or composition of matter or any new and useful improvement thereof, may obtain a patent therefor, subject to the conditions and requirements under the patent law.[25] For the first time the United States Patent Office granted a patent to Louis Pasteur on 'yeast' that is free from organic germs of disease.[26] Subsequently, in Exparte Latimer[27] a patent was claimed for fibre found in the needle of the Pinus astralis, which was rejected on the ground that even the artificially bred plants are the product of nature and hence not patentable. In the case of American Fruit Growers Inc. v. Brogdex Co.,[28] the manufacture was interpreted. The Court rejected the patent claim on coated oranges on the ground of being not sufficiently modified as no new quality or property was attributed to those coated oranges.

It was in the year 1970s when the US Patent Law regime started marching towards the grant of patent on living matter, laying down the foundation stone for biotechnology patent law. In *Diamond* v. *Chakraburty*[29], the patent claim was for a genetically modified micro-organism capable of eating crude oil spills. The inventor claimed the patent production for both, i.e., process of producing bacteria and the bacteria. It was for the first time in history that the issue popped up on the patentability of living organisms. The patent office allowed the patent for the production of bacteria, but patent on bacteria was rejected. In an appeal, the Board of Appeal reaffirmed the decision of patent office. But the Supreme Court by a majority of 5:4 overruled the above decision and laid down that patent statute is broad enough to cover the living organisms. Therefore, it can be concluded that the judiciary played a very significant role by adopting liberal approach; as compared to the legislature. The development in this field was never expected or imagined by the legislature and hence there was no provision on the same aspect.

---

24 Donald S. Chisum, *et al.*, Principles of Patent Law: Cases and Materials, University Casebook Series, 773 (Foundation Press, New York, 1998).

25 The Title 35 of the United States Code, s.101.

26 US Patent No: 141,072 granted in the year 1873.

27 December 1889, Com.pat.123.

28 283 US 1.11.51 S.ct, 328, 330, 75 L.Ed.801 (1931).

29 (1980) US SCC 447 at 303.

B. ***European Union:*** The history of the European patent legislation is marked by three significant milestones which contributed largely to the development of substantive law on patents. The Paris Convention for the protection of industrial property which was adopted in 1883 was the first milestone in the history of European law. It lays down the basic tenants of patent law in Europe.[30] Under the Paris Convention, broad meaning is given to the term 'industrial property' as it encompass agricultural and extractive industries and to all manufactured or natural products, for example, wines, grain, tobacco leaf, fruit, cattle, minerals, mineral water, beer, flowers and flour.[31] The second milestone in the history of European patent legislation is the Strasbourg Convention, which was adopted with an aim to establish a common market in Europe.[32] The convention synchronizes the substantive patent law in terms such as novelty and inventive step. The *European Patent Convention (EPC)*, 1973, was the third milestone in the history of European Patent law. The EPC provides a uniform law on biotechnology inventions[33] for all the European countries.

According to the Convention, patent will be granted to an invention only if it is new, involves and inventive step and capable of industrial application.[34] It does not grant patent protection to living beings produced through essentially biological process, but it does not prohibit living beings produced out of non-biological processes.[35] The EPC stipulates the inventions that are patentable and also the inventions which are not patentable. Article 53(b) of the Convention lays down that plant or animal varieties and essentially biological processes for the production of plants and animals are not patentable. But, this provision is not applicable to

---

[30] Lislei G. Restaino *et al.*, Patenting DNA-related inventions in the European Union, United States and Japan : A trilateral approach or a study in contrast? UCLA Journal of Law and Technology (2003).

[31] Article 1(3) of the Paris Convention on Industrial Property Rights, 1883.

[32] The Strasbourg Convention on the Unification of Certain Points of Substantive Law on Patents for Invention, 1963.

[33] Chapter VI, Rule 23B (2) of the European Patent Convention, 1973 read as follows: Biotechnology invention is defined as any invention which concern a product consisting of or containing biological material or process by means of which biological material is produced, processed or used.

[34] Article 52(1) of the European Patent Convention, 1973.

[35] Article 53 of the European Patent Convention, 1973.

microbiological process[36] or products thereof.[37] The Convention prohibits the patenting of inventions which are against public order and morality.[38] On construing the provisions of the Convention, it can be concluded that plant and animal varieties produced through essentially non-biological processes are patentable.

The European Patent Office (EPO) was in favour of grant of patent to genetically modified plants, so as to stimulate research in the industry on transgenic plants. In Ciba Geigy[39], the patent was claimed on the invention which involved the propagating material for cultivated plant, in particular, seeds of cultivated plant were treated with chemical agent, oxime derivative, in order to make it resistant to agricultural chemicals. The Technical Board of Appeal granted patent and opined that the propagating material was claimed was not the result of an essentially biological process, but was a non-natural process of treating cultivated plant with a chemical substance. The Board interpreted Article 53(b) and opined that non-natural plants do not come within the purview of exceptions and hence are patentable. Similarly, in Plants Genetic Systems[40], the patent was claimed on genetically modified plant cells and seeds, which were made herbicide resistant. The European Technical Board of Appeals discussed in detail the concept of 'public order and morality'. It held that any invention which results into breach of public peace or social order threatening the public security or is prejudicial to the environment cannot be granted patent. It was inferred from this judgment that plants produced as a result of genetic engineering were not patentable since the starting point of every such invention would be a plant variety.[41]

After this judgment, the European Union adopted a directive on biotechnology inventions in the year 1998.[42] The adoption of the directive resulted in the nullification of judgment in the Plant Genetic Systems case. The directive laid down that invention concerning plants shall be patentable if the technical feasibility of the invention is not confined to a

---

36 Chapter VI, Rule 23B (6) of the European Patent Convention, 1973 read as follows: Microbiological process is defined under the convention to mean any 'process involving or performed upon or resulting in microbiological material.'

37 Article53(b) of the European Patent Convention, 1973.

38 Article53(a) of the European Patent Convention, 1973.

39 (1984) Journal of European Patent Office 112, Tech, Bd. App.

40 (1993) 24 IIC 618.

41 T. Ramakrishna, *Biotechnology and Intellectual Property Rights*, 29 (Centre for Intellectual Property Rights and Advocacy (CIPRA), National Law School of India University, Bangalore, 2003).

42 The Directive on the Legal Protection of Biotechnological Inventions, 1998.

particular plant variety. Therefore, now genetically modified plants are allowed patents even if they encompass a plant variety.[43] The European Patent Office Enlarged Board of Appeals, again faced the question on patenting of plants in *Novartis case,*[44] it involved the claim for genetically modified plants which were resistant to fungi. The patent was granted, overruling the judgment in Plant Genetic Systems case, on the ground that it encompassed more than one variety. The Court further held that exclusion under Article 53 (b) of the EPC was applicable only where the patent claimed a plant variety per se. After this judgment, the EPC was brought in line with the European Union directive on biotechnological inventions.

VI. INDIAN BIOTECHNOLOGY & PATENT

In the latter part of the nineteenth century, new inventions in the field of art, process, method or manner of manufacture, machinery, apparatus, and other substances produced by manufacturers were on increase in India and the inventors became very much interested in getting their inventions protected.[45] The *Patents Act,* 1970, stipulates the universally accepted requirements to be fulfilled by an invention in order to obtain patent protection such as novelty, inventive step and industrial application. The invention as defined under the Act mean any new and useful art, process, method or manner of manufacture, machine, apparatus or other articles produced by a manufacturer and includes any new and useful improvement of any of them.[46] The Act does not lay down the inventions which are patentable; on the contrary it lays down the inventions which are not patentable.[47] It is to be noted that the Indian patent law does not lay down any express provision for biotechnological invention. The reason for this is that at the time of enactment of the Act, the legislature never anticipated or imagined the development of biotechnology in India. It was the effect of judicial pronouncements in US and European Union that lead to the development of biotechnology inventions in India.

---

43 Article 4.2 of the Directive on the Legal Protection of Biotechnological Inventions, 1998.

44 (1998) OJEPO 149.

45 Manish Arora, *Universal's Guide to Patents Law as Amended by the Patents (Amendment) Act, 2002,* 2(Universal Law Publishing Company Pvt. Ltd., New Delhi, 2002).

46 Section 2(j) of the Patents Act, 1970.

47 *Id* Section 3.

The major change was brought by the wave of the TRIPS Agreement which mandated the patenting of biotechnology inventions in the member states.[48] After ratifying TRIPS, India amended all its intellectual property laws including the patent law,[49] and walked ahead towards the regime of patenting biotechnological inventions.[50] In order to fulfill the obligation under the TRIPS Agreement, India amended its patent law thrice so as to grant protection to all the inventions in field of science and technology. The first amendment was in the year 1999, which was brought into effect retrospectively from 1995. The main idea behind this amendment was to provide for mailbox applications for agricultural and pharmaceutical inventions. The Amendment extended the patent protection to inventions relating to manufacture of chemical substances intended for use or capable of being used as food or the drug. This amendment helped in the prosperity of biotechnology field and resulted in various patent applications for biotechnological inventions related to pharmaceuticals and agricultural sector.

The second amendment was introduced in the year 2002[51], which brought major changes and allowed the patenting of products of chemical, biochemical and biotechnological process as well as micro-organisms. It promoted and encouraged biotechnological inventions in India, as it included almost all types of such inventions. It was the result of this amendment that, in addition to process, product was also granted protection. The third time India amended its patent law was in the year 2005. This amendment was on the lines of the Budapest Treaty, which recognizes the practice of depositing the invention in any depository recognized under the treaty, in order to compensate the written description. Also, the 2005 amendment totally omitted Section 5 of the original Act which restricted the patent protection only to the method or processes of manufacture. Due to this amendment, the latest position is that now both the products as well as processes are granted patent protection in India. Therefore, in India, both process and product patent are granted protection in the field of biotechnology. The emergence of biotechnology patent law can be traced back to the TRIPS Agreement

48 Article 27 of the Trade Related Aspects of Intellectual Property Rights Agreement, 1995.

49 Amendments were made to the Patents Act, 1970 in 1999, 2002 and 2005.

50 India was given transition period of ten years to modify its laws in order to fulfill the obligation under the Trade Related Aspects of Intellectual Property Rights Agreement, 1995.

51 The Patents (Amendment) Act, 2002.

and the amendments introduced to the patent law. In India, microorganisms are now patentable. However, the stand of India is not very clear with regard to the patenting of non-naturally produced plants and animals.

VII. GRANT OF BIOTECHNOLOGY PATENTS

Subject matters patentable are granted patents after a series of formal procedures.[52] Grant of patent translates an invention from the world of science and technology to the world of commerce.[53] The United States and Europe follow post-grant opposition procedure and India follows both post grant and pre-grant opposition procedure in granting patents. In post-grant opposition procedure patent is granted first and afterwards the same is advertised to invite oppositions and objections. However, the grant of the patent is subject to the decision in opposition proceedings. In case of pre-grant opposition procedure application is advertised first in order to invite objections and oppositions. Depending on the decision taken in the opposition proceedings patent is granted or denied. The procedure for the grant of patent is cumbersome in India. As per the procedure it takes more than five years to grant a patent unlike in the US and in Europe. In the US it takes only eighteen months to grant a patent. In Europe it takes three years to grant a patent. Patent on biotechnology invention are protected for a term of twenty years and are maintained on payment of renewal fee till the expiry of the term of twenty years.

However, in case of successful invalidity claims or surrenders of the patent by the owner himself or revocation of the patent on valid grounds, a patent cannot be maintained. In fact, the duration of patent was not uniform earlier and different countries were granting patents for different terms. With the coming into being of the *TRIPS Agreement,* the duration of the term now is twenty years throughout the world. Once granted, the patent is protected for a period of twenty years. India follows the method of pre-grant opposition unlike the USA and the European Union, in granting biotech patents. The *Patents Act,* 1970[54] governs the law on granting of biotechnology patents in India. India is a party to the Paris Convention and also to the *TRIPS Agreement.* Hence, the patent law of India is consummate with the above international agreements. In India,

---

52 Lionel Blenty and Broad Sherman, *Intellectual Property Law,* 340 (Oxford University Press, New Delhi, 2003).

53 Charlotte Waelde, *et.al., Contemporary Intellectual Property Rights,* 510 (Oxford University Press, United Kingdom, 2011).

54 The Patents (Amendment) Act, 2005.

patents applications can be filed at any branch office at Chennai, Mumbai or Delhi or at the head office in Kolkata.[55] Any person claiming to be the true and first inventor of the invention, his assignee, or his legal representatives can file an application for the grant of patent claiming a biotechnology invention. There is also the possibility of joint applications by two or more inventors in case of all of them have worked for the same invention.

VIII. ENFORCEMENT OF BIOTECHNOLOGY PATENTS

Universally, biotechnology patents are offered protection for a term of twenty years.[56] Protection is offered to the inventor as a reward of his efforts in inventing and disclosing something, which is useful to the society. As far as enforcement of biotechnology patents is concerned, the international conventions like the Paris Convention or the TRIPS Agreement does not say anything specifically. International convention leaves the enforcement of inventions to the respective states. Therefore, the respective Member state must enforce a patented invention as per its local law. The patent law of the US provides that till the expiry of the period of a patent, no other person except the owner can use or exploit the invention. If any person without the authorization of the owner happens to use the invention, he does not infringe the patent.[57] The patent law provides for certain remedies to the patent owner against infringement, in the form of injunction, damages or compensation. A suit for infringement can be filed in a district court; from which the appeal will lie before the Court of Appeal for the Federal Circuit and the highest court of appeal is the Supreme Court of America. In the European Union, EPC governs the law relating to biotechnology patents. However, enforcement of biotechnology patents is left to the respective member states of the Union. The EPC states that national law shall deal with any infringement of a European patent.[58] Neither the EPC nor the Directives on biotechnology inventions does provide for the enforcement of biotech patents. The Courts follow the principles of natural justice in adjudicating infringement suits.

---

55 Rule 20C of the Patent Rules as amended in 2002.

56 Article 27 of the Trade Related Aspects of Intellectual Property Rights, 1995.

57 Section 271 of the Title 35 of the United States Code deals with Infringement of Patent.

58 Article 64(3) of the European Patent Convention, 1973 deals with Rights conferred by a European Patent.

In India biotechnology patents are enforced against infringement under the Patents Act. The Act states that it is the owner who can exclusively use and exploit the patented invention. If any person without the authorization from the owner uses, makes, exploits, sells, offers to sell, or imports the patented invention, he does infringe the patented invention. The importation of patented products by any person from a person who is duly authorized by the patentee to sell or distribute the product also does not constitute infringement.[59] Infringement proceedings shall be instituted in any court inferior to a district court. Remedies are available in the form of injunctions, damages and account of profits. The objective behind enforcing patents against infringement is to guarantee exclusive rights on the invention to the patent owner. India has placed great importance on the development of a strong scientific sector since its early days as an independent country. Technology and science have been associated not only with culture, social progress and the import substitution paradigm, but also with political pre-eminence and even national pride. P. Ghosh affirms for instance that the commitment of the Indian government in the biotech field 'emerges out of compulsions and social commitments to minimize foreign dependence'.[60] As early as in 1983, the Long Term Plan in Biotechnology identified as top priorities self sufficiency in food, housing and clothing, as well as a balance in international trade. If statistics and forecasts on the percentage of imports are taken into account, India would be on the right track to fulfil those goals, since it has almost overcome its previous dependence. It is foreseen then that in 2012 only 10.95% of local consumption of biotechnological products will be imported. Thanks to decades of important and constant efforts on the part of Indian society, nowadays India is acknowledged for having a thriving knowledge-based sector and world-class scientific centers. What once were buoying but isolated sectors, such as those based on information and communication technologies, are presently accompanied by other dynamic sectors. At present biotechnology are a fast growing field and one of the most successful scientific and economic areas in the Indian economy.[61]

---

[59] Section Patent Convention, 1973 deals with Rights conferred by a European Patent.

[59] Section 107A of the Patents Act, 1970.

[60] Ghosh, K., 'Indian Efforts for Developing Biotechnology', 11(1) *Asian Biotechnology and Development Review* 36 (2008).

[61] Sharma, Manju., *India: Biotechnology Research and Development*, 2000, *available at*: www.icsu.org/1_icsuinscience/GMO/PDF/CG%20Sharma.pdf (Last accessed on May 15, 2015).

IX. BIOTECHNOLOGY AND PUBLIC POLICY

In a country where poverty is still a daunting reality, investing in science and technology is a deliberate pro-development choice. Although Indian knowledge-based industries do not present notable differences in terms of management and goals when compared to Western companies, in India efforts are also undertaken to turn technological innovation into goods and services which are not only useful to the economic development of the country but also accessible to the Indian public and adapted to local conditions. As the Annual Report of the Department of Biotechnology states, in India, 'balancing needs of economic competitiveness with affordable products continues to engage policy makers and the industry'.[62] The equilibrium India tries to achieve between innovation and access is important to the entire developing world. At present Indian innovation benefits numerous developing countries that share Indian climatic, logistic and economic characteristics. This has been seen particularly in the field of information and communication technologies, and in the area of pharmaceutical products. An outstanding challenge is to replicate the same success in the field of biotechnology, two good candidates being biopharmaceutical products and bioinformatics services.

The need to link Indian technological development with the economic and human development of the country has been emphasized in several relevant reports. For instance, in the specific field of biotechnology the 2004 Report of the Task Force on Application of Agricultural Biotechnology stated that biotechnology offers opportunities for converting India's biological wealth into economic wealth and new employment opportunities on an environmentally and socially sustainable basis.[63] Even more clearly, it has been stated that 'for Indian policy makers it is paramount not only to encourage excellence in high tech industries but also further inclusive pro-poor innovation'.[64]

These statements are not anecdotal. In India there is an open debate on what the priorities of the research should be. This is a debate that, in fact, requires to consider whether Indian innovation should be different- and if so, to what extent—from the innovation generated in countries

62 Government of India, *Annual Report 2008-2009* (Department of Biotechnology, Ministry of Science and Technology, 2010).

63 Swaminathan, M.S., 'Task Force on Agricultural Biotechnology', *Report of the Task Force on Application of Agricultural Biotechnology* 6 (Ministry of Agriculture, Government of India, 2004).

64 Chaturvedi, Sachin, Agricultural Biotechnology and New Trends in IPR Regime: Challenges before Developing Countries, 37 *Economic and Political Weekly* 13-19 (2002).

pertaining to the Organization for Economic Cooperation and Development (OECD). In a related way but at the other extreme of the innovation chain, questions also are posed with regard to accessibility. Thanks to countries such as China and India, products such as electronics and pharmaceuticals have become accessible to masses of people all over the world. Personal computers for less than 80 US$ or AIDS generic medications with prices ten-fold lower than branded antiretroviral have improved or saved the lives of tens if not hundreds of millions of people. It would be naïve to affirm that Indian manufacturers produce these goods at highly competitive prices with the sole goal of fostering the well-being of the masses. Nevertheless, it would also be erroneous not to establish a balance between the price of the invention and the economic possibilitics of those willing or needing to consume the invention.

As a subset of science and technology, India quickly identified the potential biotechnology had for fostering national development. The Sixth Five Year Plan, which set out the developmental priorities of India for 1980-1985, signaled out biotechnology as a useful tool to meet the health and agriculture needs of the Indian population. More precisely, it identified "tissue culture application for medicinal and economic plans; fermentation technology and enzyme engineering for chemicals; (...) emerging areas like genetic engineering and molecular biology".[65] The Council for Scientific and Industrial Research was identified as the body in charge of guaranteeing the coordination of the biotechnological initiatives undertaken by different departments. In 1982, the National Biotechnology Board was created. This was a small division within the Department of Science and Technology devoted to the management of biotechnology. More specifically, it was established to signal out priorities and oversee and plan for required manpower, integrated industrial development and large scale use of biotechnology products and processes.[66] This inter-departmental body drafted and issued in 1983 the *Long Term Plan in Biotechnology for India*, which mapped the priorities in that field for the years to come. The document was drafted taking as a reference the developmental needs of the country. Four years later, in 1986, a Department of Biotechnology was founded.[67] In fact, this new

---

65 Government of India, *Sixth Five Year Plan* (Planning Commission, 1981), *available at*: http://planningcommission.nic.in/reports/publications/pub_techsix.pdf (Last accessed on May 15, 2015).

66 Chaturvedi, S., 'Emerging Indian Entrepreneurship in Biotechnology and National Innovation System: Exploring Linkages and Prospects', 5(2) *International Journal of Technology and Globalization* 78 (2010).

67 Bhargava, P.M., 'Biotechnology in India: The Beginnings', 4 *Biotechnology Journal* 313-318 (2009).

department within the Ministry of Science and Technology resulted from the upgrading of the National Biotechnology Board. This was coincidental with the first experimental release of a genetically engineered organism into the environment as well as with the production of the first transgenic farm animal.

Since those early beginnings of biotechnology in India, it has been regarded as fundamental for the development and placed at the centre stage of the Indian development strategy. In 2001 the Vision Statement on Biotechnology affirmed that the goal of the Indian biotechnology policy was 'attaining new heights in biotechnology research, shaping biotechnology into a premier precision tool of the future for creation of wealth and ensuring social justice especially for the welfare of the poor'.[68]It can be concluded that the developments in the field of biotechnology have gained impetus in the recent past. These biotechnological inventions are beneficial for the public at large, especially in a developing country like India. But, with certain benefits of these inventions certain demerits are also attached, and hence it becomes necessary to regulate such inventions as they involve the use of flora and fauna, which needs to be protected at the same time. India is a soft target for big corporations due to various reasons; hence effective regulation is the need of the hour.[69]

X. CONCLUSION

Biotechnology, through its broad applications and infinite promise, has the potential to carry our economy into the 21st century. The benefits of biotechnology initiatives have been felt by virtually every industry in the world. Biotechnology has had its most profound impact on those industries that seek to sustain, improve and prolong our lives such as the health care, agriculture, and environmental preservation industries.[70]

However, despite biotechnology's immense potential to stimulate our economy and enhance our quality of life, the behind the scenes researchers and developers of these innovative technologies must still weather through a maze of regulatory and business issues before their

---

68 Government of India, Biotechnology-A Vision (Ten Year Perspective), 2001 (Department of Biotechnology, Ministry of Science and Technology, 2001), *available at*: http://dbtindia.nic.in/uniquepage.asp?id_pk=102 (Last accessed on April 12, 2015).

69 Reddy, K. I. Varaprasad., 'Biotech Regulation in India: Problems and Promises', 4 *Biotechnology Journal* 306 (2009).

70 Gaisford, J.D. *et al.*, 'Biotechnology Piracy: Rethinking the International Protection of Intellectual Property', 50 (1) *Canadian Journal of Agricultural Economics* 15-34 (2002).

products can ultimately reach the public. Biotechnology developers must become familiar with and comply with applicable the U.S. Food and Drug Administration (FDA), the Department of Agriculture (USDA) and the Environmental Protection Agency (EPA) regulations. At the same time, property protection mechanisms such as obtaining a patent and entering into a fair and effective licensing arrangement should be sought. Properly addressing and surmounting these issues will help to ensure that both the biotechnology developers and the public at large receive the benefits of the new technology.[71]

The biotechnology boom will undoubtly have a tremendous impact on international trade and the growth of this sector hinges on various factors such as:

a) Possibility of technology transfer
b) Protection of intellectual property rights.

Intellectual property occupies a central position in the biotechnology innovation system, which is expected to provide a source of new medicines, foods and bio-energy.[72]

There is a need to be educated in the markets and the technologies and also develop a clear understanding of the importance of IP protection in biotechnology for many people working in the biotechnology field, managing IP has become a practical necessity because the research tools they use are covered by IP protection, or they find they can't develop or apply their research outcomes in a particular direction without negotiating the use of another technology that is covered by a patent. In any event, there are specific skills and legal mechanisms that are used to achieve the benefits of IP rights, whether these benefits are seen in commercial, developmental or social terms. Intellectual property rights can be a valuable resource, even for researchers involved in public research, but like any resource have to be carefully managed to produce the desired benefits.[73] So a biotechnology researcher needs to understand how to manage IP, just as much as one need to understand the principles of IP law. It is therefore very important to think about protecting ones intellectual property while one is still in researching phase.

---

71 Ramasami, T., 'Basic and Applied Research in India: Present and future', 4 *Biotechnology Journal* 301-305 (2009).

72 Kardam, K.S., 'Patenting in the Emerging Fields of Technology', 12(1) *Journal of Intellectual Property Rights* 15-29 (2007).

73 Choudhary, B., 'Indian Biotech sets a Constitutional Challenge', 419 *Nature* 667 (2002).

Section-IV

Cybernetics, Law & Public Policy

10

Information Technology & Cyber Crimes Problems & Prospects

Syed Shamimul Hasnat Azmi

I. INTRODUCTION

Information technology has heralded a new era of Communication System. It has revolutionized the whole commercial world. The mother earth looks like a global village where people sitting thousands of miles away can talk face to face, like people sitting across the table. Business men and consumers are using computer to create, transmit and store information in the electronic form. Traditional form of paper documents are being discarded for the reason that electronic method is Cheaper, easier to store, retrieve and communicate. Though these advantages are obvious but people were reluctant to transact business in electronic form due to lack of legal frame work, validating these transactions. All the paper transactions involved writing and signature to conclude them. These writings and signatures posed a great hurdle for electronic governance and electronic commerce for validating and enforcing them. The law of Evidence is based on paper made documents which should have been signature. Since electronic commerce eliminates the need for paper based transactions, hence to facilitate e-commerce the need for legal change has become an urgent necessity. International trade, though the medium of e-commerce, is growing by leaps and bounds for the past few years. Many countries have switched over from traditional paper based commerce to e-commerce. The instantaneous means of communications through internet have been a great menace to copy right in different areas David Teather from London has reported that the International Federation of the Phonographic Industry say that the market in year 2000 was worth $36.9 billion, a fall of 1.3 per cent on the previous year. The biggest decline in the sale of C.D. singles was 39% and globally it fell by 14%. The growth in popularity of Napster and to contain the damage. *Napster* is in the process of removing copyrighted material from its site.[1] But the powers of the computer are so great that the law enforcement agencies are facing a real challenge to contain its onslaught. Internet telephony is a common sight at cyber cafe, despite the fact that it is illegal.[2] B.B. Nanda and R.K.Tewari observe that " internet paedophilia, computer network break-ins, industrial espionage, Child pornography password sniffling, spoofling, telecommunications fraud, software piracy, e- mail bombing and spamming, and the availability of illicit or unlicensed products and services are offences already making themselves felt. Emerging problems include credit card fraud, cyber terrorism, cyber laundering and criminal use of secure internet communications. The huge growth of internet will breed cyber fraud with great ease especially in the area of share-holdings of companies.[3] The present weak electronic system of payment without adequate safeguard is posing a serious risk for unauthorised withdrawals from banks and counter money laundering operations. Software piracy is a boom business and video and phonographic industries are sinking day by day globally.[4] The UNCITRAL Model law provides for equal legal treatment of users of electronic communication and paper based communication. In pursuance of a declaration made 'by Member Countries, the World Trade Organisation (WTO) is about to form a work programme to handle its work in this area including the formation of multilateral trade deals through the medium of electronic commerce. The paper discusses, briefly, the meaning of cyber space the origin and development of intemet and e commerce its uses and abuses. Certain provisions relating to *Information Technology Act,* 2000 have been briefly discussed to apprise oneself about its effectiveness in meeting the challenges posed by e commerce in different areas.

II. MEANING OF CYBER SPACE

The term cyber seems to derive its origin from cybernetics which means science of communication and control over machine and man (including animal) cyber space is used to refer to a system controlled by machine for communication of information between human beings sans geographical borders. It is referred now for online community to represent all the people connected to the internet. It is a medium through

1 David Teather, London "Pirates Sink Music Finn" *Hindustan Times* April 21: 2001.

2 Yashmi Yadv, "In Touch and Not Broke", *Hindustan Times,* March 4: 2001.

3 B.B.Nanda & R.K. Tewari "Cyber Crime : A Challenge to Forensic Science", *The Indian Journal,* April – September, 2000 102 at 103.

4 David Teather "Pines Sink Music Firms", *Hindustan Times* April 21: 2001.

which information may flow and communication may be made between the parties across the globe. It is referred now for online community to represent all the people connected to the internet. It is a medium through which information may flow and communication may be made between the parties across the globe. Network and Internet are Key Word or terms under information technology. Network refers to inter connection of computers through master computer. Thus every organisation like, trade, industry, banking services, railways, Airlines etc have their own networks for efflcient management of their own affairs. When all such networks are connected through a central system, it is called Internet. Thus internet refers to inter connection of networks that may run into millions for exchange of information. Microsoft Press Computer Dictionary deflnes it as a set of computer networks joined together by means of gateways that handle data transfer and the conversion of messages from the sending network to the protocols used by receiving network.

Now the computers are being used for communication and dissemination of information. This has brought into lime light the terms 'Programme' and 'Software'. Programme refers to steps for solving a problem by feeding information in a computer. There may be a number of programmes fed in a computer. A set of such programmes is known as software. The greatest characteristic of software information available anywhere is that it may be used locally for solving a problem through Internet. At present, for reservation of ticket through certain Airline or other problems related to that may be sorted out through internet. The sale of goods in grain markets and other fruits[5] in a profitable manner, inflow and outflow of information through internet in earthquake hit Gujarat,[6] online Banking,[7] e-mail, voice mail Health care, Internet phone service. Newspaper and magazine, Entertainment and Games etc offer immense opportunity to the people.[8] Information Technology refers to tools and techniques for origination, generation, collection, recurring, feeding, manipulation, dissemination and distribution of information. Computer is the hub around which information technology revolves.

---

5 Vishal Thaper "The Mndi Goes on Line", *Hindustan Times* March 2001.

6 Shewta Rajpal, "Aûer Shocks Hit Cyberspace Too", *Hindustan Times* H.T. Feb 3: 2001, "Online Disaster Management, Feb. 4: 2001.

7 Tania Padget "Online Bnk Winning Over More customers", *Times of India* January 30: 2001.

8 Graham Jones "How To Use Internet" (1999 Ed) at 9, For general uses of computer/ internet and its beneûts. read also Mohd. Yunus & Roshan Khayal "Glamour or Guile: The lnternet Today" lASLlC Bulletin 45(2) 2000, p.p. 83-91.

It provides magnetic media, sound media, including VCR telephone, microphone, modem, and key board. They are all interfaced with computer. The capability of computer to possess multimedia facilities for undertaking all the activities of Information technology at one stretch is really unique. Information technology deals with efficient management of information.[9]

III. ORIGIN AND DEVELOPMENT

The Internet is the result of invention by U.S. Defence Departments, Advanced Research Project Agency Network (ARPANET). It started as a defence project in 1969 in U.S.A. and in India in 1987-88 as Education and Research Network (ERNET) Videsh Sanchar Ngam Ltd (VSNL) started it in India only in 1995. The year 2000 brought great progress and prosperity in the fleld of Information Technology and the bug of Y2K proved to be a boom in disguise for Indian I.T. Industry. The proposed communication Commission of India (CCI) under a new communication Law, known as the Convergence Bill 2000, will oversee all mattes under I.T. Sector.[10] This information regulatory regime will address the growing technological convergence of telecommunications, data communication, internet, satellite and terrestrial broad casting, cable television, audio broad-casting, software and content creation.

The internet can now be surfed and radio broad casting listened using mobile phones. India will be only second to Malysia in passing this type of legislation which has enacted communications and *Multimedia Commission Act* 1998. This piece of legislation drafted by Fali S Nariman is being viewed by European Union as a model to be followed by its member countries, while drafting convergence legislation. The U.S. Federal Communications Commission is also looking to Nariman for guidance in this area.[11] However, the concern is growing over the erosion of power of CCI by MPs and MLAS who will interfere with the independence of commission. If this road block is removed, Information

---

9 Naik on Information Technology, Institute of Objective Studies, *News Letter*, September, 2000 at pp. 4-5.

10 For a Comprehensive view see Dawang Mehta "A year of Frenetic Activity", *Hindustan Times Report* Dec. 31: 2000.

11 2000See Ravi Visvesuaraya Prasad "Convergence to Untangle", *Hindustan Times* Report April 14, 2001 and Hindustan Times Correspondent "Major Policy changes. corporate Deals", *Hindustan Times* Report Dec. 31, 2000. and Ashok Das "Software Experts from Hyderabad Set to Touch Rs.18,000 Cr. This Fiseal", *Hindustan Times* Report Feb. 21: 2001, Wherein he reports that almost all the States are establishing the technological parks to spread the growth of I.T. Sector.

Technology sector will receive great boost to develop infrastructure by foreign and national investors.[12]

IV. CHALLENGES TO LAW ENFORCEMENT

The law enforcement agencies are facing the following challenges in controlling Cyber Crimes.[13]

a) Legal challenges which are dependent on the statutory provisions to be used as a tool to investigate and control the cyber crimes.

b) Operational challenges require a cohesive well trained and well equipped force of investigators operating and co-ordinating at national and International level.

c) Technical challenges thwarting the efforts of law enforcement agencie's ability to catch and prosecute the online offenders.

In order that the corridors of communication are not used as a den to promote and perpetuate crime, Government, law enforcement agencies, Industry, users and consumers all have to co-operate and coordinate in elimination thereof. While taking up the legal challenges, the *Information Technology Act* 2000 provides a legal framework for the recognition of digital signature and authentication of documents in electronic format.[14] Such documents may be authenticated by afflxing digital signatures. Any tampering with the electronic record will invalidate such signature. The identity of persons signing is authenticated through a private key and the same can be verifled by anybody who has the public key matching with such private key.[15] The provisions relating to electronic governance give legal recognition to electronic records, digital signatures and flling of information in electronic form.[16] Industry's development of digital signatures and 'watermarks' has considerable potential as a tool to prevent crimes.[17] Hence, it is hoped and expected that effective enforcement of provisions relating to secure digital signature will minimise the crimes.[18] Further, elaborate rules with regard to communication of information in electronic forms with comprehensive

---

[12] *Ibid.*

[13] B.B. Nanda & R.K.ewari Supra note 3 at 104.

[14] *See* Chapter ll of the Act.

[15] *Id* Section 3 .

[16] *Id* Chapter III.

[17] B.B. Nanda & N.K. Tewari *Supra* note 3.

[18] Section 15.

terms and conditions relating to receipt, acknowledgement and acceptance thereof have been laid down which will guide the law enforcement agencies in pin pointing the responsibilities of the parties in compliance with the formation and performance of a valid contract.[19] The two subsequent chapters deal with the procedure to be followed in administration of the Act.[20]

V. PENALTIES AND PUNISHMENTS

Chapter IX and XI deal with penalties, adjudications and punishment. Anyone who without the permission of the owner or any other person who is incharge of a computer, computer system or computer network (a) secures access, (b) down loads, copies or extracts any data, computer data base or any information; (c) introduces or causes to be introduced any computer virus or contaminant, (d) damages or causes to be damaged, (e)disrupts or causes to be disrupted (f) denies or causes the denial of access to any person illegally, (g) provides any assistance to any person to facilitate access to a computer in contravention of the provisions of this Act (h) charges the services availed of by a person to the account of any other person, shall be liable to pay damages by way of compensation not exceeding one crore rupees to the person so effected.[21]

Chart of Offences and Punishments

Section	Description of the Act/ Offence	Punishment & Fine
43	Penality for damage to computer system etc.	Upto Rupees one crore
44(a)	Penality for failure to furnish information, to Controller etc.	Penality upto one lakh flfty thousand
(b)	Not filing information within time specifled	Rupees 5000/ for each day.
(c)	Not maintaining books of accounts etc.	Rupees 10,000/- for each day.
45	Where no penality has been separately provided for contrave-ntion of any rules and regulation.	Compensation upto Rs.25,000/- to the person affected or penality upto same amount.
65	Tampering with computer source documents	Jail upto three years or fine upto Rs. 2 lakh or both

19 *Id* Chapter IV.

20 *Id* Chapter V & VI.

21 *Id* Section 43.

66	Hacking with computer system	Punishment and fine as given under S. 65.
67	Publishing of information which is obscene in electronic form	Jail upto 5 years and fine upto Rupees one lakh for first conviction and Just double for subsequent conviction.
68	Failure to comply with the direction of the Controller, for compliance with the Act.	Jail upto 3 years and a fine upto two lakh or both.
69	Failure by the subscriber in not helping any agency to decrypt information on the direction of the Controller which may be against the sovereignty or security of the State.	Jail upto seven years
70	Attempting to secure or securing access to a protected system.	Jail upto 10 years and fine.
71	Supressing or misrepresenting material fact to authorities	Jail upto 2 years or fine upto Rupees one lakh or with both.
72	Securing access to any book or record etc. which is confldential and passesiton to other person without the consent of its owner.	Jail upto 2 years or fine upto Rupees one lakh or with both.
73	Publishing Digital Signature certificate false in certain particulars	Jail & fine as given in Sections 71-72.
74	Publication of Digital Signature certificate for fraudulent purpose	Jail for 2 years or fine upto Rupees one lakh or both.
76	Any computer or other material through which the contravention of the Act is taking place may be confiscated.	Confiscation
85(1)	If there is contravention of rule or order by a company the person in whose charge the contravention took place may be liable. He may not be liable if it took place with out his knowledge or inspite of due deligence.	Punishment as per rule
85(2)	If the contravention is attributable to any other officer of the company with his consent or connivance.	Punishable according to rules.

If any person required to furnish any document return or report to the controller or the certifying authority under this Act or any rules there under does not furnish the same, he shall be liable to a penalty upto rupees one lakh and fifty thousands for every such failure or if he does not file any return or furnish any information etc within time specified, he shall be liable to a penality upto five thousand rupees for every day, till such failure continues or if he fails to maintain books of account or record, he shall be liable to a penalty upto ten thousand rupees per day, till the failure continues.[22] Any person, who contravenes rules or regulations of the Act for which no separate penalty is provided, shall be liable to pay a penalty or compensation not exceeding twenty five thousand rupees to the person affected by such contravention.[23] The punishment for tampering with computer source documents which are required to be kept or maintained by law for the time being in force, is imprisonment upto three years or fine upto rupees two lakh or both.[24] The punishment for lacking with computer system is same as given above for tampering with computer source documents. whoever with intent to cause or knowing that he is likely to cause wrongful loss or damage to public or any person, destroys or deletes or alters any information residing in a computer resource or diminishes its value or utility or affects it injuriously by any means, commits Hacking.[25]

Publication of obscene information in electronic form whose effect is such as to tend to deprave and corrupt persons who are likely to come in contact with it by reading, seeing or hearing matter embodied or contained in it will attract punishment on first conviction, imprisonment upto 5 years and fine upto Rupees one lakh and on second conviction imprisonment upto 10 years and fine upto Rupees two lakh.[26] A very interesting case has come up relating to this offence where a school boy from Air Force Bal Bharti School has been found storing pornoographic material in his recently established web site. He has been arrested for the reason that he gave undesirable details about girls boys and certain teachers of his school. This alarmed the parents of such students and the matter was reported to the police. The boy was arrested and released. Though the police investigation does not show anything undesirable about the conduct and behavior of the boy still because of this activity,

---

22 *Id* Section 44.

23 *Id* Section 45.

24 *Id* Section 65.

25 *Id* Section 66.

26 *Id* Section 67.

the career of the student may be spoiled. It has been reported that there are owners of internet sites who are storing more pornographic materials at their web site but nothing has been done to them. Why this boy only.[27]

The controller has power to direct a certifying authority or his employee in order to seek compliance with any provisions of the Act to do or refrain from doing anything, as specified in the order. Non compliance with the order will amount to an offence which may attract conviction of imprisonment up to three years or a fine up to Rupees two lakh or both.[28] The controller has been empowered to direct any agency of the government in writing to intercept any information transmitted through any computer resource in the interest of the sovereignty of India, security of the State, friendly relations with foreign states or public order or for preventing incitement to the commission of a crime. On such order, the government agency may direct the subscriber or in charge of computer resource to do the needful. Such person shall extend all technical assistance to decrypt the information. Non compliance by the person so directed will attract a punishment of imprisonment up to 7 years.[29]

The appropriate government may by declaration in the official Gazettee notify a particular computer or computer system or computer network to be protected. Anyone seeking access to it, in contravention of the order of the government will be liable to be punished for imprisonment extending upto 10 years and also a flne.[30] Any one making misrepresentation, or suppressing any material fact with the controller or certifying authority to obtain a licence or digital signature will be liable to an imprisonment extending to two years or flne up to rupees on lakh or both.[31] Similar punishment is prescribed for a person who has secured confidential information by access to electronic record etc without the consent of the person concerned and discloses such information to any other person committing breach of confidentiality and privacy.[32]

Any person publishing a digital signature certificate or making it available to any other person with the knowledge that certifying authority listed in the certificate has not issued it or the subscriber mentioned

---

27 Neeta Sharma "School boy Admits haunching porn site, Arrested", *Hindustan Times* April 27: 2001 & "Arrested Development: Dis cops go Too Far", *Hindustan Times* April 28: 2001.

28 *Id* Section 68.

29 *Id* Section 69.

30 *Id* Section 70.

31 *Id* Section 71.

32 *Id* Section 72.

therein has not accepted it or the certificate has been revoked a suspended will be punishable with imprisonment up to two years or fine up to rupees one lakh or both.[33] The same punishment has been prescribed for any person who publishes a digital signature certiflcate or makes it available to any person for any unlawful purpose.[34]

Confiscation of any computer, computer system, floppies or accessories can be made if the same is found to be used in contravention of the provisions of the Act or rules and regulations made there under. However, if the court or adjudicating offlcer is satisfied that the person in possession thereof is not responsible for the contravention of the provisions of the Act or rules and regulations made there under, he may make such order as he may deem fit.[35] The order or conflscation or other penalties will not be a bar for punishing any person liable undcr any law for the time being in force.[36]

If any provisions of the Act have been contravened by a company then the person responsible for contravention shall be held liable unless he proves to the satisfaction of the court or adjudicating officer that contravention took place without his knowledge or he exercised due deligence to prevent such contravention. If the contravention has taken place with the connivance or neglect of any other officer of the company, then he will be liable to be punished even though he was not incharge of contravening activity.[37] A chart of offences with relevant sections and quantum of punishment is given for convenience.

VI. INVESTIGATING OF CYBER CRIME

The Act empowers a police officer not below the Rank of Deputy Superintendent of Police to investigate into the matter relating to alleged offences.[38] This will ensure that only in genuine cases, the police will interfere. Such police officer or another officer of the Central or State Government may enter any premises, search or seize any material and arrest any person who is reasonably suspected to have committed any offence under the Act.[39] In this connection, what is note worthy is the professional competence of the police officer or other government officers

---

[33] *Id* Section 73.

[34] *Id* Section 74.

[35] *Id* Section 76.

[36] *Id* Section 77.

[37] *Id* Section 85.

[38] *Id* Section 78.

[39] *Id* Section 80.

who even have no basic knowledge of operating a computer which is highly desirable for such investigation. However, a customer in a cyber cafe may, by chance, click on an 'obscene web site' out of a long list of sites thrown up by a search engine. A question has been arisen whether the owner of the cafe will be liable for allowing it to come on its computer.[40] The reply lies in section 79 wherein the internet service provider is not liable if he proves that the offence or contravention has taken place without his knowledge or that he had exercised all due diligence to prevent the commission of such offence or contravention. It is submitted that in such cases where the element of mensrea is absent and where the very nature of operation permits search in good faith, nobody should be held liable for such an incidence *i.e.* neither the customer nor the Internet service provider.

We have great expertise in forensic science relating to conventional paper related offences but really lack very much in this area. The laws which were made for paper related crimes have to be changed to suit digital language. Tracking criminals relating to computer and internet offences is a difficult job, as they get sufficient time to eliminate digital evidence. "Investigating agencies in India are ill prepared to conduct a professional investigation of cyber crime and identify, handle and examine evidence that resides in digital form. This leaves a fertile ground for criminals to sprout and flourish".[41] In order to investigate the offences relating white collar crime in general and computer crime in particular, it is essential to have trained staff to handle the criminals properly and to punish them. That will have a deterrent effect and establish the credibility of law enforcing agencies. Ashok Das has observed that most policemen lack technical knowledge to effectively deal with cyber crimes. In fact very few know as to how to operate a computer. To rectify this draw back, the city police of Hyderabad had organised a workshop in association with a private bank in April 2001 to educate policemen about frauds in the banking sector and how to tackle and handle them. A cyber crime cell has also been established in Hyderabad in the City Police Commissioner's Office "With considerable success". Police Commissioner P. Ramulu has observed that there is a great need for strengthening the I.T. Act by making online crimes cognizable offence. A code of conduct for cyber cafes and Internet Service providers (I.S.P.) is also needed. He has also observed that matching the finger prints or the iris of the eye of the credit card holder could be useful in preventing frauds.[42]

---

40 B.B. Nanda & R.K. Tewari, *Supra* note 3 at 106.

41 *Id* at 102.

42 Ashokdas Hydrabad, "Think before you handover our credit card", *Hindustan Times*, April 16: 2001.

The office of the Government Examiner of questioned Document (GEQD) of BDR&D existed in Simla since 1904 and has been considered as one of the premier institutions in forensic science set ups to deal with white collar crime. Now the need is to develop Computer Forensics. Indeed in the power of internet reaching millions of people across the globe lies its deficiency also.

The Financial Action Task Force (FATF) has reported that lnternet casinos are being used as cover by criminal gangs for money laundering operation. This force has been deployed to co-ordinate international effort to combat money laundering. The force observed that ease of access, the lack of face to face contact between individuals and the speed of electronic transactions has turned the internet in an ideal vehicle for money laundering. Lars Oftedal Brock, a Supreme Court Judge in Norway also observed that "there is a whole new dimension of anonymity as to who is really behind a Computer or telephone on the internet.[43] To combat crime on the internet FATF said it had discussed requiring service providers to maintain reliable subscriber's registers with appropriate identification for six months to a year. Expert opinion has suggested ISPs keeping detailed records of visitors to their sites". This is really very effective to trace out the criminals making online purchases or commiting other fraud.[44] Another device has been introduced by Enter Oye Nok, a Web authentication service, designed by channai based Myespace, net which ensures that every internet transaction authenticates the genuineness of the user. While registering with the Myespace net for the authentication service, one has to give his mobile phone number and in turn he may be provided an eight digit authentication code, you will get a user ID to check your oye Nok enabled transaction. Every time while transacting business on the net Oye Nok calls on mobile giving the detail of the transaction ID and asks for approval. If one key in the code, the transaction is completed. Otherwise, it does not proceed. So even if some one is using one's credit card detail, he will not be able to complete the transaction in the absence of authentication code.[45] This is an excellent proposition to meet a situation where a person went to a hotel and gave his credit card to the hotel staff for payment. The staff did not steal the card but only noted the details of the card and passed it on to a computer

---

[43] Guardian News Service, London "intemet Casinos a cover for crime", *Hindustan Times Report* Feb. 2: 2001.

[44] Ashok Das, Hydrabad "Think before you handover your credit card", *Hindustan Times Report* Hindustan Times report, April 15: 2001.

[45] "Web authentication makes buying ox er internet safer", *Hindustan Times* Feb. 3: 2001.

operator, who used the details to make online purchases. To the dismay and shock of the credit card holder, the company sent a bill of Rs. 42,000/- due to cyber fraud. The other suggestion is that personal information on internet is not safe. So avoid making on line purchases with credit card.[46]

Online auctions made 78% of internet fraud in 2000, as per the report of National Consumers League, Washington, resulting in to loss $326 per victim. Internet auction fraud is also on U.S. Federal Trade Commission's (FTC) top ten onlines scams list and makes up 42% of all internet related complaints filed with the FTC. An over whelming majority of complaints is failure to deliver the goods after the buyer has sent the payment as per report of Dolores Gardner, an attorney with FTC specialising in internet auction fraud. Inspite of auction fraud, on line auctions are extremely popular among the internet users with 31% on line Americans which is 35 million. The FTC observed that a significant on line fraud was caused by dealings in computers and their accessories.[47] The research study carried out by Neilson Media suggests that there are 80 million users of online service throughout the globe and the number may increase to one billion by the year 2010.[48]

Central Government will establish Cyber Appellate Tribunals. The person eligible for appointment will be a person who is or may be eligible for appointment as a Judge of High Court or such person is or has been a member of 1st grade Indian Legal Service for at least three years.[49] It does not say anything about their qualification as a Judicial Officer dealing with cyber crime. It will be an irony of fate if a single person eligible to preside over the tribunal unaided by two members experts in cyber crimes and internet/computer operating devices *MRTP Act,* 1969 is appointed to deal with them. Further there should be a special bench dealing with cyber crimes or internet/computer software related matters in High Courts. The present generation of Judiciary, it is submitted with great respect, is not fully aware in modern technological advances in this area. This was heard from a honourable Judges of High Courts and Supreme Court in recent seminars held in Delhi in the area of Intellectual Property Right. B.B. Nanda and R.K. Tewari observe that "For successful

---

46 *Supra* note 45.

47 Washington "Online auctions Top Internet Fraud grips, repon", *Hindustan Times* Feb. 2: 2001.

48 Report on E-Commerce, Hype gives way to reality 1996; Electronic commerce feds hangover, No. 1 (Business research publications) Jan. 1996.

49 Section 49 & 50.

prosecution of the cases involving computers, it is essential that the Judiciary is made aware of the technological aspects involved to appreciate the evidence placed before them and to understand various hurdles in the path of investigators.[50]

VII. EXTRA TERRITORIAL JURISDICTION

As per the nature of crime which may be committed globally from any territory outside India, a very satutory provision has been added to the Act which is armed with extra territorial jurisdiction. It says that the provisions of the Act shall apply to any offence or contravention committed outside India by any person irrespective of his nationality if it involves a computer, computer system or computer net work located in India.[51] In other words even though the perpetrator of crime is out of the territorial limit of India, but if his acts or omissions amount to an offence or contravention of the provisions of the Act, he is liable to be punished by an Indian court. So far so good. But the flrst question arises as to how to bring the criminal or contravener to the book and enforce the judgement against such criminal. Secondly in order to prosecute a person outside India, it must be ascertained through investigation in a foreign territory that such and such person is behind such contravention or offence. Easier said than done. Then comes the question of his arrest. Both of these problems have been discussed below.

VIII. CRIME IN FORIEGN TERRITORY

As the area of operation of internet users may expand from India to Europe, America, Australia or any country in Asia, it will not be possible to control or investigate the crime through a single agency. It is the need of the hour to establish units of the well trained investigators in all the Member States of World Intellectual Property Organisation (WIPO) with its Headquarters established in National Capitals. All these Headquarters should have link with Chief Headquarters under WIPO. This Chief Headquarter should co-ordinate with the Headquarters in Member Countries. Immediately after receiving any call from any member country, WIPO Chief quarter should establish contact with other Headquarters of the country from where the criminal is suspected to be operating. The investigators should be put in action to ascertain and pin point the individuals or organisations responsible for such crime. The police force should also be brought in action to assist them.

---

50 *Supra* note 3 at 105.

51 Section 75.

The Headquarters in National Capital should have units in every state. The state units should be supported with a well equipped laboratory to provide the scientiflc support to investigation. With passage of time and expansion of internet activity in villages, branches of these units could be opened at district level. Investigation and prosecution of transborder high tech crimes requires concerted effort and co-ordination of all States, irrespective of the fact as to where the crime has been committed. Law enforcement personnel should be well equipped and trained to combat with the crime. Through research, information and telecommunication systems should be so designed as to enable the investigators to help and prevent the abuse and detect network of undesirable and illegal activities. It should be conducive to collect evidence and effectively search and trace the criminal. Police investigators have to be properly trained in computer application programmes, as great challenges lie ahead for cyber police to play a crucial role in this area. "*Dealing with Cyber Crime needs a knack, aflinity and a habit to play around with computers.* This culture has to grow among the police and forensic scientists.[52] Global protection is necessary not to allow the computer criminals to flnd shelter or refuge in certain places from where they can operate safely and launch their attack. A very well devised scheme is required to be operated with co-ordination of Member nations, taking into consideration the need of international trade relations and the liberty of the individuals.

IX. ENFORCEMENT OF JUDGEMENTS

With regard to enforcement of judgements in India delivered in foreign courts or vise versa, it is suggested that they should be enforced in India and abroad like arbitration awards[53] or alternatively as foreign judgments arising out of litigation. So far as the enforcement of a foreign award in England or an English award in a foreign country is concerned, one has to distinguish between the enforcement under *Geneva Protocol,* (1923) and *Geneva Convention,* (1927) and that under the New York Convention (195 8). Enforcement under *Geneva Protocol,* and *Convention* is regulated by the *Arbitration Act,* 1950 and these awards are known as foreign awards. Enforcement under the New York convention is possible under the Arbitration Act 1975 and these awards are known as Convention Awards. Some countries are parties to both – The *Geneva*

52 B.B. Nanda & Dr. R.K. Tewari Supre note 3 at III.

53 *See:* Schmittolfs Expon Trade (lnrernational Student Edition. 1993) "Enforcement of foreign Awards" P.P. 687 at etseq.

Convention and *New York Convention.* Where ever such a situation arises, enforcement is preferred under *New York Convention* as the same is easy to enforce. In addition to these two methods, a foreign arbitral award made in a country to which the *Foreign Judgement (Reciprocal Enforcement) Act,* 1933 is made applicable can be enforced in England and Wales upon registration, provided that it is enforceable in the country in which it is made in the same manner as a judgemment. However, enforcement of a foreign arbitral award is easier than to enforce a foreign judgment.[54]

Under *Geneva Convention,* a foreign award can be enforced in the English jurisdiction in the same manner as an English award, provided the arbitration Agreement is valid under its proper law. However, it will not be enforced if the same is contrary to English public policy. The application of these provisions depends upon reciprocity being granted by the country where the award is made. So far as law in India is concerned, the rules are similar in India. The provisions of *Geneva Protocol* (1923) and *Geneva Convention* (1927) were incorporated in the Arbitration (Protocol and convention) Act 1937. The requirements of *New York Convention,* 1958 were fulfllled by *Foreign Awards (Recognitions and Enforcement) Act* 1961. India had made two reservations while ratifying the convention that, that it would apply the convention for recognition and enforcement of award if it was made in the territory of another contracting state and it was reciprocal in nature. Second reservation related to application of the provisions of the Act to commercial awards only. The *Arbitration and Conciliation Act,* 1996 has repealed the Acts of 1937 and 1961. Subject to the provisions of section 34, an arbitral award will be enforced in India in the same manner as if it were a decree of the court.[55] Procedure For Enforcement of Awards under Conventions: Any person interested in enforcing a foreign award may apply in writing to a court of competent jurisdiction. A copy of the agreement or contract and that of award along with evidence of the fact that it is a foreign award is to be flled before the court. The court will issue notices to the parties to show cause as to why the award should not be filed. After the court is convinced that the foreign award is enforceable under the Act, it will pronounce judgement according to the award. This will be followed by a decree which is not appealable except in the cases where it is in excess of the award or is not in accordance with the award. Enforcement of award to which the Conventions do not apply:

---

[54] Schmittoft's Export Trade *op. cit. Supra* note 54 at 691.

[55] Section 36, Arbitration & Conciliation Act I996 Sec. 36.

The countries which are not parties to the *Geneva Convention* or *New York Convention,* their awards may be enforced on ground of justice, equity and good conscience.[56] The Jurisdiction of English Courts over Foreign Litigants: The English Courts have jurisdiction over claims arising from contractual relations :

1. If the defendant is resident in England and Wales and is served with a writ there.

2. If not in England (a) he has submitted to the jurisdiction of the English court or (b) The courts have assumed jurisdiction over him.

A. ***Service out of jurisdiction***: There are two different rules for persons residing outside the jurisdiction of English court but not having submitted to their jurisdiction. Para 1 of Rules of Supreme Court order II deals with service on persons living in non convention country and Para (2) with convention country. Under the first rule, the leave of the court is required not only if the contract is to be performed in England but even if it is formed in England and is to be governed by English law. But if the service is to be carried out in a convention (Hague convention) country, only the place of performance is relevant.

B. ***Non-Convention Service out of the Jurisdiction***: Assumed jurisdiction over persons in non-convention States shall only be exercised subject to fulfillment of two conditions (1) The plaintiff must have a good arguable case in his favour and (2) the court must be satisfied that it is a fit case to grant leave to serve abroad. The court is "exceedingly careful before it allows a writ to be served out of the jurisdiction".[57] The court will refuse leave if it feels that the defendant will be put to great inconvenience or if the full disclosure is not made. Where the English court assumes jurisdiction over persons and companies abroad, with full service affected thereon, the defendant must defend his case, failing which the court may grant exparte decree.

C. ***Effecting Service Abroad:*** Service abroad is effected by British Consular Authority in the country where the defendant resides or in pursuance of procedure laid down by Hague Convention on the senice Abroad of Judicial and Extra Judicial Documents in Civil & Commercial Matters of Nov. 15, 1965. This is also known as Service Convention. Under

---

[56] For detailed study see G.K. Kwatra " The Arbitration & Conciliation Law of India, Chapter VIII.

[57] Per pearson J. in societe general: *de Paris* V. *American G. & C. corporation* 1944 60 T.L.R. 265.

the convention, each contracting state has appointed a central authority which looks into requests for service from other States and executes them.

D. ***Concurrent Proceeding:*** In certain cases, more than one National court may have jurisdiction in certain matters. Here the plaintiff looks for the most beneficial forum. This is known as Forum Shopping. Thus where the plaintiff commences litigation in England as well as other foreign country, the defendant may apply to English Courts either to stop proceedings or restrain the plaintiff to proceed in a foreign court. The English court on such application may stop the proceeding, if it comes to the conclusion that the foreign court is the "Natural and Appropriate Forum" to deal with the dispute.[58]

If the English court feels that the proceedings in foreign court are oppressive to the defendant, it may grant injunction. While resolving a foreign dispute, the British court resort to the following injunction:

E. ***The Mareva Injunction:*** Where English courts have jurisdiction over a dispute, and the proceedings are either pending or contemplated thereon, an interim injunction may be obtained against the defendant freezing his assets and not to dispose of or remove them. The purpose of injunction is "simply to prevent the injustice of a defendant removing or dissipating his assets so as to cheat the plaintiff fruit of his claim.[59] Mareva Injunctions are primarily an interim conservation order granted on the undertaking of plaintiff to indemnify the defendant in case he loses the action. The court may order the defendant or other third person having knowledge of the defendant's assets anywhere in the world to furnish full information. In Mareva injunction, the rights of third party are not affected. The assets of the defendant may be frozen and the defendant may be ordered not to go abroad and surrender his passport till the case is decided.

F. ***Anton Pillar Injunction:*** This is an injunction which authorises the plaintiff to enter the premises of the defendant and to inspect and take away specified documents or property. It is named after a case *Anton Pillar K.G.V. Manufacturing Process Ltd.*,[60] and is granted by virtue of *Supreme Court Act* 1981.[61]

---

[58] The Abiden Daver (1984) A.C. 398; *Aerospatiale* V. *Lee Kui Jak* (1987) A.C. 871.

[59] Per Llyod J. in P.C.W. (undertakings) *Agencies Ltd.* V. *P.S. Dixon* (1983) 2 Lloyd's report 197, 202.

[60] (1976) Ch. 55.

[61] Section 33.

G. ***Enforcement of Judgements Abroad***: There are two methods to enforce the judgements outside the jurisdiction of the court which pronounced it: (1) A new action founded on the judgement has to commence in the foreign country in which it sought to enforce the judgements, or it may be possible to pass the judgement in foreign country and then enforce it in the same manner in England as if it were the judgements made in the foreign country.[62] As the above methods of enforcement of judgement at international level are mostly confined to commercial matters, they cannot be enforced without amending the relevant conventions and other related matters connected therewith. It will be in fltness of things that World Intellectual Property Organization (WIPO) should take a lead and co-ordinate with member countries in this area to make treaty for enforcement of national judgements in foreign courts.

H. ***Indian Law Relating to Foreign Judgements:*** The provisions of Civil Procedure Code on this point clearly state that "a judgement delivered by a foreign court of competent jurisdiction can be enforced by an Indian court".[63] However, this is subject to exceptions that they are not delivered by a competent court or are not on merits or are against International Law or Indian Law or are opposed to natural justice or are obtained by fraud or founded on breach of Indian Law.[64] Upon the production of any document, purporting to be a certified copy of a foreign judgement, the court shall presume, that such a judgement was pronounced by a court of competent jurisdiction.[65] If anybody submits himself to the jurisdiction of Indian Court, the court will have jurisdiction. It may be express or implied. A foreign judgement can be enforced by filing a suit on such judgement. The general principle of law is that in order to enforce a foreign judgement, it must be in the form of a decree of the court of that country. The decree shall be conclusive and the Indian courts cannot go into the merits of the original claim.

I. ***Execution Proceedings:*** Where a certified copy of a decree of any of the superior courts of any reciprocating territory has been filed in a District court, the decree may be executed in India as if it had been passed by that District Court. However, the judgement debtor may challenge

---

62 For a comprehensive study see Schmittotfs Export Trade, op. cit. chap. 32 "International Commercial Litigation".

63 N.C.K. Takwani, *Civil Procedure Code* "Foreign Judgements" part two, chapter IV (4th ED) at 81.

64 Section 13, *Civil Procedure Code,* 1908.

65 *Narsimha Rao* V. *Venkata Lakshmi* (1991) 3 SCC 451.

such decree under any of the grounds mentioned in Section 13 of Civil Procedure Code.[66]

X. CONCLUSIONS AND SUGGESTIONS

Computer is the hub round which electronic means of communications revolve. Software in computer is the life blood of computer. It is copyrightable under *Copyright Act,* 1957 and also *Trade Related Aspect of Intellectual Property Rights* (TRIPs) which is a vital part of World Trade Organisation (WTO). It has been observed the though computer related activities are very useful and convenient mode of communication, but have also great nuisance value and damaging effect over the life and property of others. Therefore it is the dire necessity that its activities should be regulated and monitored properly to retain and promote its advantages and gains and to curb and keep a watch to eradicate and eliminate its ugly and evil activities. This is the job of *Information Technology Act.* It deals with efflcient management of communication techniques for the greatest beneflt of human society. In so doing, it has to adopt measure which may eliminate its evil effect. In order to achieve this result, the Act has for the flrst time declared certain activities on internet as an offence which attracts penalty by way of imprisonment and flne. Where ever, a person has no knowledge or has given no consent or has exercised due diligence to avoid unlawful activities, the Act exonerates such person from liability.

In order to keep a check on criminals in cyber crimes, a well trained and equipped police force, investigators with expert knowledge in computer forensics, a well trained and knowledgeable judiciary in the fleld of cyber crime, international co-ordination in tracking the criminals and acting cautiously by individuals in relation to financial matters is very essential. With a co-ordinated effort at all levels, only the problem of elimination of cyber crimes can be tackled. The problems of the enforcement of the judgements of the court can be tackled by adopting the rules of enforcement of commercial arbitration awards or enforcement of foreign judgements with certain modifications in the old conventions and treaties which only confine its operation to commercial matter. The most effective way of enforcing them will be to make a treaty under WIPO with the co-ordination of the member countries. It should not be difficult at all as it is the need of time and all are victims of the tyranny of cyber criminals.

[66] Section 44-A CPC.

11

Copyright Protection of Content on Websites: Legal Challenges

Raman Mittal

I. INTRODUCTION

The Websites are soaked in information, much of it with varying degrees of copyright protection. In fact, the reality is that almost everything on the Net is protected by copyright law. E-business Websites are a composition of materials, often consisting of words, graphics, audio, and video that are expressed to the consumer as information content. The owners and Website developers carefully select the content to sell the company's product or service. The subject matter expressed in the site is an electronic publication of this content. Since, designing, producing, and maintaining a sophisticated Website is very expensive, protecting content ownership is extremely important. Electronic commerce will continue to be highly competitive. As Websites become more and more interactive with consumers, their creation, design, and maintenance place enormous demands on innovative marketing techniques that should be legally protected.

Never before has it been so easy to violate a copyright owner's exclusive right to copy the material. Everyone with a computer and an Internet connection creates his own Web pages and thus become a publisher. Hence the rules that once applied to only a few companies bind million of people now. Imagine having paid a Website developer hundreds of thousands of rupees to launch a killer application and acquiring millions of Rupees from a venture capitalist firm, only to discover that another e—business is using your online material. Or consider a scenario where your Website is linked to an e-business that displayed copyrighted material without the owner's consent. Could your company be liable under a theory of copyright infringement? This paper highlights the scenario when contents of your Website are exploited by others without your permission or knowledge. The discussion is centered on copyright issues involved in the practices of linking, inlining and framing technologies which are normally being used on the Internet.

II. RIGHTS OF AN E—BUSINESS

A. ***Copyright Owner***: Copyright is a bundle of exclusive rights granted to the owner by law. E- business owners of a copyright work contained in a Website have the following exclusive statutory rights which, along with other rights, collectively define the scope of the copyright.

B. ***Right of Reproduction***: Of all the people in the world the copyright owner alone has the right to reproduce the work. Copyright infringement in the online environment often involves a violation of the reproduction right that occurs by transferring data from one computer to another.

C. ***Right of Distribution***: Since a copyright is the exclusive property of the owner, the right to exercise property interests such as selling, renting or leasing the copyright, is protected by the law. A person, who does not own the copyright and makes it available on a bulletin board service, can be liable for copyright infringement.

In a U.S. case, *Playboy Enter. Inc.* v. *Frenal*[1], the "court held that when unauthorized photographs of Playboy Enterprises were downloaded to a bulletin board system by the defendant's subscribers, the plaintiff's exclusive right of distribution was infringed by customers of the defendant. The bulletin board operator, as the defendant in this case, has an obligation to monitor its system to ensure that copyrighted documents are not being displayed and "downloaded" by its customers.

In a 1997 case, *Marobie-Fl. Inc.* v. *National Ass'n of Fire Equip. Distribs.*[2], unauthorized copies of the plaintiff's electronic clip art files were placed on the defendant's Web page. The court held that this constituted an infringing distribution because the files were available for downloading by Internet users.

Since this has become a common practice, Web designers as well as managers should be careful in obtaining permission from the owner of clip art if they want to use it on their Websites.

D. ***Right of Communication to the public***: Under the *Copyright Act,* 1957 this right is defined as:[3]

---

1 839 F. Supp. 1552 (M.D. Fla. 1093).

2 9833 F. Supp. 1167 (ND. III).

3 Copyright Act, 1957. S. 2[ff].

Making any work available for being seen or heard or otherwise enjoyed by the public directly or by any means of display or diffusion other than by issuing copies of such work regardless of whether any member actually sees, hears or otherwise enjoys the work so made available. This definition covers the communication of contents of a Website on the Internet.

III. LINKING

E-business Websites often link to other sites that provide the user with merchandise, helpful information, or resources related to the product and/or service being offered. The interactive feature of the Internet's most popular information access tool, the World Wide Web, to hyperlink[4] defines its very culture distinguishing it from any other communications medium. On the Internet, a link is a selectable connection from one word, picture, or information object to another. Links usually appear as highlighted, underlined, otherwise prominent text or picture that can be selected by the user (with a mouse or in some other fashion), resulting in the immediate delivery and view of another file. The highlighted object is referred to as an anchor. The anchor reference and the object referred to constitute a link. A link is simply a connection between the content of two different files or between different parts of a single file. A link may lead either to another file in the same Website, or to a file on a different computer located elsewhere on the Internet. Internet browsers automatically decipher the instructions given by links and retrieve the specified file. A single Web page may contain many links to other Web pages. That same page may itself be the 'destination' of hundreds, or thousands of other links on other pages.

Linking is the *sine qua non* for the World Wide Web and in fact links are what make the World Wide Web a web. Links allow quick access to information that otherwise could take much time and effort to find. Consequently, if linking were disallowed or made illegal, the Web would no longer exist. Linking is of two types: Surface linking: When the home page of a site is linked it is the case of surface linking. Deep linking: When a link bypasses the home page and goes straight to an internal page within the linked site it is the case of deep linking.

The Web was built for the purpose of enabling hypertext capabilities, allowing one site to link to and access another. In most cases, the owner

---

4 On the Web or other hypertext systems, hyperlink is a synonym for both link and hypertext link.

of a Web page will desire the page to be the destination of as many links as possible because more links would mean more hits, and more hits would in turn mean wider dissemination of whatever information the page is designed to get across. To date, Website owners have made money primarily from the sale of advertising at their sites. The advertising rate is set keeping in mind the number of people who visit the site. From a revenue perspective, Website owners should encourage the practice of linking. The conventional view then has held that sites welcome linking from others because it increases traffic, advertising rates, and hence, revenue.

The problem arises only with regard to the practice of deep linking. The home page of a Website is used as the entry point to information contained within the Website and welcomes users, explains the nature of the site and offers links that allow the user to navigate through the site. Deep links defeat a Website's intended method of navigation. Further deep links may "steal" traffic from the linked site's homepage thereby decreasing the revenue that could be generated from advertising that is dependant on the traffic onto the site.

IV. JUDICIAL RECOGNITION TO LINKING

A link is just a URL, the Internet address of a Website and therefore like a street address is not copyrightable. But this technology of hyperlinking may aid in the distribution of creative material that belongs to someone else. In the *Ticketmaster Corp.* v. *Microsoft Corp.* case, the plaintiff, Ticketmaster Corporation sued Microsoft for Microsoft's practice of linking, without permission, deep within its site rather than to the home page, and claimed, among other things, that Microsoft effectively diverted advertising revenue that otherwise would have gone to the plaintiff. Ticketmaster Corporation had also entered into contracts with other firms whereby those firms had agreed to pay to link to the Ticketmaster site. Free linking by Microsoft to the plaintiff's site could have devalued those contractual relationships. Ticketmaster had also contracted to give MasterCard prominence at the Ticketmaster site. Microsoft's bypassing of the home page threatened the ability of Ticketmaster to comply with that contract. Allowing such a free link undercut Ticketmaster's fiexibility both in designing its site and in its marketing efforts and arrangements with other sites. During the pendency of the court proceedings the parties entered into a settlement agreement whereby Microsoft agreed not to link to pages deep within the Ticketmaster site and agreed that the links will point visitors interested in purchasing tickets to the ticketing service's home page.

In a Scottish case, *Shetland Times, Ltd.* v. *Dr. Jonathan Wills* the plaintiff, the Shetland Times operates a Website through which it made available many of the items in the printed version of its newspaper. The defendants also owned and operated a Website on which they published a news reporting service. Defendants reproduced verbatim a number of headlines appearing in the Shetland Times. These headlines were hyperlinked to the plaintiff's site. Clicking on the headline took the reader to the internal pages in the plaintiff's site on which the related story was found. The judge agreed that the plaintiff had presented at least a *prima facie* case of copyright infringement based upon the United Kingdom's law governing cable television program providers. He found that the articles were being sent by the Shetland Times but through the Website maintained by the defendants. In the process, the front page of the Shetland Times' site (on which paid advertisements appeared) was bypassed, significantly diminishing the value of the site to potential advertisers. The court issued an interim interdict barring defendants, without the plaintiff's consent, from copying headlines from the plaintiff's newspaper onto their Website, and creating hyperlinks from those headlines to the location on the plaintiff's site on which the article described in the headline appears.

Thereafter, the case was settled out of court by the parties whereby the defendants agreed not to deep-link into the site of the plaintiffs. The case was expected to establish a legal precedent regarding the intellectual property rights of Internet companies, as no similar lawsuit has been fully resolved in court. These two well-known cases were settled out of court, and that therefore the decisions do not represent case law, but it is reasonable to draw some conclusions regarding sensible practice when linking. There have been many cases of unwanted linking to pages. An interesting (possibly apocryphal) case was where the parents of a dead girl had created an "in memorial" Website to her memory, only to find that there was unwanted linking to the page which had a photograph of the girl from an Internet service entitled "Babe of the Week".[6]

A few courts have now held that a hyperlink violates the law if it points to illegal material with the purpose of disseminating that illegal material. In *Intellectual Reserve, Inc.* v. *Utah Lighthouse Ministry, Inc.*[7], the Plaintiff, Intellectual Reserve, held a copyright in the Church Handbook

---

5 [1997] FSR 604.

6 http://www.freepintcom/issues/O70I99.htm?FreePint_Session=89034776777142855e 2ff46bf2679c71 #feature.

7 75 F. Supp. 2d 1290(1). Utah. Dec. 6. 1999).

of Instructions. After being directed by the court to remove the Handbook from its Website, defendants posted a message on its Website that informed users that the Handbook was online. The message went on to provide users with the URLs of three Websites at which the Handbook was posted.[8] Plaintiff sought a preliminary injunction enjoining defendants from continuing to post such messages to their site, which plaintiff claimed constituted contributory infringement of its copyright in the Handbook. The court issued the requested injunctive relief and further held that by posting a message on their Website providing users with the location of infringing materials and apparently aiding a user in viewing the infringing Websites, the defendants had committed contributory infringement.

What liability is there for the content on a linked site? For example, if you link to a site that includes illegal material, could you be liable? It may be best to post a disclaimer on your site indicating that the links are for information only, and do not constitute an endorsement or approval of the material on the linked sites. A surface link to a home page does not generally require permission. This position is based on the theory that going online creates an implied license for anyone with a computer to view the Website. Simply placing a surface link is no more an infringement than the library catalogue telling you it stocks a book is an invitation to you to photocopy it in its entirety.[9] But before linking deep within a Website the prudent course would be to seek permission. And for the creators of a Website who Want that it is not linked to a pornographic or shabby site could place a prohibition in its 'terms of use' similar to, "Do not link to this site without our express consent".

V. INLINING

In-line linking enables a Web page to summon different elements from diverse pages or servers to create a new Web page. Instead of copying the elements to the composite page, the elements are linked in by "pulling in" graphic or image files from another site and displaying on the composite Web page. Thus, the composite page would consist of a series of links to other sites and servers. While browsing the composite page, the page directs the browser to get the pictures, graphics etc. from the original sources. An example would be a Web page on art that contains images stored around the world. The Web page could contain the text: "See my favourite paintings". Using an IMG link, the Web page could

---

8 http://www.phillipsnizcr.com/int-anl 76.htm.

9 Cyber Law: Text and Cases, Ferrera, lichtenstein. Reader, August, Schiano at 71 (West 2001).

then direct the visiting browser to retrieve the images of famous paintings from the Web page of various museums and place it immediately below the text. To the end-user, the integration of the two pieces of content (text and pictures) is seamless, despite the fact that they were taken from two very different sources. The viewer cannot distinguish that the image has originated at and been imported from a separate site and may never come to know that it was not created or stored at the site being visited by him. In this respect, inlining is different from deep linking where the user is usually aware that he has "changed pages", either from the different appearance of the newly accessed page, or from the change in the URL address display in the Web browser.

When the content of another page is incorporated into a page by means of an unauthorized IMG link, there is no direct copyright infringement by the creator of the link. This is because the link's creator never copies the pirated content; instead merely provides a visiting browser with instructions to retrieve the image, which is then incorporated into the overall page on the user's site. Thus the only person who copies the protected image is the final user. This does not mean that the creator of the link escapes liability. Though, inlining does not directly infringe the Web author's reproduction or distribution right, it is nevertheless aiding in the rights being implicated.[10] By inlining the 'linking site could take some elements from the linked site's multimedia settings and create it's own, thereby affecting the right of making a derivative work of the linked site because taking some elements from the multimedia setting and combining them with some other could well fit into the definition of adaptation.

Inlining brings in the question of moral rights as well. Copyrighted graphic image could be pulled into a site with its image appearing on a single page combined with other images, thus creating another work virtually new and different from the original thereby strongly implicating the right to integrity of the work. Moreover the user is confused about the original owner and hence may never come to know about the original owner, so this also affects the right to be identified as an author.

In the USA the Dilbert dispute, though did not involve the filing of a complaint or any judicial determinations, is one of the few inline controversies and thus serves as a point of discussion for these links. Dan Wallach created "The Dilbert Hack Page," a site that presented the Dilbert comic strip *via* inlining to the United Media Website, where the

[10] By virtue of s. 63 (b) of the Copyright Act. 1957 any person who knowingly infringes or abets the infringement of copyright is made liable.

comic strips were located. The images appeared on Wallach's Website via inlining. United Media, speaking for United Feature Syndicate, Inc., owner of the copyright in the comic strip, requested by letter to Wallach to discontinue the link. United Media contended that "the names or likenesses of the Dilbert comic strips and all other United Media intellectual property cannot be used—on the World Wide Web or elsewhere - without the express, written consent of UFS." United Media asserted that Wallach's inline links to copyrighted material constituted an unauthorized display of a copyrighted work, a violation of the Copyright Act. To avoid litigation, Wallach removed the page.

Even if a Web page allows others to link to it, it cannot be presumed that it has also granted permission to link to individual elements of the page. If someone were to create a composite Web page by summoning various elements from a different Website without necessary permission, it is clear that such a use would not be protected as fair use. By stripping an element of its context, you also strip many of the copyright privileges that may have been attached. It is considered a breach of net etiquette to link to anyone else image through an IMG link without permission. Consequently, one should obtain permission from the copyright owner of the image prior to creating the link.

VI. FRAMING

Web browsers allow Web authors to divide pages into "frames". A frame is an independently controllable window on a Website through which pages from another Website can be viewed. Since it is possible for a site to call a frame's contents from a different location, a programmer might "frame" another's Web content beneath his own navigation or banners. This allows him to use creative content owned by another entity to sell banner advertising on its on site. A typical use of frames is to have one frame containing a selection menu in one frame and another frame that contains the space where the selected (linked to) files appear.[11] The technology of framing was developed by Netscape and was introduced in 1996 and is now a common technology used on many Web pages, but sometimes it can lead to legal problems for those who use it. The creator of a frame does not literally "copy" the contents of the framed page but only directs the user's browser to summon content from another Website and show the same along with the content of the framing site. Since the URL of the framed Web page does not appear on the screen, the user accessing a framed site may not perceive the site as being framed and

---

[11] http://searchwebservices.teachtarget.com/sDefinition/0,,26_gic212154,00.html.

may attribute the appropriated material to the home site owner. This could implicate the right of the author to be identified as such, since the user never comes to know that he is viewing content from a different site. Since the author alone has the right to distribute the content, by making a frame, the framing site is actually aiding in the distribution of the content of the framed site and also appropriating the contents to it.

In *Washington Post Co.* v. *Total News, Inc.*[12] The Washington Post filed a complaint against an online news site, Total News, the publisher of the Website www.totalnews.com. Total News, an aggregator of web news sources, employed frame technology to display news sites from around the Web. Total News had created pages with frames that contained hyperlinks to other news Websites, such as *The Washington Post, CNN, USA Today, Time and Sports Illustrated*, etc. Web users, therefore, could use www.totalnews.com to access articles from various sources. The Total News Website generated its revenue from advertising, which it placed in a static border frame. Clicking on a hyperlink to 'The Washington Post' within the Total News Web page displayed the content of The Washington Post page within a frame that was surrounded by Total News's URL, logo, banner, advertisements and information.

Six content providers - CNN, Time-Warner, Reuters, The Washington Post, The Wall Street Journal and the LA Times, sued Total News, claiming that such framing was "the Internet equivalent of pirating copyrighted material. They also alleged misappropriation, trademark infringement and trademark dilution. The plaintiffs complained that Total News has designed a parasitic Website that republishes the news and editorial content of others 'Websites in order to attract both advertisers and users. Total News settled the case by agreeing to link to, rather than frame, the Post's Web pages of various plaintiffs and the court did not have an opportunity to decide any of the legal issues that were raised by the plaintiffs.

In, *Futuredontics Inc.* v. *Applied Anagramic Inc.*[13] Applied Anagramic, Inc., a dental services Website, framed the content of a competing site. The frames included information about Applied Anagramic as Well as its trademark and links to all of its Web pages. A district court ruled that the addition of the frame somewhat modified the appearance of the linked site and such modifications could, without authorization, amount to infringement. Despite the paucity of judicial guidance in this area it could be stated that framing could amount to copyright infringement. Therefore,

---

[12] 97 Civ 1190 (S.D.N.Y.).

[13] 1997 46 USPQ 2d 2005 (co. Calif. 1997).

the use of frames to contain linked content should only be carried out with the express permission of the owner of the framed materials.

The copyright notice consists of elements that include the copyright symbol and/or the term "Copyright", the year of copyright, and the name of the copyright holder. The © Copyright Symbol is generally the standard identifier of a Copyright Notice, and is required in many foreign countries in order for copyright protection to attach. But under Indian law putting a notice on a copyrighted work is not a requirement. As evidenced by the preponderance of Websites bearing them, it is generally a good idea to put copyright notice on a Website. In the Internet environment, varying HTML standards and browser specifications can result in transforming the nice "c-in—circle" symbol into a meaningless "#146", "& copy" or "& copr". Consequently, it is recommended that any Web copyright notice use both the symbol © and the full word "Copyright" to avoid as many of these problems as possible. In order that your Website is not unauthorized linked by some other site, it is also advisable to put a notice on your Website stating that links to this site may not be made without permission.

VII. CONCLUSION

Intellectual property laws are based on notions of sovereignty and territoriality. The Internet, in contrast, like the movement of weather within the global climate, largely ignores distinctions based on territorial borders. The Internet, the world's biggest copy machine, has been described as the greatest threat to copyright. The free flow of information that is the very culture and value of the World Wide Web conflicts with this copyright interests. Never before has it has been so easy to violate a copyright owner's exclusive right to copy the material. The intellectual property discipline is confronted with new issues generated by the emergence of the Internet. Each of them must successfully resolve these issues in order for electronic commerce to flourish.It is therefore important to adjust the legal system to respond to the new technological environment in an effective and appropriate way, and to do so quickly, because technologies and markets are evolving rapidly.

Accordingly, the goal of policy makers has been to achieve an appropriate balance in the law, providing strong and effective rights, but within reasonable limits and with fair exceptions. If this effort is successful, the result should be a positive impact from all perspectives. Copyright will prevail in the digital world as a vital instrument of cultural and economic control. The function of courts is to interpret the Copyright Act within the context of our current environment of information technology. As stated by the U.S. Supreme Court, "From the beginning, the law of copyrights has developed in response to significant changes in technology."[14] The role of the court, however, remains constant. It must maintain the delicate balance between the exclusive rights of copyright owners and the public's right to have access to information.

[14] *Sony Corp.* v. *Universal Studios*. Inc, 464 U.S. 417 (1984).

12

Regulatory Mechanism and Challenges in Controlling Cyber Crimes

Ram Prakash Sethi

I. CHALLENGES TO CYBERSPACE

The problems and prospects of copyright and information technology need to be deliberated in the context of present day jurisprudence. The subject is referable to the extensive use of information technology all over the world which has resulted in enhanced efficiency, effectiveness and optimum use of resources. The copyright law is concerned with the negative right of preventing copying of the physical material in the field of literature and arts. *Trade and Merchandise Marks Act* protects the patent, trade mark and design giving the registered proprietor an exclusive right to the registered material. The prohibition contained in rights in patent and copyright extend to the unauthorised manufacture or reproduction, so long as the exclusive right rests. Copyright has been held to be not the mere creature of the statute but a natural and civil right. The moral basis of the copyright is that the man is entitled to the fruits of its mental faculties as much as he is entitled to the fruits of his mechanical labour. The law rests on the English Commandment - *thou shall not steal*. It does not permit one man to make a profit and appropriate himself what has been produced by the labour, skill and capital of another. Blackstone in his commentaries Vol.II at page p.406 has stated:

> There is still another aspect of property and this is the right which an author may be supposed to have in his own original literary compositions: so that no other person without his leave may publish or make profit of the copies. When a man by the exertion of his rational powers has produced an original work, he seems to have clearly a right to dispose of that identical work as he pleases and any attempt to vary the disposition he has made to it appears to be an invasion of that right.

II.FOUNDATION OF COPYRIGHT LAW

The United Nations Declaration of Human Rights adopted by the United Nations on 'December 10, 1948 proclaimed the moral basis of intellectual property in Article 27 of the Declaration as follows:

1. Everyone has the right freely to participate in the cultural life of the community to enjoy the arts and to share in scientific advancement and its benefits. (2) Everyone has the right to the protection of the moral and material interests resulting from any scientific, literary or artistic production of which he is the author."

Article VI-A of *Berne Copyright Convention* signed on 9th September, 1886 analysed the moral basis of the copyright as under:

1. Independently of the author's economic rights, and even after the transfer of the said rights, the author shall have the right to claim authorship of the work and to object to any distortion, mutilation or other modification of, or other derogatory action in relation to, the said work, which would be prejudicial to his honour or reputation.
2. The rights granted to the author in accordance with the preceeding paragraph shall, after his death, be maintained at least until the expiry of the economic rights, and shall be exercisable by the persons or institutions authorised by the legislation of the country where protection is claimed. However, those countries whose legislation, the moment of their ratification of or occasion to this Act, does not provide for the protection after the death of the author of all the rights set out in the preceding paragraph may provide that some of these rights may after his death cease to be maintained.
3. The means of redress for safeguarding the "rights granted by this Article shall be governed by the legislation of the country where protection is claimed."

III. COPYRIGHT & INFORMATION TECHNOLOGY

In India the *Copyright Act* of 1957 as amended from time to time has only consolidated the already prevalent law relating to copyright. The importance of copyright has assumed great significance in the present day system based upon the information technology and its on-going rapid development. Computers, internet, convergence technology, electronic mail, video conferencing, fascimile machines, etc., have provided the ability to process large volume data with speed and accuracy by exchange of useful information between different locations facilitating higher quality decision making process. The information technology development can well be held to be a information revolution which is likely to tackle enormous problems being faced in various fields of economic activity of the society. It can help in solving the enormous problems facing the judiciary due to arrears, backlog and delays by resorting to automation in the courts.

The *Law Commission of India* in its 121st Report has taken note of the importance of information technology by devoting a whole chapter to technological advancements and its use in the context of judicial appointments. The administrative system has been computerised in the Supreme Court. The query system introduced facilitates the litigants anywhere in the country in obtaining information on the status of a case filed in the Supreme Court through NICNET. Various High Courts in the country have adopted a comprehensive case management system with the help of computers and internet technology. The use of the computers can improve the case management, file management and docket management in the courts.

The Indian Institute of Management, Bangalore, in its Background Paper has pointed out that the following are the areas where computers can facilitate in enhanced productivity and reduction in delays.

a) Legal Information Data Bases.

b) On line query system for precedents, citations, codes, statutes, etc.

c) Generation of Cause Listing and on line statistical reports.

d) On line Caveat matching

e) On line updating of data, monitoring and "flagging" of events.

f) Pooling of orders and judgments

g) Daily List generation with historical data of each case.

h) Word processing with standard templates including generation of notices/processes.

i) Access to international data bases.

j) Feed back reports for use at various Levels.

Various countries in the world particularly the USA and UK have been extensively using information technology for creating initial court records for registering a case, issuance of summons, storing electronic copies of evidence, generating cause lists, updating records and maintaining court diary, etc.

IV. CHALLENGES OF CYBER CRIME

Cyber crimes and regulatory mechanism is a challenge of the 21st Century. The word "Cyber" has its origin in the word "Cybernetics" which means the science of communications and automatic control of systems in both machines and living things. The present day modern life is just unimaginable without the modern systems of communications. Since the time immemorial the communication has remained the part and parcel of human life. In the Stone Age the people used to communicate with each other by gestures and used to send messages from one place to another with the beat of drums. Later on, when the mankind learnt the art of writing, the written communications took over the beats of drums and with the passage of time came the telephone system. Now in this jet age new ways of communication such as computer, internet, cell phones, fax, etc. have replaced the old systems. These new systems are known as cyber-systems as they are controlled by machines.

It is true that the progress of the information technology has placed the mankind with positive results, however, it is equally true that with the advent of the systems based upon information technology, the anti-social elements and criminals have changed their style of functioning by resorting to the criminal activities by using the information technology facilities and finding out innovative ideas to commit the crimes. By sending messages on internet the criminals send their messages in absolute confidentiality. It has become very difficult for the law enforcement agencies to keep a track on the criminal activities. It is the need of the hour to find out ways and means to combat these problems and make these systems society-friendly.

V. ENFORCEMENT OF CYBER CRIME

It has become essential for our law enforcement agencies to learn the art of collecting materials by the use of these very systems and use the said material as evidence against the criminals. We need to train our investigators to learn the complexity of these systems and the way to trace information and collect evidence so that the guilty could be brought to book. In these types of crimes the first and foremost problem which comes in the way is the jurisdiction of the agency as these crimes do not recognise the boundaries of countries. A criminal can commit a crime in another country while sitting in one country by using the electronic media. For this we have to change our laws and the legal system will have to be moulded in such a fashion that these crimes can be brought to book and guilty punished in accordance with law. To this direction India has taken a step by enacting the *Information Technology Act*, 2000 which is based on the UNCITRAL Model recommended by the General Assembly of the United Nations by a Resolution dated 30th January, 1997. Chapter 9 of this enactment deals with the civil wrongs committed by a person and there is a provision of paying damages by way of compensation for wrong doings against the computers and wrong doings by means of computers.

The crime relating to computers have been dealt with in Chapter 11 of the *Information Technology Act,* 2000. Tampering with computer documents, hacking of computer systems, publication of obscene information in electronic form, breach of confidentiality and privacy, misrepresentation and suppression of material before the controller or certifying authorities and publication of digital signature certificates, without such certificate have been issued by the authority or accepted by the person and use of digital signature certificates for a fraudulent purposes have been declared as serious offences under the Act. Section 75 of the Act deals with extra territorial operation by making it applicable to an offence or contravention committed outside India by any person if the act or conduct constituting the offence or contravention involves a computer, computer system or computer network located in India. A police Officer not below the rank of Deputy Superintendent of Police or any other officer of the Central or State Government have been duly authorised and empowered to enter any public place for the purpose of seizure and arrest without a warrant for the purposes of keeping a check on these crimes. Section 81 gives the Act overriding effect.

With the enactment of *Information Technology Act,* 2000 a lot of problems coming in the way of bringing the cyber offenders to book will come to an end but still we have to go a long way in nipping these evils in the bud as we have to train our personnel to unearth the criminal activities by using these very systems to help the society in eradicating the evils from the system so that the mankind can take benefit and march towards the way of development and prosperity. The problem of copyright and information technology requires solutions and remedies beneficial to the humanity all over the globe.

Appendices

APPENDIX-A: NATIONAL INTELLECTUAL PROPERTY RIGHTS POLICY, 2016

EXECUTIVE SUMMARY

Creativity and innovation have been a constant in growth and development of any knowledge economy. There is an abundance of creative and innovative energies flowing in India. India has a TRIPS compliant, robust, equitable and dynamic IPR regime. An all-encompassing IPR Policy will promote a holistic and conducive ecosystem to catalyse the full potential of intellectual property for India's economic growth and socio-cultural development, while protecting public interest. The rationale for the National IPR Policy lies in the need to create awareness about the importance of IPRs as a marketable financial asset and economic tool.

VISION STATEMENT

An India where creativity and innovation are stimulated by Intellectual Property for the benefit of all; an India where intellectual property promotes advancement in science and technology, arts and culture, traditional knowledge and biodiversity resources; an India where knowledge is the main driver of development, and knowledge owned is transformed into knowledge shared.

MISSION STATEMENT

Stimulate a dynamic, vibrant and balanced intellectual property rights system in India to:

- foster creativity and innovation and thereby, promote entrepreneurship and enhance socio-economic and cultural development, and
- focus on enhancing access to healthcare, food security and

* Government of India, Ministry of Commerce and Industry, Department of Industrial Policy & Promotion, 12th May, 2016.

environmental protection, among other sectors of vital social, economic and technological importance.

The Policy lays down seven Objectives which are elaborated with steps to be undertaken by the identified nodal Ministry/department. The Objectives are briefly mentioned below.

OBJECTIVE 1: IPR Awareness: Outreach and Promotion - *To create public awareness about the economic, social and cultural benefits of IPRs among all sections of society:* The 21st century belongs to the knowledge era and is driven by the knowledge economy. A nation-wide program of promotion should be launched with an aim to improve the awareness about the benefits of IPRs and their value to the rights-holders and the public. Such a program will build an atmosphere where creativity and innovation are encouraged in public and private sectors, R&D centers, industry and academia, leading to generation of protectable IP that can be commercialized. It is also necessary to reach out to the less-visible IP generators and holders, especially in rural and remote areas. The clarion call of the program would be the holistic slogan

"Creative India; Innovative India: रचनात्मक भारत; अभिनव भारत."

OBJECTIVE 2: Generation of IPRs - *To stimulate the generation of IPRs:* India has a large talent pool of scientific and technological talent spread over R&D institutions, enterprises, universities and technical institutes. There is a need to tap this fertile knowledge resource and stimulate the creation of IP assets. A comprehensive base line survey or IP audit across sectors will enable assessment and evaluation of the potential in specific sectors, and thus formulate and implement targeted programmes. Focus will be placed on facilitating researchers and innovators regarding areas of national priority. The corporate sector also needs to be encouraged to generate and utilize IPRs. Steps also need to be taken to devise mechanisms so that benefits of the IPR regime reach all inventors, especially MSMEs, start-ups and grassroot innovators.

OBJECTIVE 3: Legal and Legislative Framework - *To have strong and effective IPR laws, which balance the interests of rights owners with larger public interest:* The existing IP laws in India were either enacted or revised after the *TRIPS Agreement* and are fully compliant with it. These laws along with various judicial decisions provide a stable and effective legal framework for protection and promotion of IPRs. India shall remain committed to the *Doha Declaration on TRIPS Agreement and Public Health.* At the same time, India is rich in traditional medicinal knowledge which exists in diverse forms in our country, and it is important to protect it from misappropriation.

OBJECTIVE 4: Administration and Management - *To modernize and strengthen service-oriented IPR administration:* The Offices that administer the different Intellectual Property Rights (IPOs) are the cornerstone of an efficient and balanced IPR system. IPOs now have the twin challenges of making their operations more efficient, streamlined and cost effective, with expanding work load and technological complexity on one hand, and enhancing their user-friendliness by developing and providing value added services to the user community on the other. The administration of the *Copyright Act,* 1957 and the *Semiconductor Integrated Circuits Layout-Design Act,* 2000 is being brought under the aegis of DIPP, besides constituting a *Cell for IPR Promotion and Management* (CIPAM). This will facilitate more effective and synergetic working between various IP offices, as also promotion, creation and commercialization of IP assets.

OBJECTIVE 5: Commercialization of IPR - *Get value for IPRs through commercialization:* The value and economic reward for the owners of IP rights comes only from their commercialization. Entrepreneurship should be encouraged so that the financial value of IPRs maybe captured. It is necessary to connect investors and IP creators. Another constraint faced is valuation of IP and assessment of the potential of the IPRs for the purpose of marketing it. Efforts should be made for creation of a public platform to connect creators and innovators to potential users, buyers and funding institutions.

OBJECTIVE 6: Enforcement and Adjudication - *To strengthen the enforcement and adjudicatory mechanisms for combating IPR infringements:* There is a need to build respect for IPR among the general public and to sensitize the inventors and creators of IP on measures for protection and enforcement of their rights. At the same time, there is also a need to build the capacity of the enforcement agencies at various levels, including strengthening of IPR cells in State police forces. Measures to check counterfeiting and piracy also need to be identified and undertaken. Regular IPR workshops/colloquia for judges would facilitate effective adjudication of IPR disputes. It would be desirable to adjudicate on IPR disputes through specialised commercial courts. Alternative Dispute Resolution mechanism may also be explored.

OBJECTIVE 7: Human Capital Development - *To strengthen and expand human resources, institutions and capacities for teaching, training, research and skill building in IPRs:* In order to harness the full potential of IPRs for economic growth, it is essential to develop an increasing pool of IPR professionals and experts in spheres such as policy and law, strategy development, administration and enforcement. Such a reservoir of experts will facilitate in increasing generation of IP assets in the country and their utilization for development purposes.

IMPLEMENTATION

The present IP Policy aims to integrate IP as a policy and strategic tool in national development plans. It foresees a coordinated and integrated development of IP system in India and the need for a holistic approach to be taken on IP legal, administrative, institutional and enforcement related matters. While DIPP shall be the nodal point to coordinate, guide and oversee implementation and future development of IPRs in India, the responsibility for actual implementation of the plans of action will remain with the Ministries/ Departments concerned in their assigned sphere of work. Public and private sector institutions and other stakeholders, including State governments, will also be involved in the implementation process.

❑❑❑

NATIONAL INTELLECTUAL PROPERTY RIGHTS POLICY, 2016

INTRODUCTION

Creativity and innovation have been a constant in growth and development of any knowledge economy. There is an abundance of creative and innovative energies flowing in India. The evolution of the film and music industry; the contribution of the Indian pharmaceutical sector in enabling access to affordable medicines globally and its transformation to being the pharmacy of the world; a strong and dynamic software industry; a considerably diverse handicraft and textile industry; richness and versatility of the Indian systems of medicines such as *Ayurveda, Unani, Siddha* and *Yoga;* the advances made in the Indian space programme and the pioneering role of our scientists in keeping it cost effective; these are but a few examples of these energies.

While India has always been an innovative society, much of the intellectual property (IP) created remains unprotected both on account of lack of awareness and the perception that IP protection is either not required or that the process to obtain it is unnecessarily complicated. The rationale for the National IPR Policy lies in the need to create awareness about the importance of intellectual property rights (IPRs) as a marketable financial asset and economic tool.

India has robust IP laws and a strong IP jurisprudence. The legal framework does reflect the underlying policy orientation and national priorities, which have evolved over time, taking into account development needs and international commitments.

An all-encompassing IPR Policy will promote a holistic and conducive ecosystem to catalyse the full potential of intellectual property for India's economic growth and socio-cultural development, while protecting public interest. Such a Policy will nurture the IP culture, guiding and enabling all creators and inventors to realize their potential for generating, protecting and utilizing IPRs which would contribute to wealth creation, employment opportunities and business development.

This policy shall weave in the strengths of the Government, research and development organizations, educational institutions, corporate entities including MSMEs, start-ups and other stakeholders in the creation of an innovation-conducive environment. It will complement the strengths of our substantive laws with transparent, predictable and efficient administrative and procedural mechanisms as also well-informed adjudicatory structure.

OVERVIEW

The concrete measures taken by the Government in the last two decades in consonance with national development priorities and in conformity with international treaties, conventions and agreements to which India is a party has created and established a TRIPS compliant, robust, equitable and dynamic IPR regime. The continuous and unending improvements alongwith the sweeping and far-sighted changes at the legislative and administrative levels has resulted in strengthening the administration, management and enforcement of IPRs.

The statutes governing different kinds of IPRs in India are *Patents Act,* 1970; *Trade Marks Act,* 1999; *Designs Act,* 2000; *Geographical Indications of Goods (Registration and Protection) Act,* 1999; *Copyright Act,* 1957; *Protection of Plant Varieties and Farmers' Rights Act,* 2001; *Semiconductor Integrated Circuits Layout-Design Act,* 2000 and *Biological Diversity Act,* 2002.

The Department of Industrial Policy and Promotion (DIPP) is entrusted with matters concerning the specialised UN agency on IPRs, the *World Intellectual Property Organisation* (WIPO), including coordination with other concerned Ministries or Departments.

The *Controller General of Patents, Designs and Trade Marks* (CGPDTM) under the Department of Industrial Policy and Promotion, Ministry of Commerce and Industry is entrusted with the responsibility of administering the laws relating to Patents, Designs, Trade Marks and Geographical Indications within the territory of India. The CGPDTM presently functions through Patent Offices at four locations (Chennai, Delhi, Kolkata, and Mumbai), Trademarks Offices at five locations (Ahmedabad, Chennai, Delhi, Kolkata, and Mumbai), a Geographical Indications Registry at Chennai and a Designs Wing at Kolkata. The Office of CGPDTM is also in charge of the Rajiv Gandhi National Institute of Intellectual Property Management at Nagpur.

Copyrights were administered by the Ministry of Human Resource Development. The Copyright Act is comprehensive and with the recent amendments, the rights of creators have been strengthened.

The *Protection of Plant Varieties and Farmers' Rights Act,* 2001 is a *sui generis* legislation in India providing protection for plant varieties and rights of farmers and is under the aegis of the Ministry of Agriculture.

The Department of Information Technology was responsible for Semiconductor Integrated Circuits Layout-designs; the first registration under the *Semiconductor Integrated Circuits Layout-Design Act* was granted in October 2014.

The preservation of biological diversity in India is under the Ministry of Environment and Forests; the Biological Diversity Act 2002 provides mechanism for regulating access and ensuring fair and equitable sharing of benefits arising out of the use of biological resources and associated traditional knowledge.

India has always been conscious of its obligations in the international arena, and has acceded to a number of international conventions to further the cause of IPRs globally. India was the first country to ratify the *Marrakesh Treaty* 2013 for Access to published works by visually impaired persons. The accession to the *Madrid Protocol* in 2013 is a step towards global alignment for proprietors of marks. The Indian Patent office has been recognized as an *International Search Authority* and an *International Preliminary Examination Authority.*

The IPR regime in India has adequate safeguards in the form of judicial review and appellate provisions. Indian courts have consistently enforced IPRs, with judgements clearly expressing the intent and purpose of our laws. The *Intellectual Property Appellate Board* hears appeals arising from the decisions of Controllers of Patents as also Registrars of Trade Marks and GIs.

In a slew of initiatives, the IP offices under the CGPDTM have been modernized and there is a perceptible change for the better. Conscious efforts have been made to develop a robust e-service delivery system, including real-time public dissemination of dynamic IP knowledge through e-enabled innovative tools.

VISION STATEMENT

An India where creativity and innovation are stimulated by Intellectual Property for the benefit of all; an India where intellectual property promotes advancement in science and technology, arts and culture, traditional knowledge and biodiversity resources; an India where knowledge is the main driver of development, and knowledge owned is transformed into knowledge shared.

MISSION STATEMENT

Stimulate a dynamic, vibrant and balanced intellectual property rights system in India to:

- Foster creativity and innovation and thereby, promote entrepreneurship and enhance socio-economic and cultural development, and

- Focus on enhancing access to healthcare, food security and environmental protection, among other sectors of vital social, economic and technological importance.

OBJECTIVES

The Policy lays down seven Objectives which are elaborated with steps to be undertaken by the identified nodal Ministry/ department. The implementing or Nodal Ministry/ Department shall coordinate with all other concerned stakeholders, including other Ministries/ departments, towards attaining the objectives.

OBJECTIVE 1: IPR Awareness: Outreach and Promotion - *To create public awareness about the economic, social and cultural benefits of IPRs among all sections of society:* The 21st century belongs to the knowledge era and is driven by the knowledge economy- an economy that creates, disseminates and uses knowledge to enhance its growth and development. Traditionally, monetization of knowledge has never been the norm in India. While laudable and altruistic, this does not fit with the global regime of zealously protected IPRs. Hence, there is a need to propagate the value of transforming knowledge into IP assets. This requires a major paradigm shift of how knowledge is viewed and valued - not for what it *is,* but for what it can *become.*

Many IP holders are unaware of the benefits of IP rights or of their own capabilities to create IP assets or the value of their ideas. They are often discouraged by the complexities of the process of creating defendable IP rights. Conversely, they may be unaware of the value of others' IP rights and the need to respect the same. The policy proposes to tackle both perspectives through outreach and promotion programs.

A nation-wide program of promotion should be launched with an aim to improve the awareness about the benefits of IPRs and their value to the rights-holders and the public. Such a program will build an atmosphere where creativity and innovation are encouraged in public and private sectors, R&D centers, industry and academia, leading to generation of protectable IP that can be commercialized.

It is also necessary to reach out to the less-visible IP generators and holders, especially in rural and remote areas. Emphasis would be laid on creating awareness regarding the rich heritage of India in terms of our Geographical Indications, Traditional Knowledge, Genetic Resources, Traditional Cultural Expressions and Folklore.

The immediate economic rationale for individuals and the community, as well as the pride in being innovative, should be conveyed effectively to the public. The clarion call of the program would be the holistic slogan:

"Creative India; Innovative India: रचनात्मक भारत; अभिनव भारत."

The steps to be taken towards attaining this objective are outlined below:

1.1. Adopt the national slogan "Creative India; Innovative India" and launch an associated campaign on electronic, print and social media, including by linking the campaign with other national initiatives such as "Make in India", "Digital India", "Skill India", "Start Up India", "Smart Cities" and other new initiatives in the future;

1.2. Create a systematic campaign for promotion of India's IP strengths by conveying to all stakeholders the value and benefits of IP by:

1.2.1. Customizing programs for specific needs o f industries, MSMEs, start-ups, R&D institutions, science and technology institutes, universities and colleges, inventors and creators, entrepreneurs;

1.2.2. Reaching out to the less visible and silent IP generators and holders, especially in the rural and remote areas, through campaigns tailored to their needs and concerns. These would include small businesses, farmers/ plant variety users, holders of traditional knowledge, traditional cultural expressions and folklore, designers and artisans;

1.2.3. Including case studies of successful use of IPRs in campaigns to create value in the respective domains;

1.2.4. Promoting the idea of high quality and cost-effective innovation as a particularly Indian competence leading to competitive advantage;

1.2.5. Involving eminent personalities as 'ambassadors' to spread awareness and importance of IP in India;

1.2.6. Using audio/ visual material in print/ electronic/ social media for propagation;

1.2.7. Creating moving exhibits (e.g. a train with a theme that will crisscross the nation, road shows) that can travel to all parts of the country;

1.2.8. Creating materials for IP promotion in multiple languages and pictorial form for those who cannot read;

1.2.9. Studying best practices and success stories in other countries to design and launch public outreach programs.

1.3. Create awareness programs specifically targeting industry and R&D entities, both private and public by:

1.3.1. Providing scientists/researchers with a deeper level of understanding about the need to protect their inventions even before publishing;

1.3.2. Engaging public funded research organizations and the private sector to create campaigns highlighting the process of IP creation and the value generated therefrom;

1.3.3. Encourage multi-national corporations and other large corporate entities to develop IP programs for their employees and adapt and propagate them to the public;

1.3.4. Creating materials for MSMEs highlighting special support mechanisms for them to develop and protect IP.

1.4. Create well-publicized events and ongoing programs to emphasize the importance of IP by:

1.4.1. Partnering with industry bodies, large corporations and institutions of R&D and higher learning for such events, and consider establishment of Innovation, Creativity and IP museum(s);

1.4.2. Announcing with the help of State governments, Innovation and IP Days especially in major industrial, innovation and university clusters; celebrate 'World IP Day' in different cities and institutions;

1.4.3. Setting up India's 'Hall of Fame' to celebrate IP innovators and creators;

1.4.4. Instituting prizes and awards to encourage IP creation activity in specific sectors.

1.5. Create suitable course materials for:

1.5.1. Educational institutions at all levels to emphasize the importance of IP rights;

1.5.2. Online and distance learning programs for all categories of users;

1.5.3. Including IPRs in school curriculum at appropriate level.

1.6. Engage with the media to sensitize them regarding IP related issues.

OBJECTIVE 2: Generation of IPRs - *To stimulate the generation of IPRs:* The profile of IP filings and registrations/grants is one of the parameters, though not the only one, to assess the current status and potential of IP creation in a country. In India, the number of patent filings has increased in the last few years, but the percentage of filings by Indians is relatively low. In the case of trademarks, India is among the top five filers in the world, w i t h the majority being filed by Indians. The number of design applications filed is nowhere near India's potential, given its vast pool of designers, artisans and artists. India has a large talent pool of scientific and technological talent spread over R&D institutions, enterprises, universities and technical institutes. There is a need to tap this fertile knowledge resource and stimulate the creation of IP assets.

GIs is an area of strength and optimism for India, where it has accorded protection to a number of hand-made and manufactured products, especially in the informal sector. The copyright based sector contributes significantly to the Indian economy and its future potential is immense. In the area of plant varieties and farmers' rights, the number of filings and registrations are very encouraging. There is considerable unexplored potential for developing, promoting and utilizing traditional knowledge, which is a unique endowment of India. Activities for promotion of traditional knowledge have to be conducted with effective participation of holders of such knowledge.

A comprehensive base line survey or IP audit across sectors will enable assessment and evaluation of the potential in specific sectors, and thus formulate and implement targeted programmes to tap this vast potential and help develop new technologies, products and solutions. This would include strengthening and spread of IPR facilitation centres and incubators, amongst other measures. Focus will be placed on facilitating researchers and innovators regarding areas of national priority. The corporate sector also needs to be encouraged to generate and utilize IPRs. It is also desirable to introduce IPRs as part of academic curriculum in educational institutions, especially universities, law and technical institutions.

Steps also need to be taken to devise mechanisms so that benefits of the IPR regime reach all inventors, especially MSMEs, start-ups and grassroot innovators. Incentives may be built-in to encourage filing by such targeted users. These may include schemes to facilitate domestic IPR filings, for the entire value chain from IPR generation to commercialization. R&D needs to be promoted through tax benefits available under various laws, through simplification of procedures for availing direct and indirect tax benefits.

The ambit of Traditional Knowledge Digital Library (TKDL) should also be expanded, while the possibility of using it for further R&D shall be explored.

The steps to be taken towards attaining this objective are outlined below:

2.1. Use the campaign "Creative India; Innovative India" to propagate the value of creativity and innovation, and the resultant benefit to the public; to create a mindset and culture that encourages knowledge generation and its application through IP;

2.2. Carry out a comprehensive IP audit or base line survey in various sectors in cooperation with stakeholders to assess and evaluate areas of strength and potential, prioritize target groups of inventors and creators, develop specific programs to address their needs, provide resources to enable them to create IP assets and utilize them for their own and social benefit;

2.3. Undertake studies to assess the contribution of IP content in different industries on the economy, employment, exports and technology transfer;

2.4. Focus on improving IPR output of National Research Laboratories, Universities, Technology Institutions and other researchers by encouraging and facilitating the acquisition of Intellectual Property Rights by them;

2.5. Encourage researchers in public funded academic and R&D institutions in IPR creation by linking it with research funding & career progression;

2.6. Encourage researchers in public funded academic and R&D institutions by having uniform guidelines for division of royalties between the organizations and individual researchers and innovators;

2.7. Include IP creation as a key performance metric for public funded R&D entities as well as Technology Institutions, and gradually extend such evaluation from Tier-1 to Tier-2 Institutions;

2.8. Provide guidance to researchers and innovators about national priority areas to focus on, for instance in energy and food security, healthcare and agriculture, as well as specific sectors such as biotechnology, data analytics, nanotechnology, new materials and ICT;

2.9. Encourage public funded R&D institutes and industry to develop affordable drugs relating to neglected diseases;

2.10. Encourage R&D including open source based research such as Open Source Drug Discovery (OSDD) by the Council of Scientific and Industrial Research (CSIR) for new inventions for prevention, diagnosis and treatment of diseases, especially those that are life threatening and those that have high incidence in India;

2.11. Establish and strengthen IP facilitation centers as nodal points especially in industrial and innovation university clusters;

2.12. Create an industry-academia interface for encouraging cross-fertilization of ideas and IPR-driven research and innovation in jointly identified areas;

2.13. Stimulate large corporations, both Indian and foreign, that have R&D operations, to create, protect and utilize IPRs in India;

2.14. Improve a wareness of the value of copyright for creators, the importance of their economic and moral rights;

2.15. Introduce support systems for MSMEs, start-ups and grass root innovators to reduce transaction costs linked to IP creation for the entire value chain from IPR generation to commercialization, including schemes to facilitate domestic IPR filings;

2.16. Consider incentives to promote R&D, including the following steps:

2.16.1. Promote R&D through tax benefits available under various laws, through simplification of procedures for availing direct and indirect tax benefits;

2.16.2. Consider financial support for a limited period on sale and export of products based on IPRs generated from public funded research;

2.16.3. Creation of an effective and simple loan guarantee scheme in order to encourage start-ups and cover the risk of genuine failures in commercialization based on IPRs as mortgage-able assets;

2.17. Promote 'infusion of funds to public R&D units' as a part of Corporate Social Responsibility to foster a culture of open innovation;

2.18. Provide special incentives for creation of IPRs in green technologies and manufacture of energy efficient equipment;

2.19. The ambit of Traditional Knowledge Digital Library (TKDL) should also be expanded to include other fields besides *Ayurveda, Yoga, Unani* and *Siddha;*

2.20. Public research institutions should be allowed access to TKDL for further R&D, while the possibility of using TKDL for further R&D by private sector may also be explored, provided necessary safeguards are in place to prevent misappropriation;

2.21. Document oral traditional knowledge, taking care that the integrity of the said knowledge is preserved and traditional ways of life of communities are not compromised;

2.22. Introduce IPRs as part of academic curriculum in educational institutions, especially universities, law and technical institutions;

2.23. Increase awareness of international mechanisms and treaties (*e.g.* PCT, Madrid, Hague) to encourage creation and protection of IPRs by Indian individuals and entities in global markets;

2.24. Encourage and incentivize IP generation and utilization among students at all levels, use awareness programs and educational materials to inculcate an appreciation for the value of IP;

2.25. Encourage innovations in the agriculture and pisciculture sector through application of IP for higher sustainable agricultural production;

2.26. Encourage the registration of Geographical Indications (GIs) through support institutions; assist GI producers to define and maintain acceptable quality standards, and providing better marketability;

2.27. Encourage creation of design related IP rights by identifying, nurturing and promoting the aspects of innovation protectable under the design law and educating designers to utilize and benefit from their designs; involve the NIDs, NIFTs and others institutions in sensitization campaigns;

2.28. IPR generation for ICT technologies, including those relating to cyber security for India, will be encouraged;

2.29. Take steps to increase domestic filings of patent applications;

2.30. Promote India's rich heritage of traditional knowledge with the effective involvement and participation of the holders of such knowledge. Traditional knowledge holders will be provided necessary support and incentives for furthering the knowledge systems that they have nurtured from the dawn of our civilization.

OBJECTIVE 3: Legal and Legislative Framework - *To have strong and effective IPR laws, which balance the interests of rights owners with larger public interest:* It is an acknowledged fact that a strong and balanced legal framework encourages continuous flow of innovation and is among the bare necessities to fuel a vibrant knowledge economy. India recognizes that effective protection of IP rights is essential for making optimal use of the innovative and creative capabilities of its people. India has a long history of IP laws which have evolved taking into consideration national needs and international commitments. The existing laws were either enacted or revised after the *TRIPS Agreement* and are fully compliant with it. These laws along with various judicial decisions provide a stable and effective legal framework for protection and promotion of IPRs. India will continue to utilize the legislative space and flexibilities available in international treaties and the *TRIPS Agreement,* even as it continues to engage constructively in the negotiation of such international treaties and agreements. India shall remain committed to the *Doha Declaration on TRIPS Agreement and Public Health.*

At the same time, India is rich in traditional medicinal knowledge which exists in diverse forms in our country. Amongst them, well developed systems like Ayurveda, Yoga & Naturopathy, Unani, Siddha, Sowa-Rigpa and Homeopathy have immense economic value. It is important to protect such knowledge, be it oral or in codified form, from misappropriation, while providing space and environment for dynamic development of traditional knowledge for benefit of mankind.

Since it is difficult to predict the reach of existing laws in a changing and dynamic knowledge field, it becomes necessary to carry out legislative changes, as may be required from time to time. For this purpose, stakeholder consultation shall be done to keep the laws updated in consonance with national needs and priorities. The legal framework may also be utilized to enhance transparency and efficiency in the administration and enforcement of IPR laws.

The steps to be taken towards attaining this objective are outlined below:

3.1. Review existing IP laws, where necessary, to update and improve them or to remove anomalies and inconsistencies, if any, in consultation with stakeholders;

3.2. Engage constructively in the negotiation of international treaties and agreements in consultation with stakeholders; examine accession to some multilateral treaties which are in India's interest; and, become signatory to those treaties which India has *de facto* implemented to enable it to participate in their decision making process;

3.3. Continue to engage actively and constructively in the deliberations at various international fora to develop legally binding international instrument(s) to protect Traditional Knowledge (TK), Genetic Resources (GR) and Traditional Cultural Expressions (TCE);

3.4. Pursue transfer of clean technology and know-how from developed countries to India, as per the provisions of Article 4 of the UNFCCC, in order to meet the objectives of reducing anthropogenic emissions of GHGs and support activities of climate change adaptation;

3.5. Review and update IP related rules, guidelines, procedures and practices for clarity, simplification, streamlining, transparency and time bound processes in administration and enforcement of IP rights;

3.6. Undertake an in-depth study to determine the appropriateness and extent of a pplying the existing laws to protecting TK, GR and TCE, and to propose changes required, if any;

3.7. Indian *Cinematography Act,* 1952 may be suitably amended to provide for penal provisions for illegal duplication of films;

3.8. Identify important areas o f study and research for future policy development, such as (the list is indicative, and not exhaustive):

3.8.1. Interplay amongst IP laws; and between IP laws and other laws to remove ambiguities and inconsistencies, if any;

3.8.2. IP interface with competition law and policy;

3.8.3. Guidelines for authorities whose jurisdictions impact administration or enforcement of IPRs such as patents and Biodiversity;

3.8.4. Protection of Trade Secrets.

3.9. Examine the issues of technology transfer, know-how and licensing relating to SEPs on fair and reasonable terms and provide a suitable legal framework to address these issues, as may be required.

OBJECTIVE 4: Administration and Management - *To modernize and strengthen service-oriented IPR administration:* The Offices that administer the different Intellectual Property Rights (IPOs) are the cornerstone of an efficient and balanced IPR system, administering laws, granting or registering IP rights, providing IPR related services to users, including dissemination of IPR related information for the benefit of research & development and furthering of innovation in the country, as also serving as a bridge between the government, IP support institutions and the user community. As IPRs increase in significance and contribute to economic development, the importance and role of IP administration and management has also expanded. The IPR infrastructure is one of the key elements of enhanced competitiveness in the globalized international economic paradigm. This in turn, influences the organization, structure and functions of modern IPOs.

IPOs now have the twin challenges of making their operations more efficient, streamlined and cost effective, with expanding work load and technological complexity on one hand, and enhancing their user-friendliness by developing and providing value added services to the user community on the other. Steps will continue to be taken towards modernization of various IP offices, including improvement of ICT infrastructure. Aiming towards a service oriented regime at IPOs, steps would be taken to fix and adhere to timelines for disposal of IPR applications. There is also need to augment manpower after analyzing the projected workload.

Sensitization of IPR officials at all levels with regard to the objects and reasons of our laws and international obligations; their continuous education and training and regular audit of their work will ensure a vibrant and service oriented IPR regime. The Rajiv Gandhi National Institute of Intellectual Property Management, Nagpur (RGNIIPM) needs to be strengthened to cater to the training needs in an evolving IP environment. Measures should also be taken to promote interaction between the IP Offices and various R & D organizations and Universities.

The administration of the *Copyright Act,* 1957, hitherto under the Department of Higher Education, and the *Semiconductor Integrated Circuits Layout-Design Act,* 2000, hitherto under the Department of Electronics and Information Technology, is being brought under the aegis of the Department of Industrial Policy and Promotion leading to synergetic linkage between various IP offices under one umbrella, streamlining processes, and ensuring better services to the users. To facilitate promotion, creation and commercialization of IP assets, a Cell for IPR Promotion and Management (CIPAM) should be constituted under the aegis of DIPP.

Continued efforts should be made for promotion of technical cooperation with IP offices in other countries in areas such as capacity building, human resource development, training, access to databases, best practices in search and examinations, use of ICT and user oriented services.

The steps to be taken towards attaining this objective are outlined below:

4.1. The administration of the *Copyright Act* 1957 alongwith the office of the Registrar of Copyrights, under the Department of Higher Education, is being transferred to the Department of Industrial Policy and Promotion;

4.2. The administration of the *Semiconductor Integrated Circuits Layout-Design Act* 2000 alongwith the office of the Semiconductor Integrated Circuits Layout-Design Registry (SICLDR), under the Department of Electronics and Information Technology, is being transferred to the Department of Industrial Policy and Promotion;

4.3. Restructure, upgrade and modernize IPOs taking into account the rapid growth and diversity of IP users and services, higher responsibilities and increased workload;

4.4. Augment manpower after analyzing projected workload, speedy liquidation of backlog, requirements of global protection systems and productivity parameters;

4.5. Study and review the organizational and cadre structure, processes of recruitment, training, career development, performance based incentives to attract and retain the best talent to enhance efficiency and productivity;

4.6. Modernize further the physical and ICT infrastructure taking into account the expanding needs of the IPOs and to accelerate e-filings, e-processing and other e-services;

4.7. Promote interaction between various IP offices and public R&D institutions for sensitization of personnel and scientists;

4.8. Collaborate with various R&D Institutions, Universities, Funding Agencies, Chambers of Industry and Commerce in providing advisory services to improve IP creation, management and utilization;

4.9. Make efforts to include TKDL as a part of PCT minimum documentation;

4.10. Establish close cooperation between IPOs and create a common web portal for ease of access to statutes, regulations, guidelines and for better coordination;

4.11. Promote cooperation with IP offices in other countries in areas of Capacity Building, Human Resource Development, Training, Access to Databases, Best Practices in search and examinations, use of ICT and user oriented services;

4.12. Introduce approaches and mechanisms so that benefits of the IP system reach all inventors including MSMEs, informal innovators and holders of traditional knowledge;

4.13. Create a Cell for IPR Promotion and Management (CIPAM) under the aegis of DIPP to facilitate promotion, creation and commercialization of IP assets;

4.14. Explore the possibility of expedited examination of patent applications to promote manufacturing in India;

4.15. Enhance international and bilateral cooperation and coordinate with Indian Missions abroad to follow IP developments and advice on IP related matters;

4.16. Office of the Controller General of Patents Designs and Trademarks.

The office of CGPDTM, which administers patents, designs, trademarks and GIs, has undergone a sea change in the past few years, in up gradation and use of ICT. These changes shall be further advanced through such measures as:

4.16.1. Fix and adhere to timelines for grant of registrations and disposal of opposition matters;

4.16.2. Adopt best practices with respect to filing and docketing of documents, maintenance of records and digitizing the same including document workflow and tracking systems;

4.16.3. Create a service-oriented culture to make the IP office user friendly;

4.16.4. Take steps t o expedite digitization of the Design office and enable online search and filing;

4.16.5. Ensure that public records in the IP office are easily available and accessible both online and offline;

4.16.6. Conduct periodic audits of processes being adopted in IP administration for efficient grant and management of IP rights;

4.16.7. Implement quality standards at all stages of operations with the aim to obtain ISO certification;

4.16.8. Establish effective coordination between its office and National Biodiversity Authority to enable harmonious implementation of guidelines relating to grant of patents on inventions using biological resources and associated TK;

4.16.9. Provide continuous training to staff of the IP Office to update them of developments in procedures (especially search and examination), substantive laws and technologies, with the Rajiv Gandhi National Institute of Intellectual Property Management, Nagpur (RGNIIPM);

4.16.10. Remove disparities, if any, among different branches of the trademark registries and patent offices and adopt standardized procedures in examination/grant of applications including maintenance of rights;

4.16.11. Implement centralized priority field-wise on a national basis for patent applications;

4.16.12. Examine joining Centralized Access for Search and Examination (CASE) and WIPO Digital Access Services (DAS);

4.16.13. Existing guidelines published by the Patent Office shall be reviewed periodically and revised to reflect legislative provisions;

4.16.14. Value added services in the form of helpdesks, awareness and training materials, ease of remote access of the international patent search mechanisms and other IP related databases;

4.16.15. Implement incentives for MSMEs and grass root innovators to encourage filing by the said sector;

4.16.16. Conduct patent and trademark agent examinations at regular intervals; arrange training programs and involve them in capacity building activities.

4.17. Office of Registrar of Copyrights: The office will:

4.17.1. Take measures to expedite modernization of the Copyright Office in terms of office space and infrastructure, organizational structure, e-filing facility including e-applications, processing and issue of final extracts of registrations;

4.17.2. Digitize copyright records and introduce on-line search facility; Provide necessary manpower and adequate training facilities to personnel in the Copyright Office;

4.17.3. Take urgent measures for effective management and administration of copyright societies to ensure transparency and efficiency in the collection and disbursement of royalties in the best interest of the right holders;

4.17.4. Provide user friendly services in the form of helpdesks, awareness and training materials;

4.17.5. Streamline the processes to grant copyright permissions to individual creators, enterprises and institutions for their creative work.

4.18. The Protection of Plant Varieties and Farmers' Rights Authority will:

4.18.1. Support increased registration of new, extant and essentially derived varieties of plants and streamline procedures;

4.18.2. Facilitate development of seeds and their commercialization by farmers;

4.18.3. Establish links between the Authority and Agricultural Universities, Research Institutions, Technology Development & Management Centers and Krishi Vigyan Kendras;

4.18.4. Coordinate with other IPOs for training, sharing expertise and adopting best practices;

4.18.5. Augment awareness building, training and teaching programs;

4.18.6. Modernize office infrastructure and use of ICT.

4.19. Registrar of Semiconductor Integrated Circuits Layout Design

4.19.1. The Registrar will study the reasons for lack of interest in filings under the *Semiconductor Integrated Circuits Layout Design Act,* 2000 and suggest appropriate remedial measures;

4.19.2. Liaise with the concerned Group in the Patent office and Design wing under the CGPDTM for further working.

4.20. National Biodiversity Authority

4.20.1. The Government will formalize a consultation and coordination mechanism between the NBA, IPOs a n d o t h erconcerned Ministries/departmentslik eAYUSH, with a view to harmonious implementation of guidelines for grant of IP rights and access to biological resources and associated traditional knowledge and benefit sharing;

4.20.2. The NBA will streamline approvals for expeditious grant of IP rights, monetary and non-monetary benefit-sharing and introduce efficient and user friendly mechanisms for a meaningful interface between the NBA and applicants.

4.21. Re-designate the institution of the Controller General of Patents, Designs and

Trademarks as Controller General of Intellectual Property Rights to reflect its mandate in view of the proposed change in its scope of responsibilities.

OBJECTIVE 5: Commercialization of IPR - *Get value for IPRs through commercialization:* The value and economic reward for the owners of IP rights comes only from their commercialization. A concerted effort should be made for capitalizing the existing IP assets in the country. Entrepreneurship should be encouraged so that the financial value of IPRs may be captured. Existing mechanisms including Incubators and Accelerators set up to promote entrepreneurship should be strengthened with IP-oriented services.

Financing is a major impediment for entrepreneurs and therefore it is necessary to connect investors and IP creators. Another constraint faced is valuation of IP and assessment of the potential of the IPRs for the purpose of marketing it.

There is an urgent need to take stock of existing IP funding by different departments and bodies of the Government like BIRAC, NRDC and TIFAC, and take measures to consolidate the same, scaling up successful models while avoiding duplication of efforts. Public - funded research laboratories, academia and other institutions should stimulate commercialization of their research outcomes. They ought to be suitably state-supported in the development and deployment of their IPRs.

While certain larger organizations have the intent and capabilities to commercialize their technology/ IPRs, several others do not. Hence, it becomes imperative to establish facilitative mechanisms that can address such limitations, especially in terms of MSMEs, academic institutions and individual innovators. One of the effective ways of achieving this would be by synergizing the activities of IP facilitation centres with the industry, especially industrial clusters. This would also include sensitization regarding licensing arrangements.

Efforts should be made for creation of a public platform to function as a common database of IPRs. Such a platform can help creators and innovators connect to potential users, buyers and funding institutions. It would also be helpful in scouting the technology landscape to identify white spaces and thereby help promote innovative activities in uncovered areas. Significant potential for innovation exists in new and emerging technologies like nano-technology, biotechnology, agri-biotech, life sciences, green technologies, telecommunications, new materials, space technologies, etc.

The steps to be taken towards attaining this objective are outlined below:

5.1. CIPAM shall also undertake the following tasks:

5.1.1. Provide a platform for IPR owners and users of IPRs byacting as a facilitator for creators and innovators to be connected with potential users, buyers and funding agencies;

5.1.2. Undertake a study to examine the feasibility of an IPR Exchange;

5.1.3. Establish links among different organizations for exchange of information and ideas as also to develop promotional/ educational products and services;

5.1.4. Facilitate access to databases on Indian IP and global databases of creators/ innovators, market analysts, funding agencies, IP intermediaries;

5.1.5. Study and facilitate implementation of best practices for promotion and commercialization of IP within the country and outside;

5.1.6. Promote public sector initiatives for IPR commercialization;

5.2. Promote licensing and technology transfer for IPRs; devising suitable contractual and licensing guidelines to enable commercialization of IPRs; promote patent pooling and cross licensing to create IPR based products and services;

5.3. Provide support for MSMEs, Individual Inventors and Innovators from the informal sectors with enablers like facilitation centers for single window services to help them commercialize their IPRs;

5.4. Incentivize Indian inventors, MSMEs, start-ups to acquire and commercialize IPRs in other countries also;

5.5. Examine availability of Standard Essential Patents (SEPs) on fair, reasonable and non-discriminatory (FRAND) terms ;

5.6. Identify opportunities for marketing Indian IPR-based products, especially GIs, and services to a global audience;

5.7. Promote collaborative IP generation and commercialization efforts between R&D institutions, Industry, Academia and Funding Agencies;

5.8. Ensure enhanced access to affordable medicines and other healthcare solutions by (a) encouraging cross-sector partnerships between public sector, private sector, universities and NGOs; (b) promoting novel licensing models, and (c) developing novel technology platforms;

5.9. Streamline regulatory processes to ensure timely approval for manufacturing and marketing of drugs while maintaining safety and efficacy standards;

5.10. Make efforts to reduce dependency on active pharmaceutical ingredients (API) imports, including incentivizing manufacture of APIs in India and revitalizing public sector undertakings in health care sector;

5.11. Support the financial aspects of IPR commercialization by:

5.11.1. Enabling valuation of IP rights as intangible assets by application of appropriate methodologies and guidelines; facilitating securitization of IP rights and their use as collateral by creation of enabling legislative, administrative and market framework;

5.11.2. Facilitating investments in IP driven industries and services through the proposed IP Exchange for bringing investors/ funding agencies and IP owners/users together;

5.11.3. Providing financial support to the less empowered groups of IP owners or creators like farmers, weavers, artisans, craftsmen, artists etc. through financial institutions like rural banks or cooperative banks offering IP friendly loans;

5.11.4. Providing financial support for development and commercialization of IP assets through links with financial institutions including banks, venture capital funds, angel funds, crowd funding mechanisms;

5.11.5. Utilizing Technology Acquisition and Development Fund under the Manufacturing Policy for licensing or procuring patented technologies;

5.11.6. Taking stock of all IP funding by the Government and suggesting measures to consolidate the same to the extent possible; scaling up the funding as needed and avoiding duplication; enhancing the visibility of IP and innovation related funds so that utilization is increased; performance based evaluation for continued funding;

5.12. Promote use of Free and Open Source Software along with adoption of open standards; possibility of creating Indian standard operating environments will be examined;

5.13. Promote going-to-market activities by:

5.13.1. Creating mechanisms to help MSMEs and research institutions to validate pilots and scale up through market testing;

5.13.2. Providing seed funding for marketing activities such as participating in trade fairs, industry standards bodies and other forums;

5.13.3. Providing guidance and support to IPR owners about commercial opportunities of e-commerce through Internet and mobile platforms;

5.13.4. Encouraging enterprises to create brand equity from their IP rights, such as trademarks and GIs.

OBJECTIVE 6: Enforcement and Adjudication - *To strengthen the enforcement and adjudicatory mechanisms for combating IPR infringements:* IP rights are essentially private rights. The primary obligation of protecting IP rights is on the IPR owners who can seek legal remedies for enforcement of their rights. Along with providing an effective mechanism for enforcement of IP rights, it is equally important to balance the rights of the public in a manner conducive to social and economic welfare and to prevent misuse or abuse of IP rights.

There is a need to build respect for IPR among the general public and to sensitize the inventors and creators of IP on measures for protection and enforcement of their rights. At the same time, there is also a need to build the capacity of the enforcement agencies at various levels, including strengthening of IPR cells in State police forces.

Measures to check counterfeiting and piracy also need to be identified and undertaken. In this regard, the definitions of "counterfeit trademark goods" and "pirated copyright goods" as referred to in the footnote of Article 51 of the *TRIPS Agreement* shall serve as the guiding principles.

Regular IPR workshops/colloquia at judicial academies and other fora for judges would facilitate effective adjudication of IPR disputes.

Multi-disciplinary IP courses/modules for other stakeholders are also needed.

It would be desirable to adjudicate on IPR disputes through specialised commercial courts. Alternative Dispute Resolution mechanism may also be explored.

The steps to be taken towards attaining this objective are outlined below:

6.1. Create awareness of the value of IP and respect for IP culture by:

  6.1.1. Educating the general public, especially the youth and students, on ills of counterfeit and pirated products;

  6.1.2. Engaging with all levels of industry, including e-commerce, in order to create respect for IP rights and devise collaborative strategies and tools;

  6.1.3. Sensitizing inventors, creators of IP on measures for protection and enforcement of their rights.

6.2. Take strong measures against attempts to treat generic drugs as spurious or counterfeit;

6.3. Undertake stringent measures to curb manufacture and sale of misbranded, adulterated and spurious drugs;

6.4. Public awareness as also legal and enforcement mechanisms, including technology based measures, will be reinforced to combat offline and online piracy;

6.5. Small technology firms will be supported in safeguarding their IP rights; for instance, support for IPR in ICT focus areas will be provided through easy-to-use portals;

6.6. Assistance to smaller firms for protection of their IPRs internationally will be enhanced, such as DeitY's Support for International Patent Protection in Electronics and IT (SIP-EIT);

6.7. Pursue incidents of misappropriation of TK, GR and TCE in other countries vigorously;

6.8. Strengthen the enforcement mechanisms for better protection of IP rights by:

  6.8.1. Enhanced coordination between the various agencies and providing direction and guidance on strengthening enforcement measures; coordinating with and sharing of intelligence and best practices at the national and international level; studying the extent of IP violations in various sectors; examining the implications of jurisdictional difficulties among enforcement authorities; and introducing appropriate technology based solutions f or curbing digital piracy;

6.8.2. Working closely with state governments for establishment of IP cells for curbing IP offences;

6.8.3. Augmenting manpower, infrastructure facilities and technological capabilities of the enforcement agencies and building capacity to check proliferation of digital crimes;

6.8.4. Providing regular training, including refresher training, for officials in the enforcement agencies at their academies;

6.8.5. Encouraging application of technology based solutions in the enforcement of IP rights;

6.8.6. Initiating fact-finding studies in collaboration with stakeholders concerned to assess the extent of counterfeiting and piracy and the reasons behind it as well as measures to combat it;

6.8.7. Taking up the issue of Indian works and products being pirated and counterfeited abroad with countries concerned;

6.9. Licensing practices or conditions that may have an adverse effect on competition will be addressed through appropriate measures, including regulation of anti-competitive conduct in the market by the Competition Commission of India;

6.10. Facilitate effective adjudication of IP disputes through different measures including:

6.10.1. Adjudicate IP disputes through Commercial Courts, set up at appropriate level;

6.10.2. Creating IP modules including case laws for the benefit of judges who deal in IP; conducting regular IP workshops / colloquia at the judicial academies;

6.10.3. Promoting ADRs in the resolution of IP cases by strengthening mediation and conciliation centers, and developing ADR capabilities and skills in the field of IP;

OBJECTIVE 7: Human Capital Development - *To strengthen and expand human resources, institutions and capacities for teaching, training, research* *and skill building in IPRs:* The IPR scenario is dynamic and fast changing with increasing globalization, advancement of technologies, digital environment, development imperatives and global public policy issues. It is important to build national capacity for providing thought leadership in the IPR field. Continuous policy research is also needed on empirical and topical IPR areas of relevance with an interdisciplinary perspective at the national and international level. This research would enrich the process of policy, law, strategy development and international negotiations at the government and organizational levels. While apex level institutes or bodies exist for most sectors of national importance, such an institution has yet to be established for intellectual property rights development.

In order to harness the full potential of IPRs for economic growth, it is essential to develop an increasing pool of IPR professionals and experts in spheres such as policy and law, strategy development, administration and enforcement. IPR expertise would thus need to be developed and increased in industry, academia, legal practitioners, judiciary, IP users and civil society. In addition, there will be enhancement of multidisciplinary human and institutional capacity for policy development, teaching, training, research and skill building. Such a reservoir of experts will facilitate in increasing generation of IP assets in the country and their utilization for development purposes.

The steps to be taken towards attaining this objective are outlined below:

7.1. Strengthen and empower RGNIIPM, Nagpur to conduct training for IPR administrators and managers in industry and business, academicians, R&D institutions; IP professionals; inventors and civil society; train the trainers and develop training modules; develop links with other similar entities at the international level; provide legal training for examiners;

7.2. Strengthen IP Chairs in educational institutes of higher learning to provide quality teaching and research; develop teaching capacity and curricula and evaluate their work on performance based criteria;

7.3. Introduce multi-disciplinary IP courses/ modules in all major training institutes such as Judicial Academies, National Academy of Administration, Police and Customs Academies, Institute for Foreign Service Training, Forest Training Institutes; Dehradun.

7.4. Making IPR an integral part of the curriculum in all legal, technical, medical and management educational Institutions, NIFTs, NIDs, AYUSH Educational Institutes, Agricultural Universities, centres of skill development and the like;

7.5. Strengthen existing and create new IPR cells and technology development and management units in NIDs, NIFTs, Agricultural Universities, Technology and Management Institutes and centres of skill development;

7.6. Encourage formulation of institutioal IP Policy/Strategy in Government Departments, Higher Education, Research and Technical Institutions;

7.7. Progressively introduce IP teaching in Schools, Colleges and other Educational Institutions and centres of skill development;

7.8. Facilitate Industry Associations, Inventor and Creators Associations and IP Support Institutions to raise awareness of IP issues and for Teaching, Training and Skill Building;

7.9. Develop distance learning and on-line courses on IP for all categories of users; strengthen IP teaching in open universities and centres of skill development;

7.10. Strengthen IP Teaching, Research and Training in collaboration with WIPO, WTO, other International Organizations and reputed Foreign Universities;

7.11. Encourage and support capacity building am on g Women Creators, Innovators, Entrepreneurs, Practitioners, Teachers and Trainers.

IMPLEMENTATION

Intellectual property in India is regulated by several laws, rules and regulations under the jurisdiction of different Ministries/ Departments. A number of authorities and offices administer the laws. The legal provisions need to be implemented harmoniously so as to avoid conflict, overlap or inconsistencies among them. It is necessary that the authorities concerned administer the laws in coordination with each other in the interest of efficient administration and user satisfaction. Legal, technological, economic and socio-cultural issues arise in different fields of IP which intersect with each other and need to be addressed and resolved by consensus in the best public interest. International, regional and bilateral negotiations require developing a common national position in consultation with different Ministries, authorities and stakeholders.

The present IP Policy aims to integrate IP as a policy and strategic tool in national development plans. It foresees a coordinated and integrated development of IP system in India and the need for a holistic approach to be taken on IP legal, administrative, institutional and enforcement related matters.

Thus, the Department of Industrial Policy and Promotion shall be the nodal point to coordinate, guide and oversee implementation and future development of IPRs in India. The responsibility for actual implementation of the plans of action will remain with the Ministries/ Departments concerned in their assigned sphere of work. Public and private sector institutions and other stakeholders, including State governments, will also be involved in the implementation process.

Appendices

APPENDIX-B: DRAFT TEMPLATE ON INTELLECTUAL PROPERTY POLICY FOR HIGHER EDUCATION INSTITUTIONS (HEIs)*

CONTENTS

---

http: //www1.msuiit.edu.ph/research_extension/downloads Draft % 20 IP % 20 Policy % 20 of % 20 Aug % 2026

7.2 Return of Ip to Inventors

7.3 Commercialization and Protection of the University's IP

7.4 Distribution of Commercialization Benefits

Article 8. RESEARCH COLLABORATIONS WITH EXTERNAL PARTIES

8.1 General Statements

8.2 Research Collaborations with Non-Commercial Parties

8.3 Research Collaborations with Industry

8.4 General Policies on Other Terms in Research Agreements

Article 9. GENERAL OBLIGATIONS

9.1 Confidentiality

9.2 Disclosure of Conflicts of Interest

Article 10. CONSULTANCIES/DIRECTORSHIP IN COMPANIES

10.1 Consultancies

10.2 Conflict of Interest

10.3 Directorship of Companies (Including University Spin-Off Companies)

Article 11. GENERAL PROVISIONS

11.1 Interpretation

11.2 Waiver of Policy

11.3 Commencement and Application of IP Policy

11.4 Amendment of the Rules and Guidelines of the IP Policy

ANNEXES

ANNEX A : Invention Disclosure Form

ANNEX B : Declaration of Mandatory Disclosure

ANNEX C : Letter Agreement for Return of IP to Inventors

The University Intellectual Property (IP) Policy is hereby promulgated as follows:

ARTICLE 1

INTRODUCTION : General Statement

1.1 The University conducts research in the pursuit of knowledge for enriching the minds and lives of university staff and students, and for the benefit of society as a whole.

1.2 As the University becomes increasingly active in research, technology transfer, and as university staff and students actively participate in ensuing entrepreneurial activities, there is a need for the University to promulgate a "Policy on Intellectual Property, Technology Transfer and Research Collaboration".

1.3 The University largely depends upon financial support primarily from the government and from local and international organizations for its research activities. Consistent with this premise, the University seeks to ensure that any resultant intellectual property is administered and protected in the public interest. (This provision is generally applicable to SUCs).

1.4 The IP Policy seeks to provide guidelines that can be consistently applied to facilitate the commercialization of research outputs and to arrive at hbequitable solutions to possible IP issues relating to the conduct of research, technology transfer and commercialization.

ARTICLE 2

POLICY OBJECTIVES

2.1 Promote, preserve, encourage and aid scientific investigation and research;

2.2 Facilitate the transfer of technology from the University to industry in order that research conducted at the University results in applications that would benefit the public;

2.3 Establish and maintain an innovation fund for research and innovation;

2.4 Enhance the prestige of the University as an academic research institution and as a member of society by pursuing the highest ideals of scholarship and teaching and by conferring the benefits of that scholarship and teaching on the University community and society.

2.5 In its broad discretion and consistent with its overall mission, encourage, assist and provide mutually beneficial rewards to the

University and members of the University community who transfer University intellectual property to the public through commercial channels under this IP Policy;

2.6 Establish standards for determining the rights and obligations of the university and creators of intellectual property; and

2.7 Ensure compliance with applicable laws and regulations and enable the University to secure sponsored research funding at all levels of research;

2.8 Generally ensure filing of protection for the IP prior to any publication.

ARTICLE 3

Coverage

3.1 **Personnel Covered.** This IP Policy applies to all University personnel i.e academic and research staffs, staff members, students who participate in research project at the University's main campus and satellite campuses unless the University specifies other arrangements in such person's letter of appointment with the University.

3.2 **IP Rights Covered.** This IP Policy shall cover all types of intellectual property rights under relevant IP Laws of the country, such as:

- Copyright and Related Rights;
- Trademarks and Service Marks;
- Geographic Indications;
- Industrial Designs;
- Patents;
- Utility Models;
- Lay-out Designs (Topographies of Integrated Circuits); and
- Undisclosed Information; and
- New plant varieties, as provided in Republic Act No. 9168.

ARTICLE 4

Definition of Terms or Expressions

4.1 **"Academic & Research Staff"** include all faculty, academic staff, visiting faculty, emeritus faculty while at the university and affiliate and adjunct staff members, fellows and other researchers carrying out research at the University, whether part-time or full-time.

4.2 **"Breeder"** means the University personnel or student who bred, or discovered and developed a new plant variety; or the person who is the employer of the aforementioned person or who has commissioned the work; or the successors-in-interest of the foregoing persons as the case may be; or the holder of the Certificate of Plant Variety Protection.

4.3 **"Confidential Information"** means any information or data of a confidential nature, including all oral and visual information or data, and all information or data recorded in writing or in any other medium or by any other method, and all information and data which the University is under an obligation, whether contractual or otherwise, not to divulge.

4.4 **"Copyright"** is the legal protection extended to the owner of the rights in an original artistic or literary work.

4.5 **"Creator"** means the University personnel or student (covered under Article 3.1 of this IP policy) who is considered the legal owner of literary, scholarly, scientific and artistic works or has made creative or authorship contributions.

4.6 **"Geographical Indication (GI)"** is a name or sign used on certain products which corresponds to a specific geographical location or origin (e.g. a town, region or country). The use of a GI may act as a certification that the product possesses certain qualities, or enjoys a certain reputation, due to its geographical origin.

4.7 **"IP Code"** means Republic Act 8293 or the Intellectual Property Code of the Philippines and its amendments.

4.8 **"IP Policy"** means the University's "Policy on Intellectual Property, Technology Transfer and Research Collaboration" as may be amended from time to time.

4.9 **"Intellectual Property" or "IP"** means any patentable invention, utility model, industrial design, undisclosed information or know-how, copyright, layout design of integrated circuits, tangible research property, rights relating to computer software, trade mark and any other industrial or intellectual property rights, registrable, registered or otherwise, including tangible research property.

4.10 **"Inventor"** means the University personnel or student (covered under Article 3.1 of this IP policy) who is considered the legal inventor of the work under relevant IP laws.

4.11 **"Industrial Design"** is any composition of lines or colors or any three-dimensional form, whether or not associated with lines or colors; Provided, that such composition or form gives a special appearance to and can serve as pattern for an industrial product or handicraft.

4.12 **"Know-how"** means any methods, techniques, processes, discoveries, inventions, innovations, non-patentable processes, specifications, recipes, formulae, designs, plans, documentation, drawings, data and other technical information.

4.13 **"Layout Design of Integrated Circuits"** is an original topography (picture of a place) of elements, at least one of which is an active element, and of source or all interconnections of an integrated circuit, or such three-dimensional disposition prepared for an integrated circuit intended for manufacture.

4.14 **"Mark"** means any visible sign capable of distinguishing the goods (trademark) or services (service mark) of an enterprise and shall include a stamped or marked container of goods.

4.15 **"Patentable Invention"** means any technical solution of a problem in any field of human activity which is new, involves inventive step and is industrially applicable. Non-patentable inventions are those enumerated under Section 22 of the IP Code.

4.16 **"Plant"** includes terrestrial and aquatic flora

4.17 "**Staff member"** includes all administrative staff, non-researchers or any other persons employed by the university participating in research projects, whether part-time or full-time.

4.18 **"Student"** means all matriculated undergraduates, student employees and higher degree students i.e. graduate students, candidates for masteral and doctoral degrees, post doctoral fellows at the University.

4.19 **"Tangible Research Property"** shall mean research results that are in a tangible form and that include items such as materials, drawings, integrated circuit chips, computer software, computer and other databases, processes, prototypes and circuit diagrams.

4.20 **"Utility Model"** means any technical solution of a problem in any field of human activity which is new and is industrially applicable. A utility model does not involve an inventive step.

4.21 **"University Personnel"** means all academic and research staff as well as staff members covered by this IP Policy under Article 3.1

4.22 **"University resources"** are defined as all tangible resources provided by the University to inventors, including:

i) Facilities such as office, lab and studio space and equipment;

ii) Computer hardware and software;

iii) Support and secretarial services;

iv) Research teaching, and lab assistants;

v) Supplies;

vi) Utilities;

vii) Funding and reimbursement for research and teaching activities, including travel.

University resources do not include salary, insurance or retirement plan contributions paid to or for the benefit of Creators.

4.23 **"Undisclosed information or trade secrets"** shall mean information which is secret in the sense that it is not, as a body or in the precise configuration and assembly of its components generally known among or readily accessible to persons within the circles that normally deal with the kind of information in question; has commercial value because it is secret; and has been subject to reasonable steps under the circumstances to keep it secret, by the person lawfully in control of the information.

4.24 **"Works"** are original intellectual creations in the literary and artistic domain protected from the moment of their creation and shall include in particular:

i) Manuscripts, educational course materials and academic papers;

ii) Books, pamphlets, articles & other writings;

iii) Periodicals & newspapers;

iv) Lectures, sermons, addresses, dissertations prepared for oral delivery, whether or not reduced in writing or other material form;

v) Letters;

vi) Dramatic or dramatic-musical compositions, choreographic works or entertainment in dumb shows;

vii) Musical compositions, with or without words;

viii) Works of drawing, painting, architecture, sculpture, engraving, lithography or other works of art; models or designs for works of art;

ix) Original ornamental designs or models for articles of manufacture, whether or not registrable as an industrial design, and other works of applied art;

x) Illustrations, maps, plans, sketches, charts and three-dimensional works relative to geography, topography, architecture or science;

xi) Drawings or plastic works of a scientific or technical character;

xii) Photographic works including works produced by a process analogous to photography; lantern slides;

xiii) Audiovisual works and cinematographic works and works produced by a process analogous to cinematography or any process for making audio-visual recordings;

xiv) Pictorial illustrations and advertisements;

xv) Computer programs; and

xvi) Other literary, scholarly, scientific and artistic works.

4.25 **"Variety"** means a plant grouping within a single botanical taxon of the lowest known rank, that without regard to whether the conditions for plant variety protection are fully met, can be defined by the expression of the characteristics resulting from the given genotype or combination of genotypes, distinguished from any other plant groupings by the expression of at least one (1) characteristics and considered as a unit with regard to the suitability for being propagated unchanged. A variety may be represented by seed, transplants, plants, tubers, tissue culture plantlets and other forms.

ARTICLE 5

INTELLECTUAL PROPERTY OWNERSHIP

5.1. **Copyright of Works**

a) Copyright ownership of Works by University Personnel or Students shall vest in the Creator, except under the following circumstances:

i) If the Work is created in the course of or pursuant to an agreement between the University and an external party, copyright ownership is subject to the terms on IP ownership set out in the relevant agreement; or

ii) If the Work is created by a non-academic University Personnel or Student in the course of his or her employment with the University; or

iii) If the Work is commissioned by the University or is created at the direction of the University for a specific University purpose; or

iv) If the Work is created using funds provided by or through the University for such purpose.

b) Copyright with respect to software is dealt with as per other IP rights under Article 5.1 above.

c) The University shall also have the right to use, publish and reproduce such Works in whatever form, electronic or otherwise, for its teaching, research and academic purposes with appropriate notification to the owner.

d) If the owner of the copyright is other than the University, prior consent is required from the owner before any compilation, distribution and sale can be made.

5.2 IP Ownership by the University of Patent and other IP Rights

a) Rights in IP made or created by the University personnel or students are owned by the University when either of the following applies:

i) The IP was developed in the course of or pursuant to University Research. University Research includes:

A. in the case of a University Personnel, all research conducted in the course of his/her employment with the University as part of his/her duties or in fulfillment of his/her contract of employment;

B. in the case of Students, all research for which the Student receives financial support in the form of wages, allowances, salary, stipend or grant from funds whether or not administered by or through the University; and

C. all research conducted pursuant to a research agreement between the University and an external party, subject to the terms on IP ownership set out in the relevant research agreement

ii) The IP was developed with substantial use of University's resources. The following shall be deemed to be substantial use of the University's resources:

A. Where University funds are used to specifically support the development of the IP;

B. Where there has been use of resources at the University that are not ordinarily available to most University personnel or Student. The use of office, library, computers and storage servers constitutes resources that are ordinarily available to University Personnel and Students and do not constitute substantial use of University's resources.

b) All IP developed by University Personnel or Students in their own personal time, which are neither connected to University Research nor developed with substantial use of University's resources, shall belong to such University Personnel or Students as Inventors.

5.3 **Trademarks**

The University shall be the sole owner of the university logo and shall have it registered with the Intellectual Property Office of the Philippines. Any use of the university logo shall require prior license or permission from the university.

5.4 **Tangible Research Property (TRP) or research results** as defined in Article 4.19 which cannot be the subject of any other kind of intellectual property protection are presumptively owned by the University. In no case shall biological material in any form be the subject of patents or any form of acquisition.

5.5 **Student Thesis/Dissertation**

a) A Student shall own the copyright of his or her thesis/dissertation subject to any agreement with the University or external parties. The Student shall grant to the University a royalty-free permission to reproduce, publish and publicly distribute copies of the thesis, in whatever form, electronic or otherwise.

b) If a thesis/dissertation contains information on an invention that may be patentable, the thesis may be required to be withheld in accordance with the procedures below:

i) The College/Department may withhold public access to the Student's thesis/dissertation containing information on patentable invention until such time a patent application is filed by the TLO.

ii) If the TLO or IP Unit decides not to pursue a patent protection in accordance with Article 7.1 c, the thesis/dissertation may be released in accordance with the procedures adopted by the University.

iii) If the Inventors' request for the return of the IP under Article 7.5 and wishes to pursue patent protection for the invention themselves, the Inventors may request the College/ Department to withhold the thesis/dissertation for not more than three (3) months from the date of return of the IP in order for the relevant patent application to be filed.

ARTICLE 6

ADMINISTRATION

6.1 Creation of the Technology Licensing Office (TLO)/Intellectual Property Unit (IP Unit)

To supervise the implementation of the IP Policy and commercialization of University IP assets, a Technology Licensing Office (TLO) or Intellectual Property Unit (IP Unit) shall be created with the following functions and responsibilities:

i) Administer and monitor the implementation of the IP Policy;

ii) Evaluate the potential of the works and/or inventions submitted for commercialization;

iii) Negotiate with University personnel with respect to the development of independently owned technologies after a determination of their commercial potential for purposes of registration, licensing or joint venture agreements;

iv) Manage the University's patent portfolio including the drafting, filing and prosecution of applications with the Intellectual Property Office of the Philippines (IP Philippines) as well as the maintenance of granted patents and registered trademarks;

v) Administer the funds allocated for patenting and activities related to the protection and commercialization of the University IP;

vi) Negotiate and manage contracts for the production, distribution and marketing of the University's IP assets;

vii) Spearhead the preparation of business and marketing plans, and in securing financial assistance for any commercialization project activity.

viii) Administer payments derived from any commercialized IP assets.

ix) Negotiate all license agreements for the University IP.

6.2 Staffing of TLO or the IP Unit

The TLO or IP Unit may have the following personnel, the number of which depends on the volume of activities that will be handled:

i) **Technology Licensing Officer** - who shall direct and supervise the day-to-day operation.

ii) **Associate Technology Licensing Officer** - who shall evaluate patentability and commerciability of University IP assets submitted to the TLO.

iii) **Financial Operations Staff** - who shall handle financial matters of the TLO.

iv) **Marketing Officer** - who shall be responsible in locating suitable commercial development partners.

v) **Legal Officer** - who shall handle legal matters and issues relating to University IP assets.

vi) **Office Operations Staff** - who shall provide administrative support to the staff member of the TLO.

6.3 Creation of the Intellectual Property Management Committee (IPMC)

The University administration supervising the operation of the TLO or IP Unit may be placed under the ___________ or opt to create an IPMC with the following suggested functions:

i) The IPMC shall serve as the oversight committee that will oversee the management of the University's IP by the TLO or IP Unit.

ii) The IPMC will be responsible for resolving any dispute that may arise from the interpretation of this IP Policy. If the matter cannot be resolved at the IPMC, such matter shall be referred to the University President for his decision, which will be final and conclusive.

iii) The IPMC will also review and endorse license agreements negotiated by the TLO or IP Unit as well as periodically review the patent management and licensing practices of the University.

ARTICLE 7

DISCLOSURE, EVALUATION AND COMMERCIALIZATION OF UNIVERSITY IP

7.1 IP Disclosure and Evaluation Process

a) If an Inventor has developed any IP, the ownership of which is vested in the University under Article 5, or pursuant to any obligation to disclose such IP under any agreement the University may have with an external party, the Inventor(s) must promptly disclose the full details of the IP to the TLO or the IP Unit by submitting a Technology Disclosure Form with a copy to his/her Dean of School.

b) The TLO or the IP Unit will evaluate the commercial potential and patentability of the IP. The TLO or the IP Unit may consult with other University Personnel or independent experts who are competent in the field to assist in the evaluation if appropriate or necessary.

c) The TLO or the IP Unit shall, within three (3) months from the date of receipt of the Technology Disclosure Form, confirm in writing to the Inventor(s) whether or not the University will pursue patenting and/or commercialization of the IP, subject to any obligations that may be owed to external parties [see further Article 7.1 (e)].

Failure of the TLO to act within the period as stated herein shall be deemed as a waiver by the University of its right to patent and/or commercialize.

d) The TLO or the IP Unit generally will seek patent protection in order to pursue commercialization of the invention and/or protect scientifically meritorious inventions.

e) If there are obligations owed to an external party under the terms of a grant or research agreement in respect of the IP, the TLO or the IP Unit will contact the external party and proceed with the management of the IP in accordance with the terms of the agreement with such party.

f) The Inventor(s) shall at all times maintain confidential the details of the invention in accordance with the Confidentiality policy set out in Article 9.1 below, in particular during the period when the TLO or the IP Unit is assessing the viability of commercialization and/or patenting the invention. Any publication (even verbal disclosure) which describes an invention prior to filing for a patent may jeopardize the patenting process. During the evaluation process, the inventor is obliged to delay public disclosure until patent application has been filed. The University must endeavor to minimize delays in publication.

g) All Inventors shall disclose to the TLO or the IP Unit the identity of any party interested in the commercial exploitation of the IP in sufficient detail and as soon as practicable after the relevant facts have come to their knowledge. All Inventors are also required to disclose any conflict of interest as set out in 9.2 below.

h) Prior to any patent filings or commercialization by a University Personnel in respect of IP deemed owned by the University Personnel under Article 5.2(b) above, the University Personnel shall make full and truthful disclosure to the University by submitting the Declaration of Mandatory Disclosure.

7.2 Return of IP to Inventor(s)

a) The TLO shall within 3 months return the IP to the inventors for commercial exploitation where:

   i) The TLO has informed the Inventor(s) that it does not wish to pursue the commercial exploitation and patenting of the IP under Article 7.1(c); or

   ii) The TLO does not inform the Inventor(s) within 3 months of the acknowledgment of receipt of the Technology Disclosure whether it wishes to pursue commercial exploitation and/or patenting of the IP; or

   iii) The University has not commercialized the IP after 3 years from the date of receipt of the Technology Disclosure and there are no on-going discussions with any interested parties.

7.3 Commercialization and Protection of the University's IP

a) The University shall be entitled to approach, negotiate and enter into any binding IP agreement with any third party on such terms and conditions as the University, being the legal and beneficial owner of such IP, shall in its sole and absolute discretion deem fit.

b) The University shall be entitled to assign rights or grant licenses, whether exclusive or not, in respect of the IP for such periods as it shall deem fit, or make such other arrangements relating to such IP as it may deem appropriate in order to facilitate technology transfer while protecting the rights of the University and the Inventors.

c) The University will not negotiate contracts for consulting services for individual Inventors as part of a license arrangement. Individual Inventors are free to negotiate such contracts on a personal basis.

d) The University may use any means whatsoever, as it shall in its sole and absolute discretion deem fit, to protect any IP owned by it, including but not limited to instituting proceedings concerning infringement of IP rights and breach of license agreements.

e) The support and cooperation of the Inventors are usually critical for successful commercialization. The Inventor(s) shall provide all information and render all assistance to the University in any phase as may be required from time to time.

7.4 Distribution of Commercialization Benefits

a) The University shall share with the Inventor(s) of the IP any Net Revenue [as defined in Article 7.4 (b) below] received by the University in the following ratio:

University (___%):

Inventor(s) (___%)

b) Net Revenue is defined as the gross consideration (including all royalties, fees and other benefits) received from the commercialization of the IP less all Expenses incurred in the commercialization of that IP. Expenses shall include all patent filing and legal fees, marketing and licensing costs, administrative expenses and fixed overhead costs and any other expenses necessarily incurred for patenting and commercializing the IP.

c) If the University receives shares in a company in exchange for a license or assignment of the IP to the company, the shares the University obtains will be held by the University and the proceeds from the liquidation of the shares shall be distributed to the Inventor(s) according to the same ratio as set out in Article 7.4(a). An Inventor may also request to hold his/her portion of the shares in his/her own name, in which case such Inventor shall no longer be entitled to any proceeds from the liquidation of the remaining shares by the University.

d) The Inventors' share of Net Revenue under Article 7.4(a) will be distributed equally among any joint Inventors unless the University has been previously notified in writing of any different sharing arrangement agreed upon between the joint Inventors.

e) It is the responsibility and obligation of each Inventor to keep the University updated of his/her current contact number and address in order for the University to distribute his/her share of the Net Revenue.

f) The University's share of the Net Revenue shall be distributed as follows:

College/Department (___%)

Administration of IP (___%)

Innovation Fund (___%)

Where there are multiple Inventors from different Colleges/ Departments, the College's/Department's share of Net Revenue will be distributed amongst the College/Department in accordance with the number of Inventors from each College/ Department.

g) The University shall distribute to the Inventor(s) the proportion of the Net Revenue due to them in such manner and at such times the University shall, in its sole and absolute discretion, deem fit.

b) Where the University returns the IP to Inventor(s) under Article 7.2 above, the Inventor(s) shall sign a Letter Agreement, which shall include the following terms and conditions for the return of the IP:

i) The Inventor(s) shall be entitled to file for patent rights in their own name and at their own expense.

ii) The University shall be entitled to a percentage of any benefits received by the Inventor(s) from the commercial exploitation of the IP as follows:

A) The Inventor(s) shall account to the University ___% of any Net Revenue that the Inventors receive for the commercial exploitation of the IP. Net Revenue in this context shall mean the gross consideration (including all royalties, fees and other benefits, but excluding shares in a company), received less all Expenses incurred in the commercial exploitation of the IP. Expenses in this context shall mean all patent filing, licensing, legal, and any other reasonable and necessary expenses incurred for patenting, enforcement of rights and commercially exploiting the Invention.

B) Where the Inventor(s) receive shares in a company in return for the license or assignment of the IP to the company, the University shall be entitled to ____% of the Inventors' shares. Such percentage may be reviewed on a case-by-case basis.

Where the Inventor(s) will be receiving shares in a start-up company that the Inventor(s) found, the University or its nominee will further have a first right to invest in up to ____% of the total equity of the company at the initial formation of the company.

The University's share of the said Net Revenue shall be distributed as per Article 7.4 (f) above.

iii) The Inventors shall submit to the University an annual report, and will keep the University informed of the status of each and every patent application filed in connection with the IP.

iv) The Inventor(s) shall disclose, furnish or otherwise make available to the University all information relating to or in connection with such patent application(s) and/or the commercial exploitation of the IP as and when requested by the University.

v) The University may, but is not obligated to, request for the IP to be returned back to the University if the Inventor(s) fail to commercialize the IP after 3 years from the date the IP is returned to the Inventor(s).

ARTICLE 8

RESEARCH COLLABORATIONS WITH EXTERNAL PARTIES

8.1 Research Collaborations with Non-Commercial Parties

a) Non-commercial parties include other universities, research institutions, government agencies and non-governmental organizations.

b) In a collaboration with non-commercial parties, IP will generally be jointly owned where both parties have jointly developed the

IP (i.e. where employees/students of both parties are involved in creating, developing or generating the IP). Usually the parties will have the right to jointly commercialize the jointly-owned IP.

c) Where the IP is solely developed by the University, the University will retain the ownership of the IP but the non-commercial party will have free internal use of the subject IP. The terms and conditions of any commercial use of IP shall be subject to negotiations.

8.2 Research Collaborations with Industry

a) Collaborations with industry arc encouraged as interaction with industry ensures that research at the University remains relevant and they also provide exposure to students to possible future employers. Companies will also benefit as they obtain access to the University's expertise, facilities and resources not otherwise available elsewhere.

b) The guidelines below lay down the factors that are taken into consideration in determining the IP terms in order to provide consistency in decision-making. The guidelines also recognize the different types of projects that can be undertaken with industry, which can range from exploratory research (where the application is not known), technology development (where the application is known) to product design and problem solving. The guidelines also provide for recognition of the University's contributions in the form of license fees payable by the Company as the Company obtains commercial benefits from IP generated with the help of the University.

c) The following guidelines on IP ownership and commercial use and licensing of the subject IP will apply to all research projects with industry:

i) Sole Ownership of IP by the University

A. This will be the default position taken for all research collaborations with industry unless the scope of the project and the contributions by the Company can be shown to fall under (i) or (iii) below.

B. The Company will have a first right to negotiate either a non-exclusive or exclusive fee-based license on commercial terms. An exclusive license may not be available where a key platform technology is involved.

ii) Joint Ownership of IP by the University and the Company

A. The University will consider joint ownership where the Company will be contributing background IP to the project or will have intellectual contribution to the IP, that is, employees of the Company are also involved in creating or generating the IP together with the University. The Company must also be providing funding for a significant portion of the total project costs.

B. As a joint-owner which has contributed significantly to the development of the IP, the Company will have a non-exclusive royalty-free right to commercially exploit the IP. As the Company is free to commercially exploit the project IP on its own without accounting to the University, the University will also retain the right to give out non-exclusive licenses without accounting to the Company.

C. The Company will have the right to license the IP non-exclusively to third parties but is required to account to the University a percentage of any licensing revenue it receives.

D. If the Company wishes to commercially exploit the IP exclusively, the Company will also have a first right to negotiate a royalty-bearing exclusive license with the University on commercial terms.

iii) Sole Ownership of IP by the Company

A. The university will consider the sole ownership by the Company if the project meets the following criteria:

1. The project is focused mainly on product development or improvements to the Company's existing products or services and only the Company's background IP is involved;

2. The project has unambiguous known objectives and the Company lays down a defined way of performing the study;

3. The University's existing IP is not involved as the Company requires mainly access to the expertise and know-how of the University's staff members;

4. The University must benefit from the project and acquiring relevant industry experience through the exposure provided by working with the Company.

B. The Company will be required to bear the full project cost, which includes full University manpower and facilities/ equipment costing.

C. The Company's ownership of IP, will, however, be limited to the Company's Field of Application as specified in the project agreement. The University will reserve ownership of any project IP generated in the fields of application not specified in the project agreement and will be free to exploit the IP in those other fields of application.

8.3 General Policies on Other Terms in Research Agreements

a) **Publications**

The University reserves the right to publish or present the findings of the project, subject to only the right of the external party to require the delay of any publication or presentation in order to remove any of its confidential information or for the filing of any patents in accordance with the term of the research agreement for the project.

b) **Warranties**

As the research is only conducted on a reasonable efforts basis, the results are provided "as-is" and without any representation or warranty of merchantability or fitness for any particular purpose or any warranty that any use will not infringe or violate any patent or other proprietary rights of any other person.

c) **Indemnities**

The University requires the external party to indemnify the University from any claim, loss, cost, expense or liability of any kind that may be incurred by the University due to the external party's use (commercial or otherwise) of the results or IP generated from the project.

d) **Overhead Charge**

i) A ______ percent (__%) overhead charge will apply to all research projects to take into account the overhead costs in providing the facilities and resources to carry out research at the University. The overhead charge shall be distributed in the following ratio:

University (__%) :

College/Department (__%)

ii) The overhead charge will be imposed on all direct funding received from the external party.

iii) The overhead charge does not apply to unrestricted or outright grants or to government grants that do not allow such overhead charges. Usually for such grants, no specific results are required or expected from the sponsor and no rights to any IP accrue to the sponsor.

ARTICLE 9

GENERAL OBLIGATIONS

9.1 Confidentiality

a) All University Personnel and Students shall at all times maintain confidential all information as defined herein, whether made/ developed on his/her own, in collaboration with University colleagues, or acquired through discussions (whether formal or informal) with University colleagues.

b) The above confidentiality obligations shall not apply in any of the following circumstances:

i) Where disclosure is required by law or any government agency;

ii) Where the information is in the public domain or becomes generally available to the public; or

iii) Where disclosure is made with the prior consent of the University.

9.2 Disclosure of Conflicts of Interest

a) All Inventor(s)/Creator(s) who have any interest, whether directly or indirectly, in any party interested in the commercial exploitation of University IP, shall make full and honest disclosure of the nature and extent of their interest to the University, as soon as practicable and to the best of their knowledge. Without prejudice to the generality of the foregoing, an Inventor shall be deemed to have an interest if he/she (or a person over whom he/she has control) is a director of, or a shareholder with a material shareholding in the organization or company interested in the commercial exploitation of the University IP.

b) In addition, all University Personnel shall make full and honest disclosure and seek the approval of the University in the event of any situation where a conflict of interest may arise, as highlighted by 10.2 below.

c) Failure to declare his/her interest in the commercial exploitation of the University IP and/or to seek approval from the University as required in 9.2 (a) and (b) above shall subject the University Personnel liable to disciplinary or other actions which the University shall, in its sole and absolute discretion, impose.

ARTICLE 10

CONSULTANCIES/DIRECTORSHIP IN COMPANIES

10.1 Consultancies

a) University Personnel entering into consultancy work pursuing the commercialization of the IP shall commit not to disclose or transfer to external party any IP belonging to the University. They shall also ensure that a separate agreement is entered into with the appropriate College/Department for the use of University facilities, equipment or resources for such consulting work.

b) In any consulting service, University Personnel shall not breach the confidentiality obligations to which they are subject by virtue of being employees of the University. They shall not disclose any Confidential Information which relate to University IP or any research which is being carried out at the University.

10.2 Conflict of Interest

a) Conflicts of interest may arise in various situations relating to technology transfer interactions with industry. To minimize or prevent such conflict of interest situations, University Personnel must make full and honest disclosure to, and seek approval of, the University in the following situations:

i) Undertaking sponsored or collaborative research with a company that has licensed IP from the University, where the research is related or in the same area as the IP licensed;

ii) Deployment of Students by the University Personnel to do product and/or process research and development for a company in which the University Personnel has an interest. In cases where a University Personnel supervises final-year projects and higher degree students, this includes working on thesis topics in which the University Personnel has a commercial interest in the research area;

iii) Transmitting to company information that is not generally available to the public. This includes withholding or reducing publications after transferring technology to the company, or failing to attend to industry visitors from competing companies;

iv) Undertaking or changing the orientation of the University Personnel's research (whether supported by University funds or external grants) to serve the research, product development or other needs of a company;

v) Use of the University Personnel's position in the University to participate in company activities;

vi) Purchasing of equipment, instruments, materials or other items for University teaching and/or research from a company in which the University Personnel has an interest;

vii) Engaging in consultation with a company in which the university personnel or any person related to him (including without limitation, his parent, spouse, brother, sister, son, daughter, or any person who is holding legal title for the benefit of the university personnel) has an interest, whether legal, beneficial or otherwise.

10.3 Directorship of Companies (Including University Spin-Off Companies)

Subject to the conditions as laid down by the University for academic staff to undertake external consultation and specialist work (including Non-Executive Company Directorship), University Personnel may be given approval to accept appointment to non-executive directorships in companies, including companies to be formed, that will commercialize their inventions.

ARTICLE 11

GENERAL PROVISIONS

11.1 Interpretation

The Intellectual Property Code of the Philippines (Republic Act No. 8293), the Plant Variety Protection Act of 2002 (R.A. 9168), the Agriculture and Fishery Modernization Act (R.A. 8435), the Philippine Fisheries Code of 1998 (R.A. 8550), the Wildlife Act (R.A. 9147), Indigenous People Rights Act (IPRA Law), the Inventor's and Invention Incentives Act (R.A. 7459), the Magna Carta for Scientists, Engineers, Researchers and other Science and Technology Personnel in Government (R.A. 8439), the Administrative Code of

1987 (E.O. 292), and the respective charters of agencies under the University, and other relevant laws and their corresponding amendments, implementing rules and regulation are deemed written into the IP Policy.

11.2 Construction

In the event of doubts in the interpretation of this IP Policy, the provision should be construed in favor of the University/generator of IP. (Please choose)

11.2 Waiver of Policy

The University shall have the discretion to waive or vary any or all of the provisions of these rules in a particular case. A waiver on one occasion and for a particular case shall not be deemed to be a waiver or variation of the same or any other provision on a future occasion or for a future case.

11.3 Commencement and Application of IP Policy

This Policy is effective from ____________ and shall be applicable to all University IP licensed after the effective date. The rules set out in the IP Policy are subject to the terms of any agreement with external parties that the University may enter into.

11.4 Amendment of the Rules and Guidelines of the IP Policy

The rules and guidelines set out in the IP Policy may be amended by the University from time to time. The University shall undertake to notify University Personnel and Students as soon as is practicable of the amendments so made. In any case, the amendments shall be in full force and effect on the date the amendments have been announced by the University to take effect.

ARTICLE 12

PENALTIES

Any person found to have violated any of the provisions of this IP Policy shall be dealt with in accordance with the provisions of the faculty, staff, administrative or applicable employment manual. Any violation of these policies shall be considered as a disciplinary offense.

FSC
www.fsc.org
MIX
Papier | Fördert
gute Waldnutzung
FSC® C083411

Kolibri 360 GmbH
Ferdinand-Jühlke-Straße 7
99095 Erfurt, Deutschland
produktsicherheit@kolibri360.de